THE MAKING OF *THE GOLDEN BOUGH*

The Golden Bough (1834) by J. M. W. Turner, described in Frazer's opening paragraph. From 1847 to 1929 this hung in the National Gallery in London. It was then transferred to the Tate Gallery, where it now hangs.

THE MAKING OF
THE GOLDEN BOUGH

THE ORIGINS AND GROWTH OF AN ARGUMENT

ROBERT FRASER

St. Martin's Press   New York

© Robert Fraser 1990

First published in the United States of America in 1990

Printed in Great Britain

ISBN 0–312–04205–1

Library of Congress Cataloging-in-Publication Data
Fraser, Robert.
    The making of *The Golden Bough*: the origins and growth of an
argument/Robert Fraser.
        p.   cm.
    Includes bibliographical references.
    ISBN 0–312–04205–1
        1. Frazer, James George, Sir, 1854–1941.—*The Golden Bough*.
    2. Mythology.   3. Religion, Primitive.   4. Magic.   I. Title.
BL310.F62   1990   89–29260
291—dc20   CIP

FOR BENEDICT JOSEPH FRASER

PREFACE

THE VERSION of Sir James Frazer's *The Golden Bough* familiar to many readers is the one-volume abridgement of the Third (1906–15) Edition which Frazer himself made in 1922. Always ready to popularise his researches for those not strictly scholars, Frazer made modest claims for this redaction, which he viewed as a *propylaea* into the precincts of the temple rather than a complete ground-plan, still less a comprehensive guided tour. Shorn of footnotes as well as some of the author's more striking theories, it serves as a port of entry for honest inquirers, and I have kept it constantly in mind while writing this book. It is none the less essential for those who would confront the full scale of Frazer's achievement to recognise that *The Golden Bough* in any of its three full-length editions is a structure of altogether nobler proportions.

To play Ariadne to the reader's Theseus it is necessary not simply to retrace the labyrinth back to its beginnings but to follow the course of its successive transformations through the mind of the master builder. Frazer's working-method, consistent throughout his life, was to start with the germ of an idea, which he then cultivated into more and more extensive growths until the end product of his labours issued in a work of many volumes. The genesis of *The Golden Bough* may well lie in a footnote to Frazer's concurrent edition of the travels of the second-century Greek physician Pausanias. When, a mere fourteen months after its inception, a two-volume work appeared under the now-familiar title, the theories which were to make it famous presented themselves in advanced embryo. This was the version read by Hardy and Yeats, but it remains a sketch, and those familiar with later versions will easily recognise lacunae, *non sequiturs* and places where Frazer's argument provides no more than an elegant skin over matters as yet uncertain.

The beginnings of Frazer's expansion upon, and refinements to, this early version can be observed in the marginalia he made in his personal copy and incorporated in subsequent versions. The Second Edition marked perhaps the boldest departure, with its unsettling theories concerning the crucifixion of Christ and its introduction of the tripartite division of man's cultural evolution into the stages of Magic, Religion and Science. Frazer promised himself another edition within a few years, but fifteen were to pass before the eventual completion of the Third, the several parts of which had in the interval appeared by fits and starts, and by no means in the order of its numbered volumes. It is a version now more usually dipped into than read, but it is Frazer's definitive statement, and in it the theory of the King of the Wood appears in a radically new guise. Supplemented in 1936 by *Aftermath*, an addendum Frazer dictated after his blindness to his amanuensis R. Angus Downie, the whole can profitably be compared to a palimpsest in which the first marks on the parchment have been overlaid by decades of thought and painstaking accretion. It may also be compared to the final state of an engraving, provided it is remembered that the plate has been successively enlarged, and that Frazer like any artist constantly rethought the nature of his conception.

It is to examine the genesis and transformation of Frazer's argument that I have written this book. It is not a biography in the orthodox sense of the term. For those who wish to inform themselves about Frazer the man, a ready account lies to hand in Robert Ackerman's *J. G. Frazer: His Life and Work* (1987). It is one hundred years since *The Golden Bough* first burst upon the world. To mark the event Frazer's publishers are issuing this study together with a collection of essays by various hands entitled *Sir James Frazer and the Literary Imagination*. Together the two books compose a head of Janus, one face looking back to key figures and influences in Frazer's past, the other forwards to the writers and thinkers he in his turn influenced.

Acknowledgements are due to the British School at Rome for their hospitality and the use of their matchless library; to Trinity College, Cambridge, for accommodating a conference on Frazer's work; to the English Department of Royal Holloway and Bedford New College, London, for an Honorary Research Associateship during which the college became in large measure my own Trinity; and to the staff of two other libraries – the Wren Library, also at Trinity, and the British Library in London – for their unfailing courtesy and support. For permission to quote from Frazer's letters and notebooks as well as to reproduce a page from Frazer's own copy of the First Edition with its marginalia, I am indebted to the Master and Fellows of Trinity College, Cambridge. Frazer's letters to George Macmillan are quoted by kind permission of the British Library. Turner's painting *The Golden Bough* is reproduced by courtesy of the Trustees of the Tate Gallery. I would also like to tender my personal gratitude to Graham Eyre for his editorial work on the typescript and to Alan MacCormick of the Castle Museum, Nottingham, for permission to reproduce the map of Nemi. Lastly I would like to thank my wife and son for living with me during periods when I was thinking about the King of the Wood and not about the lunch.

ROBERT FRASER

London – Andros – Kuwait

CONTENTS

LIST OF ILLUSTRATIONS

Frontispiece: The Golden Bough (1834) by J. M. W. Turner, described in Frazer's opening paragraph.

Map 1 (see p. 4): Nemi and its surrounding area, showing towns and peoples of the Latin League.

Plate 1 (see opposite p. 196): Page in the First Edition (II, 286) on which Frazer refers to mistletoe cut in June.

"Hoc nemus, hunc" inquit, "frondoso vertice collem
(quis deus incertum est) habitat deus."
                                    Virgil, *Aeneid*, VIII. 351–2

Πάντα ῥεῖ καὶ οὐδὲν μένει is as true of man (and
therefore of his mind, for the mind is the man) as it is
of nature. You seem to think that man stands for ever
on the same spot in the river and sees it speeding past
him. It is not so; he is borne aloft on the current. There
is no absolute way of looking at the world.
              James Frazer to Henry Jackson, 22 August 1888

When Frazer begins by telling the story of the King of
the Wood at Nemi, he does this in a tone which shows
that something strange and terrible is happening here.
And that is the answer to the question "why is this
happening?": because it is terrible.
                            Ludwig Wittgenstein, *Remarks on
                                    Frazer's Golden Bough*

CHAPTER I

PROSPECT: "DIANA'S MIRROR"

LEAVING the Aureleian Walls by the Porta Sebastiano, the old Appian Way strikes across the Campagna south-east of Rome flanked to either side by the sepulchres of the illustrious dead. Past the Sepolcro di Anna Regilla and the Catacomb of Saint Callisto it flies straight as an arrow until on the horizon the smooth vertebrae of the Alban Hills appear in the distance, much as the Pentland Hills do on the southerly road going from Edinburgh. Gradually the road ascends until the traveller finds himself on the tip of a declivity looking down at the clear pool of Lake Albano below. It was here, every Ides of August, that grateful female pilgrims, healed of their distempers by the huntress goddess, came carrying torches for the festival of lights at the grove of Diana at Nemi, under the protection then of the Senate and people of Aricia (modern Ariccia). Passing through Ariccia itself and then Genzano, the road swerves to the left skirting the periphery of Lake Nemi until, dominated by the round turret of its castle, the village of Nemi appears on the crest of a spur at the north-east corner of the lake from which the pool – "Diana's Mirror" – is glimpsed, an irregular ellipse nestling in the lap of a volcanic decline below.

It is after this manner that James George Frazer's epic study of an antique rite begins: with a vivid sense of place. Yet in Frazer's time as now, little was to be seen of the former Roman road which dropped down from Genzano toward the valley bottom until, bending northwards, it approached the precincts of Diana's sanctuary by way of a colonnaded stoa. For our clearest impression of what ancient votaries may then have seen, we must go to the Greek geographer Strabo:

> After Mount Albanus comes Aricia, a city on the Appian Way; it is one hundred and sixty stadia distant from Rome. Aricia lies in a hollow, but for all that it has a naturally strong citadel. Above Aricia lies first, on the right-hand side of the Appian Way as you go up from Aricia, the Artesium, which they call Nemus. The temple of Aricia, they say, is a copy of the Tauropolis. And in fact a barbaric and Scythian element

1

predominates in the sacred usages, for the people set up as a priest a runaway slave who has slain with his own hand the man previously consecrated to his office: accordingly the priest is always armed with a sword, looking around for attacks, and ready to defend himself. The temple is in a sacred grove and in front of it is a lake which resembles the open sea, and round it in a circle lies an unbroken and very high mountain brow that is hollow and deep. You can see the springs, it is true, from which the lake is fed (one of them is Egeria, as is called after a certain deity), but the outflows at the lake itself are not apparent, though they are pointed out to you at a distance outside the hollow, where they rise to the surface.[1]

Inundated by such streams, it was the rich volcanic soil of the region which gave Nemi its economic importance in classical times, as it does today, when the eastern shore of the lake is overspread with plantations of olive, vine and strawberry. The area encompassing the shrine is today covered by a congeries of agricultural smallholdings, the proprietor of one of which has hung beside his gatepost Cicero's salute to a noble profession:

Nihil est agri cultura melius, nihil uberius
nihil dulcius, nihil homine libero dignius.[2]

(Nothing surpasses agriculture, nothing is more fruitful, more pleasant, more worthy of a free man.)

The position of the sanctuary lies about two hundred yards inland, now almost smothered by the market gardens which stretch beyond it to the lakeside.[3] All that is visible from the road below is a containing wall of some twenty feet in height which in classical times supported the western flank of the enclosure. For many centuries after the cult fell into desuetude the temple's whereabouts were a matter of fervent speculation. Not until the seventeenth century of our era did the tentative explorations of two local landowners, the Marchesi Frangipani, bring to light votive statuettes and an effigy of the goddess together with a number of inscriptions published by Bishop Tomasini in Padua in 1654.[4] In the following century and a half the vogue for classical themes brought several artists to Nemi, including Turner, who visited the place at least once and set two paintings there, though not, *pace* Frazer, alas, *The Golden Bough*, whose lake is an imaginary Lake Avernus. Despite, or perhaps because of, Frazer's mistake about the setting of the picture, Turner's painting is better known than Thomas Jones's sideways view of the ruins of 1777, or Domenichino's vision of priestesses indulging in the pleasures of the hunt, now in the Palazzo Borghese.[5]

More systematic investigation of the site had to await the development, towards the end of the nineteenth century, of a scientific archaeology.[6] Elsewhere – in Schliemann's Mycaenae for example, or Evans's Knossos – this was the domain of full-time professionals, many of them German. In the English-speaking community in Rome, among whom the incentive to excavate Nemi occurred, it was still the province of the desultory amateur. Three such men were the moving spirits behind the British and American Archaeological Society, a gathering of enthusiasts which met for the first time towards the end of 1882: the painter Arthur Strutt; the architect Richard Popplewell Pullan; and as Vice-President John Savile Lumley (later Lord Savile), career diplomat, patron of the fine arts and Ambassador from the Court of St James to the fledgling Italian government.

Blessed with independent means and a wide-ranging curiosity, Savile had served his country in St Petersburg, from which the outbreak of the Crimean crisis had released him, and in Washington, Madrid and Berne before in 1883 at the apex of his career he was created a Privy Councillor and Her Majesty's Ambassador in Rome, where the temperamental disinclination of Lord Salisbury to consult his emissaries abroad left him free to gratify his taste for picture-collecting and archaeological exploration. In the October of the year following his appointment he purchased an estate on the Alban Hills beneath which lay the ruins of the imperial villa of Antonius Pius, and after digging up the vineyard published the results of his investigations in 1886. Meanwhile his associate Arthur Strutt had paid a visit to the castle at Nemi, owned by one Prince Orsini, and, inspired by the possibilities of so important a site lying beneath the very escarpment the castle overlooked, communicated his zeal to Savile. Later Savile was to claim that the identification of the site and the initiative behind the ensuing excavations were his alone. There is little doubt, however, that both Strutt and he knew of Tomasini's inscriptions, which were clearly reproduced in Canon Lucidi's *Memorie Storiche* of Ariccia, published in 1796. Be that as it may, Savile soon negotiated a contract with the Prince according to which, in exchange for access to the site for a preliminary period, he was to cede Orsini one

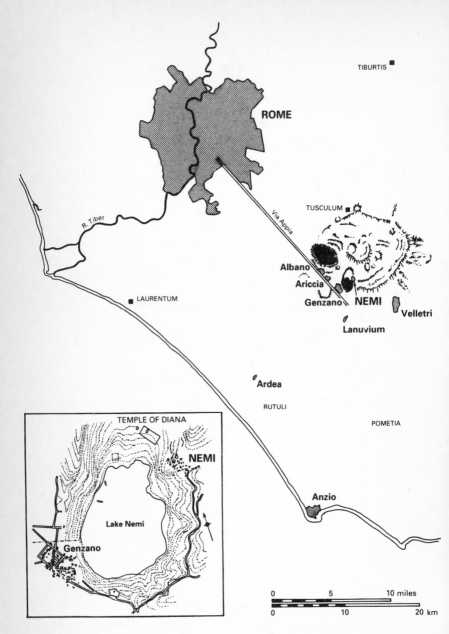

Nemi and its surrounding area, showing towns and peoples of the Latin League. Inset: location of the Temple of Diana. (Drawing by Alan MacCormick.)

half of the finds together with an option of extending the agreement for
a further period at a price more advantageous to the princely purse.

Looking down, prior to commencing work, on the location of the
temple from the ridge lying immediately above it, Savile could discern
an immense terrace of some 4,400 square metres, hemmed in by irregular
patches of wall. Concentrating on a small area on the far side from the
lake shore, he decided to dig five trenches. The first of these yielded a
trove of votive offerings similar to those discovered by the Marchesi
Frangipani two hundred years previously. It is these which Frazer
mentions in the first chapter of *The Golden Bough* as dedicated to Diana
in her manifestation of healer and protectress, "as blessing men and
women with offspring, and granting expectant mothers an easy delivery".[7]
From apertures in the back of each and a number of nails (now in the
Villa Giulia in Rome) unearthed in the excavations, Savile supposed these
offerings to have been suspended from the sanctuary walls on nails
provided for the purpose. He further imagined that the quarry of
offerings on which the team had alighted consisted of the overspill of
such objects interred at the orders of the temple officialdom, to prevent
them from further cluttering the inner walls of the enclosure.

Subsequent discoveries proved just as illuminating, even if Frazer for
reasons of his own declines to mention them. Mosaics were unearthed,
together with three Doric drums buried close to a set of matching
capitals, both presumably belonging to a temple which from nearby
inscriptions could be identified as Diana's. In the south-east extremity
lay a row of alcoves and vaulted chapels which Savile thought adjoined
the living-quarters of the priestesses. In one of these a head of the
Emperor Tiberius was discovered, in another fragments from a sculptor's
workshop, in the third the terracotta head of a horse. The last trench of
all disclosed a large circular slab and connecting sluice which had
presumably served as some kind of sacrificial table. The position of this
to the east of the temple foundations led Savile to conclude that it had
served as an abattoir for the sacrificial animals, portions of which were
then carried into the main temple buildings to be offered on the altar
within.

The most suggestive find of all was among the smallest. In the vicinity
of the temple compound Savile's workmen happened upon the curved
handle of a sacrificial ladle, the terminating hook of which resembled a
serpent's head.[8] Along its surface was inscribed the name DIANA in
letters of so archaic a style as to date the implement some centuries
earlier than the principal written sources on which most previous accounts
of the site had relied. Indeed, from the primitive form of the letters

alpha and *delta*, it was Savile's opinion that the ladle dated from the beginning of the third century BC, though possibly before. These facts suggested to Savile, as they were to suggest to Frazer, that in the grove of Diana at Nemi we have a religious foundation far older than Strabo or Ovid who describe it, older that the Latin League, older perhaps than the gathering and slow evolution of the peoples who were to form Roman civilisation as we understand it.

Weeks after these discoveries the season broke and, despairing of obtaining fairer terms from Orsini, Savile ordered his team to fill in the trenches. They have never since been disturbed.[9] If any further physical evidence exists as to the nature of the cult of Diana as it once flourished here in the cradle of the Alban Hills, it lies buried beneath the strawberry fields. Savile's discoveries were dispersed to his native Nottinghamshire (where many of them still lie in the Nottingham Castle Museum), while Orsini's went to a number of Italian museums, including the Villa Giulia, where they lie alongside the no less perplexing legacy of the Etruscans. The results of the excavation were written up in a number of Italian learned periodicals,[10] and in the British weekly *The Athenaeum*,[11] where they were perused by a young Fellow of Trinity College, Cambridge, called James George Frazer. Four years later he was reading about the pattern of succession of certain kingdoms in the southern tip of India[12] when his attention was attracted by a number of affinities with the Arician rite, with which he was already familiar from literary sources. In 1890, five years after Savile first turned the sod at Nemi, Frazer published the first two-volume edition of a work entitled *The Golden Bough*. The book was an immediate success, lending anthropological studies a popularity and a notoriety they had not until then possessed, and which they have rarely enjoyed since. The cult of Diana at Nemi, and certain atavistic and inscrutable rites connected therewith, suddenly seized the imagination of the reading public in a manner from which it has scarcely even now recovered.

But why Nemi? For a scholar interested in the early religious history of man there were in the 1880s many possible starting-points, both in the known cultures of the Graeco-Roman world and in the multitude of non-Western societies opened up to a curious public by the rampages of colonialism. Frazer's earlier researches into the origins of totemism had familiarised him with much that had recently been discovered concerning Stone and Iron Age cultures beyond Europe: he was already in touch with many of those currently looking into the aboriginal cultures of Australia and in active correspondence with ethnographers the world over. He was also a classical scholar of the first rank who had already embarked on a definitive edition of the second-century Greek traveller Pausanias. True, the excavations at Nemi had attracted widespread international attention, but they were far from representing the only front of advance in that archaeologically active decade. Besides, though familiar with the accounts of the excavations in the learned journals, Frazer's indebtedness to these is selective enough, and his combination of them with the accounts of the cult in classical literature sufficiently distinctive to lead us to suspect that there were strong pressures of another kind emanating from a different quarter. From Frazer's point of view Nemi was both unique and uniquely interesting: the problem is to work out exactly wherein that uniqueness lay.

Part of the answer must surely lie in the surprising antiquity of the site. Strabo, Ovid[13] and Statius[14] describe the shrine as it flourished in their own day, but nothing that could be gleaned from these authorities suggested that the shrine was prehistoric. Servius in his fourth-century commentary on Virgil speaks of the legends surrounding the cult as part of the long-established folklore of the Latin peoples, but just how long-established is not clear.[15] All of these commentators speak of a religious emporium of some magnificence, staffed by a college of priestesses and possibly of priests, and dedicated for the most part to the healing of sickness, and more especially of gynaecological complaints. Behind it all seems to have lurked a recognition by the various tribes that made up the Latin League that here was a focus for their difficult collective affiliation, and the cult of Diana, who was also worshipped on the Aventine Hill, seems therefore to have become something of a state religion, with her feast day on 13 August an important public holiday.

By the time of the early Caesars this national prominence seems to have converted Nemi into a place of pilgrimage with all its attendant disadvantages. Julius Caesar built a villa near the spot: the fashionable and the affluent turned up in their droves, and with them the impecunious and needy. In his fourth satire Juvenal describes the execrations hurled by the beggars at the conveyances sweeping the rich uphill on their homeward progress from the shrine,[16] while the speaker in Persius's sixth satire is so irritated by the fecklessness of his young heir that he threatens to disinherit him and bestow his legacy on one of these same mendicants.[17] By the time of Caligula the proximity of the temple precinct to the out-of-town residences of the affluent patricians had threatened to become something of a public nuisance. The peevish young emperor moored two pleasure barges on the margin of the lake not two hundred yards from the entrance to the shrine, near enough to the priest's lair for Rex Nemorensis, the King of the Wood, to upstage him. So Suetonius tells us that he dispatched a strong man along the shoreline to challenge the priest's reputation for pugilistic prowess,[18] though whether the emissary succeeded in putting him down and succeeding to his office we are not told. Caligula's barges were excavated in the 1920s under Mussolini, only later to be blown up by the retreating German army, but their very existence, together with the observations of the classical commentators, is sufficient to suggest that by the first century AD the Artesium at Nemi combined the attributes of a spa, a centre of homage and a tourist trap: a blend of Bath, Rocamadour and Lourdes. None of this is inconsistent with the most venerable antiquity, but neither does it tempt us to look further than the end of our historical noses. Prior to Frazer scholars had rested content with the assumption that the temple by the lake was the creation of the Latin League for its own socio-cultural purposes, a deliberately created and meticulously maintained national shrine. It was Frazer's business to look further.

To start him on his way there was the most enticing reference to the site in the whole of ancient literature. When in the spring of 1889 Frazer commenced work on *The Golden Bough*, he had already devoted several years of his life to the project which more than any other was to establish his reputation among classicists: a monumental edition of the travels of Pausanias, which, together with its accompanying translation, was by the time of its publication in 1898 to extend to six volumes. When matters anthropological first absorbed the larger part of Frazer's attention in 1887, he was obliged temporarily to lay Pausanias aside, but not before he had noted a vital reference in the second book. Pausanias was a doctor from Asia Minor, a Roman citizen and Hellenophile who wrote in Greek and addressed his remarks to the educated Greek-speaking world. It is not clear whether his work is complete, for his peregrinations as charted in his *Description of Greece* are confined to the Peloponnese and central Greece, whereas in fact he probably wandered further afield, as his habit of constant cross-reference makes clear. He knew the eastern Mediterranean well, and as a Roman citizen was fascinated by Roman accretions to Greek legend. At one stage, when in the vicinity of Corinth, he visits the shrine at Epidauros dedicated to the ancient world's patron saint of medicine Asclepios, whom the Romans called Aesculapius. There he finds an inscription commemorating one of the better-known episodes in local mythology: that according to which Hippolytus, dragged to death by chariot horses, was raised from the dead by Aesculapius and then transported to Italy. The incident and its legendary aftermath were inscribed on a tablet standing within the enclosure at Epidauros, Pausanias's description of which Frazer translates:

> Apart from the others stands an ancient tablet with an inscription stating that Hippolytus dedicated twenty horses to the god. The people of Aricia tell a tale which agrees with the inscription on this tablet. They say that Hippolytus, done to death by the curses of Theseus, was raised from the dead by Aesculapius, and that being come to life again, he refused to forgive his father, and disregarding his entreaties went away to Aricia in Italy. There he reigned and there he dedicated to Artemis a precinct, where down to my time the priesthood of the goddess is the prize of victory in a single combat. The competition is not open to free men, but only to slaves who have run away from their masters.[19]

When Frazer's edition of Pausanias eventually saw the light of day in 1898 his commentary on this passage was modest: "I have suggested an explanation of this custom in *The Golden Bough*."[20] In reality his indebtedness ran deeper, for, as Pausanias's more recent editor Peter Levi trenchantly observes, "This institution was the starting point of Frazer's *Golden Bough*,"[21] "Starting point" may itself be an understatement, for, although much later Frazer was to speak of the priest at Nemi as a "puppet" for other ideas, all the signs are that in 1889 it was the lurid enigma of the priestly succession that attracted him. Nor were medicinal and curative functions of the shrine of primary interest to him: it was what Strabo called its "barbarous and Scythian element" that drew him. Indeed, in certain respects Savile's and Frazer's views of the shrine run counter to one another. Savile was not especially interested in the priestly duel, for which he had found no evidence whatsoever in 1885. Deprived of any clear archaeological evidence concerning the cult of the murderous priest, Frazer was thus obliged to fall back on the literary evidence. More especially did he fall back on Pausanias, who is the only commentator to imply having witnessed the contest. Pausanias states that the hand-to-hand duel between the priest and his successor was held "in my time" – that is, in the second century, the empire of the Antonines, one of the more sophisticated civilisations known to man. A whole century later than Caligula, two hundred years after Ovid, at a time of rarefied decadence when Rome lay poised on the edge of the long slope of her decline – even this late, amid the sophisticated ennui of the imperial palaces – the Priest of Diana defended his anachronistic title.

"Rex Nemorensis" was a throwback to an age of barbarity and darkness.

To put it in a nutshell, Nemi was important because it was incongruous. It was incongruous first because it seemed somehow not to be in keeping with the period in which it evidently still flourished. It was incongruous secondly because a spa settlement dedicated to the gentle arts of healing seems to consort ill with a deadly hand-to-hand combat between a man defending life and limb and a fugitive from justice staking everything on the outcome. If, ten miles distant in Rome, the roars from the Coliseum were occasionally overheard in the sedate precincts of the Vestal virgins in the Forum nearby, the two institutions were at least distinct. Here in Nemi, if the classical accounts were to be believed, the nun-like priestesses went about their tasks within sight of the sombre priest prowling sword in hand by his tree.

The ancients had noted this incongruity and had their own explanation. The image of Diana in the shrine, they said, had come from Tauropolis, the Scythian capital of what is now the Crimea, whence it was stolen by Iphigenia; she had taken refuge there after Jupiter had saved her from the executioner's knife when she was about to be sacrificed to secure fair sailing for the Trojan expedition. After killing his mother Clytemnestra, Orestes sought refuge there. But the Scythian custom was that all fugitives from justice should be sacrificed to the image, so Iphigenia smuggled her brother out of the Tauric Chersonese and over to Aricia together with the image of the goddess. This they took to Aricia, where they re-established the cult.[22]

There is of course absolutely no historical evidence for any of this, but the invention is easy to understand. In the ancient world the Scythians had a bad press. Herodotos says that they wore the skins of wild beasts and pledged themselves out of the hollowed-out skulls of their enemies.[23] They blinded their slaves and until Darius put them down were at constant war with their neighbours. Even in Shakespeare's day the "barbarous Scythian" was a byword for savagery,[24] though for the Hellenic world it was probably sufficient that they were βάρβαρος, which is to say non-Greek. According to Herodotos they held Greek customs in abhorrence and did away with any of their kings who had the audacity to copy them. More pertinently, their treatment of slaves was notorious. What more natural than to suppose that their custom of sacrificing runaway slaves to Artemis had somehow been translated to Italy, where it was commuted into a kind of trial by ordeal? That way the fugitive was given a chance and the Italians could flatter their moral vanity with the illusion of clemency.

This mythological sleight-of-hand may have satisfied the Romans, but the nineteenth century was more sceptical. If Pausanias was right, the gruelling contest had continued well into the second century AD in the very precincts of what was in effect a convent hospital. This juxtaposition was too much for the archaeologists; the temple of Rex Nemorensis just had to be a separate foundation situated elsewhere. In 1817 the Italian archaeologist Antonio Nibby, an earlier translator of Pausanias, unearthed the remains of a very much smaller temple on the other side of the ridge just beneath the town of Ariccia.[25] Not only was this temple clearly dedicated to Artemis, but an effigy of Diana Taurica was found nearby. The scale of this temple, and the probable connection with the image, made its identification as the sanctum of Rex Nemorensis an attractive possibility. Savile for one was persuaded of it, since it relieved him of the anxiety of having failed to discover something by the lakeside which otherwise ought to have been there. In his catalogue entry to the collection he deposited at Nottingham Castle, he seizes eagerly on the idea:

> That the temple in which the idol was placed must have been a small one is evident from the fact that its duties were performed by a single priest, generally a fugitive slave, who obtained the post by slaying the incumbent, and who himself was compelled to be on his guard to defend his life against similar conditions for the priesthood until, as Strabo relates it, a more savage ruffian than himself succeeded "in depriving him of his life and office, a truly barbarous and Scythian custom".[26]

This theory had the advantage that it placed the site of the shrine very much closer to Strabo's positioning of it "on the right-hand side of the Appian Way as you go up from Aricia". Unfortunately Strabo then complicates things by saying that the shrine fronted the lake. Savile's way of getting round this is to suggest that at the period in question water was siphoned off to the other side of the crater to bring the lake down to an acceptable level, and that it is this subsidiary reservoir to which Strabo is referring. Now, Frazer not merely rejects this possibility but overlooks it entirely – less, one suspects, because of its intrinsic improbability than because of its inconsistency with his own line of argument. Frazer needed the shrine to be where tradition had placed it if his theories were to hold. If Nibby's theory was correct, then any incongruity in the ambiance of the shrine was explained away. Frazer needed the shrine to be as incongruous as possible. It was incongruity in which he was interested.

There is one other solution to the difficulty, and it is on this that Frazer fastens. It is just possible that the institution of the fugitive king was original to the lakeside shrine and that everything else had accumulated piecemeal around it. This would account for the plethora of subsidiary dieties who were worshipped at the site – Hippolytus, Virbius, Egeria – and for the fact that so grisly a provision for the succession to the kingly office was maintained at all costs, and very much against the grain. The priestesses dared not meddle with it since its age endowed it with a legendary status; besides, it was the fount from which everything else, including their own curative powers, flowed. Roman life was full of these extraordinary rituals which were honoured with painstaking persistence though their meaning had long since been forgotten. In his *Fasti*, a poetic gloss on the sacred days of the Roman year which Frazer later translated and edited, Ovid mentions several of them. Why did the Flamen Dialis, the High Priest of Jupiter who resided on the Capitoline Hill, wear a peaked cap, and why had his wife on certain days of the year to refrain from combing her hair?[27] Why on the feast day of Mars did the Salii or dancing priests parade around the city carrying *anciliae* or figure-of-eight shields and leaping up and down in their progress like so many Morris dancers? Not even Ovid could work it out:

> Quis mihi nunc dicet, quare caelestia Martis
> arma ferant Salii Mamuriumque canant?[28]

Why were straw men thrown from a bridge into the Tiber on 14 May? Ovid said they commemorated certain exiles from the Argolid who requested at their death to be thrown into the sea so that their bodies might drift back to the Aegean, but this is obviously wishful thinking.[29] These things were difficult to explain because they dated from a time long before the draining of the marshes which lay beneath the Forum, long before the Empire, the Republic, or even the Kingdom. In all probability, like Rex Nemorensis himself, they were a survival from prehistory.

The word "survival" here is of the essence. For, though common enough in our own adumbrations of cultural development, in the academic vocabulary of the 1880s, when Frazer was first lured into the field of anthropology by the writings of Edward Burnett Tylor, the term bore the unmistakable mark of a distinct school of thought. Nineteenth-century historiography had been dominated by two opposing interpretations of man's erratic progress towards modernity. The first and older stated that man had started from a state of perfection and had simply run to seed. This was the biblical view, the view of the writer of Genesis, but it could also be found in Hesiod and achieved perhaps its most memorable expression in Virgil's fourth eclogue. It could also be extracted from a simplified reading of Rousseau, and its modishness in the later eighteenth century had been increased by the speculations of men such as Lord Monboddo,[30] who considered the orang-utan a pattern of gentility, and Thomas Malthus, who thought that the increases in population were bit by bit depriving man of his livelihood.[31] The deteriorationist line of argument is puckishly parodied by Thomas Love Peacock in *Headlong Hall* in the person of Mr Escot:

the human race is undergoing a process of diminution in length, breadth and thickness. Observe this skull. . . . The frame this skull belonged to could scarcely have been less than nine feet high. Such is the lamentable progress of degeneracy and decay. . . . You all know the fable of the buried Pict, who bit off the end of a pickaxe, with which sacrilegious hands were breaking open his grave, and called out with a voice like subterranean thunder, *I perceive the degeneracy of your race by the smallness of your little finger!* videlicet, the pickaxe.[32]

Because of its religious implications the view had found stout defenders within the Church, notably Bishop Richard Whately, who four years before Darwin's *Origin of Species* had published an influential tract entitled *On the Origin of Civilization* in which he sought to assert Eternal Providence and justify the ways of God to scientifically minded man.[33]

Whately's view was that Genesis contained a parable of decline from a state of Stone Age virtue. It was a way of looking at history that had received some support from language theory. Since 1780, when William Jones first turned his attention to the origins of European languages, linguists had been intrigued by the mirage of an original Aryan tongue older than any spoken Western or Asiatic language, older even than Sanskrit yet common ancestor to all, in relation to which the existing family of Indo-European languages represented both an elaboration and a decline. Such thinking had found a powerful advocate in Max Müller, the German Indologist resident in Oxford, whose university extension lectures popularised the view.[34] The theory was all the more powerful since it interlocked with an interpretation of the origins of myth according to which all mythology was a falling-away from religious truths which had previously been expressed with more cogency, but without metaphor. The "disease of language" theory, as it became known, fell right into the hands of those eager to refute the sacrilegious implications of the new evolutionism. With the adoption of Darwinism as a model for historical development by social theorists such as Herbert Spencer, the debate flowed straight into the fabric of the emerging social sciences, where it served as a persistent challenge for those attempting to reconstruct the course of man's collective past.

Between the two camps there were, however, negotiators. As the new Darwinism gained the upper hand there were still those who saw complementary virtues in the older school of degeneration. There were, moreover, still facts to be explained, kinks in the historical chain, fossils which did not fit easily into the orderly strata of progress. It was in order to reconcile the two schools of thought and to defend the overall scheme of evolution against persistent evidences of degeneration that in 1871 Edward Burnett Tylor wrote his *Primitive Culture*.[35] The kingpin of this highly influential book was the Theory of Survivals, according to which human history was an eddying movement whose prime impetus was forwards but which occasionally filtered off into untypical sidetracks. When these sidetracks were found they could be regarded as "survivals" from previous phases of development which had obdurately resisted the impulse of change.

A useful way of imaging this theory is by way of one of the Victorians' – and Frazer's – favourite historical metaphors: the movement of the tides. History was like foam dithering on the margins of the sea as the tide rose. Occasionally pockets of water were siphoned off to the rear of the main gravitational pull. These isolated rock-pools were what Tylor called survivals. By sifting their waters we could learn much not merely about the factors trapping them into relative stagnation, but also about the nature of the tide itself.

It is clear that Tylor's view owed much to Victorian science with its emergent vision of a zigzagging but essentially upward pull from remote beginnings. It was a view very much in the air in the third quarter of the nineteenth century. Just as Edmund Gosse's naturalist father had sifted the contents of the rock-pools around Torbay in the 1860s hoping for manifestations of the earliest life on earth, so Tylor hoped to understand the purport of human history by staring at the backwaters abandoned during man's arduous ascent towards modernity.

Such a backwater was Nemi. Frazer's introduction to anthropology had been by way of Tylor's book, which the psychologist James Ward had lent him while on a walking-tour of Spain in 1883.[36] The book set a new light in his eyes, not simply because it introduced him to a new field, but because it supplied him with a fresh way of regarding the classics. Much of Frazer's classical work had to do with survivals of one sort or another. Pausanias's purpose had been to describe the monuments and shrines surviving in the Greece of his day, and his work is still invaluable to archaeologists attempting to piece together the surviving fragments of those same monuments. Indeed, the whole of classical scholarship, which Mark Pattison described as the "remains of literature", may from one point of view be regarded as a study of a body of survivals whose often ill-treated ruins it is the business of the scholar to reassemble and construe. The legends concerning the King of the Wood at Nemi were a prime example of this, and Diana's priest was just such a kink in the chain of historical events as Tylor had described.

It was because Tylor's theories depended crucially on a study of anachronistic patches in mankind's cultural development that they were to prove of such irresistible fascination to Frazer. Fully to comprehend the force of that fascination we have first to appreciate much not only about the ambiance of Europe at the time, but about Frazer's own immersion in the Scottish intellectual tradition. Frazer was a product of his times, but also of a strange collation of influences both within his immediate environment and beyond it. He was Scottish and a polymath (indeed, as any graduate of a Scottish university will affirm, this is no contradiction); he was curious and restrained by odd inhibitions; he was adventurous and conservative; daring and discreet; tactful and audacious in one breath. He was a nineteenth-century man whose principal stylistic and literary affinities lay in the previous century; an agnostic who yearned for faith; a scientist steeped in the humanities; a controversalist whose main line of attack lay in an irony often so subtle as to be almost invisible.

In one thing alone was he fairly typical of his generation: having sloughed off the trapping of religious affiliation, he spent his life attempting to reconcile himself to the change, seeking by scientific inquiry to assuage the wound. To see him as a sabre-toothed atheist or else complacent agnostic is a complete misunderstanding. The roots of Frazer's religious predicament lie deep, and we shall have to journey long and far before we find them. There is, however, one opening clue to which we shall return. The Victorian age had many ways of bodying forth its sense of religious loss, but few passages achieve the effect with more consummate a poignancy than the echo of the dying "Angelus" that wafts across the concluding paragraphs of *The Golden Bough*:

Once more we take the road to Nemi. It is evening, and as we climb the long slope of the Appian Way up to the Alban Hills, we look back and see the sky aflame with sunset, its golden glory resting like an aureole of a dying saint over Rome and touching with a crest of fire the dome of St Peter's. The sight once seen can never be forgotten, but we turn from it and pursue our darkling way along the mountain side, till we come to Nemi and look down on the lake in its deep hollow, now fast disappearing in the evening shadows. The place has changed but little since Diana received the homage of the worshippers in the sacred grove. The temple of the Sylvan goddess, indeed, has vanished and the King of the Woods no longer stands sentinel over the Golden Bough. But Nemi's woods are still green, and as the sunset fades above them to the west, there comes to us, borne on the swell of the wind, the sound of the church bells of Rome ringing the Angelus.[37]

This is the version in the Third Edition written in 1914, thirteen years after Frazer's first visit to Nemi in the January of 1901. When he included that image of the dying bells in the First Edition of 1890 he had neither heard those sounds nor seen that sight. Both were figments, and readers were not slow to point out that Nemi is too far from the outskirts of Rome for any footsore traveller to have heard that particular swell of sound subsiding like a plagal cadence on the wind. But despite the blunder Frazer stuck to it, intensifying the pathos with each successive edition. The first ends with the words *vive le roi!*; the third with the words *Ave Maria!* The image of bells itself comes, as we shall discover, from Ernest Renan,[38] and Frazer retained it because, though impossible, it meant much to him. It evoked, as the panoply of facts accumulated elsewhere through the many volumes of this much revised, much pondered-over work could not, certain intimations he meant ultimately to convey. It is crucial to his vision; but then as now, over the margins of the lake at Nemi, the bells of Rome do not sound.

CHAPTER II

THE EBBING TIDE

CHURCH BELLS, however, were very much a feature of Frazer's childhood. In the little lochside town of Helensburgh, where Daniel Frazer, the anthropologist's father, bought an out-of-town home in the 1860s whither at weekends the Frazers would flee the Glasgow streets, the Sabbath, rigorously maintained in the Frazer household, was punctuated by pealed invitations to worship and a round of prayer, Bible-reading and the singing of hymns. "The sound of sabbath bells, even in a foreign land," wrote Frazer at the age of seventy-nine, thinking of Spain and perhaps too of Nemi, "still touches a deep chord in my heart."[1] In later years Daniel Frazer drew in his horns and lived entirely in his little house by the Gareloch, where twice a Sunday the peals would ricochet across the lake.

The existence of Frazer *père* possessed twin poles, each stubbornly respected and, in the Calvinist ethos of the Lowlands, complementary. The first was the unremitting weekly grind of the Glasgow pharmacy which Daniel's elder brother had established on a family footing in 1830. Its principal branch was at 113, Buchanan Street, close to the rapidly expanding commercial heart of the city, a district of which Daniel Frazer himself left an affectionate, avuncularly anecdotal memoir.[2] The other was an adamant and completely trusting adherence to the beliefs and self-denying ordinances of the Free Church of Scotland, that plucky but now partially reconciled[3] splinter movement from the established Kirk, whose inauguration at the great Disruption of 1843 was to transform the religious map of Scotland for eighty years.

Commerce and faith, realism and soul-searching are impulses which run through the pages of Scottish history like a contrapuntal motif. In order to appreciate the compulsive pull exercised by these impulses over an entire people, we need to look back to before the Victorian age to movements which shook Scottish opinion in the wake of the Reformation, and through the seventeenth and eighteenth centuries. The Scottish Reformation of the mid sixteenth century was less, like the English Reformation which preceded it, the result of regal disaffection with the restraining hand of the papacy than a popular movement, incisively led though demotic in character, against a native-born but increasingly alienated crown. When John Knox parleyed with Mary, Queen of Scots, on the morrow of her return from France, over the rights of dissenting ministers and Her Majesty's persistence in celebrating the Mass in the chapel of the Palace of Holyroodhouse, he did so in the name of the Scottish people and in the face of leanings which were felt to militate against the forthright temper of the national mind. From the outset a major bone of contention was the celebration of what Knox had termed "the abominable idolatry of the Mass".[4]

"That the sacraments of the New Testament ought to be administered as they were instituted by Christ and nothing added or taken away from them": this was the peremptory demand of reformers inspired at one remove by Calvin and his insistence on the unencumbered workings of Grace. To later Scots, whether sceptics like David Hume, or like Andrew Lang inclining to sentimental archaism, this unwonted dedication to the austere essence of the faith was sometimes apt to appear extreme. Such later bifurcations of opinion, however, possessed their own kind of extremity. In the eighteenth century, with Edinburgh in the full flood of the Scottish Enlightenment, Hume could rail against "that hypocrisy and fanaticism which long infested the kingdom".[5] Fanaticism, sometimes spelt Enthusiasm, was a good Enlightenment word. A mere century later, with his head full of the Oxford Movement, Andrew Lang in his biography of Knox could rhapsodise, "He awoke to a passionate horror of his old routine of 'mumbled masses', of 'rites of human invention', whereof he had never known the poetry and the mystic charm. Had he known them, he could never have denied and detested them."[6] Yet deny these mysteries Knox did, and with them much of the ritual of the old faith, which, in the eyes of the Presbyterian Church he helped found, came ever after to reek of superstition, of that which had "stood over" from the ages of Rome's domination. Politically viewed – like the schisms which were to rend Daniel Frazer's world – the Scottish Reformation was a reaction against privilege in high places. Spiritually it was a reaction against the ritualistic elaboration of ancient custom and belief in favour of clarity, forthrightness and light.

From Frazer's point of view, it is the Humean inheritance which is important.[7] Frazer edited Addison and Cowper, and was addicted to the eighteenth century. Clarity, forthrightness and light are Enlightenment ideals, and nowhere had the lustre of eighteenth-century letters shone more brightly than in Edinburgh, which Smollett could describe in the 1760s as a "hotbed of genius". Brightest of all shone Hume, whose writing did more than anything to determine the Scottish philosophical tradition for the next hundred years. As a historian Hume had charted the consequences of religious enthusiasm in the England of the Stuarts, and received scant thanks from Whig or Tory in consequence. As a philosopher he was entranced by the problem of how we come to believe what we believe, and what justification can be found for so doing.

For Hume truth was a relative matter, even if his later Scottish disciples sometimes liked to make it appear otherwise. James Boswell has left us an unforgettable sketch of Hume dying in his house in St Andrew Square with all the stoical serenity of the perfect sceptic: "He said he had never entertained any belief in Religion since he had began to read Locke and Clarke. . . . I asked him if the thought of Annihilation never gave him any uneasiness . . . he said not in the least."[8]

It was this amiable and accommodating temperament which thirty. years earlier Hume had applied in his *Treatise of Human Nature* to the pitfalls of human belief and human credulity. For belief was still belief, and non-belief still non-belief, whether in Heaven or in the behaviour of billiard balls. It was to the billiard balls that Hume preferred to apply himself. Why when we cannon off a stationary ball do we expect a necessary and inevitable deflection? Just because we expect it. The grand determinant of belief is custom. Custom is governed in its turn by the Association of Ideas, a concept Hume borrowed from Hartley but made his own.[9] Ideas are derived from impressions, imprints left on the mind by the minutiae of experience. For one idea to give rise to another three conditions must be met, either singly or in combination: "contiguity" (that is, proximity), "resemblance" and "cause and effect". Belief was what occurred when the peculiar permutation of such conditions in a given train of thought gave rise to a sensation of conviction, which might be justified or not depending on the strengths of the links in the chain. Justified belief was founded on a correct perception of cause and effect regularly occurring. Thus the repeated experience of observing the impact of a cannoning billiard ball would give rise to a justified expectation as to its behaviour when struck again. Looser combinations of ideas, to which in his *Treatise* Hume gave the name "credulity", were formed by proximity or resemblance unsupported by any causal inference. It is highly significant that the lion's share of the examples Hume cites of such credulity are taken from the realm of religion, and more especially of Catholic ceremonial.

Between Hume's explanation of the way convictions lodge themselves in the mind and Frazer's conception of magic, which he took to be the guiding principle of all primitive belief, the connections run far and deep.

Frazer had studied Hume's *Treatise* at Glasgow University in the 1860s under the tutelage of John Veitch. From Veitch the line runs back unbroken to Hume, since Veitch edited the philosophical lectures of Sir William Hamilton, who had in his turn published the definitive edition of Thomas Reid, whose so-called "Common Sense school" represented a pragmatic application of Hume's teaching purged of its scepical and solipsistic overtones. Like Hume, all these men were preoccupied with how we get to know things. And, even if in the intervening century they had come to modify the sublime iconoclasm of some of Hume's conclusions, the vocabulary of the Association of Ideas is common to all of them.

Vital as it is to stress Frazer's dependence on his teachers, it is still more important to recognise his indebtedness to the classic formulations of eighteenth-century empiricism. It would be no exaggeration to state that, without the theory of knowledge which Frazer derived from Hume, the whole carefully laid structure of *The Golden Bough* would fall to the ground. Hume was concerned with the question of how polite eighteenth-century man made sense of his environment. Frazer in his turn was concerned with how early man made sense of his, whether in Nemi, in ancient Egypt or in Buganda. It was essential that the principles established should be the same in all cases, as Frazer was attempting to understand *Homo sapiens*, not any particular local variant of man. To provide the necessary uniformity Frazer needed a coherent and consistent epistemology or theory of knowledge. This theoretical underpinning to his work, which grew in prominence with successive editions, Frazer found fully formed – or almost fully formed – in Hume.

"If my analysis of the magician's logic is correct," wrote Frazer, "its two great principles turn out to be merely two different misapplications of the association of ideas."[10] The two principles as Frazer expounds them are the Law of Similarity and the Law of Contact, and both are forms of illusion. The Ojebway Indians inflicted injuries on the effigies of their enemies because the effigy and the enemy resembled one another;[11] the Australian aborigines thought that any harm which befell an extracted tooth would of necessity be passed on to the owner, since the tooth had once been in intimate contact with his gums.[12] Both are mistakes, but, because the mental habits on which they depend are commonplace, both are comprehensible. Each proceeds from a simple-minded confusion of elementary logical relations, on which the magician then proceeds to erect a superstructure of equal mistaken sorcery. Frazer sets out these faulty logical relations in a table. To illuminate the origins of his system, it will be instructive to set his table[13] alongside another illustrating Hume's:

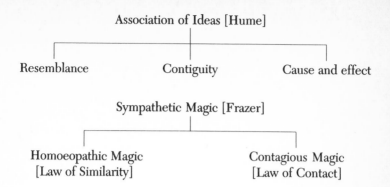

Association of Ideas [Hume]

Resemblance   Contiguity   Cause and effect

Sympathetic Magic [Frazer]

Homoeopathic Magic   Contagious Magic
[Law of Similarity]   [Law of Contact]

Frazer's Laws of Similarity and Contact are none other than Hume's resemblance and contiguity under a new guise. The only condition missing is cause and effect, since Frazer believed this to be the bedrock of science, and science had not begun its reign until the fallibility of magic had become apparent, and the claims of religion, which followed magic, had likewise dissolved.

From Hume Frazer inherited both a system of knowledge and a habit of irony based on a conviction of the profound folly of the generality of mankind. Both men share the second of these characteristics with Edward Gibbon, whose urbanely witty accounts of the early Christian Church are similarly barbed. If Frazer's irony occasionally possesses a sharper edge, it is because he was heir not only to the polite scepticism of his Enlightenment forebears, but also to the nineteenth century's more confident assurance of its own powers. The Scottish philosophical tradition in particular had grown tighter and less tolerant as Hume's conception of causality, which was no more than a modified form of uncertainty, had hardened into the mechanistic determinism of the Victorians. Hume's delicate, almost whimsical poise was out of fashion. "He must be either a fool," growled Thomas Reid, "or want to make a fool out of me, that would reason me out of my senses."[14] And, while William Hamilton held the ultimate to be unknowable, he was quite sure that our perceptions of the world we inhabit are grounded on *terra firma*. At Glasgow Frazer had studied physics at the feet of the magisterial Lord Kelvin,[15] who had bequeathed him a "conception of the physical universe as regulated by exact and absolutely unvarying laws of Nature expressible in mathematical formulas" which he was never inclined to question. It is in contrast to such certainties that the practical wisdom of ancient man occasionally struck him as pitiful. Pitiful it may have been, but it was a variety of applied knowledge none the less: botched mechanics we might call it. It is this conviction of certain tramways of thought tunnelling beneath the operations of the human intelligence at different levels and in diverse contexts which ultimately unites Frazer with the founders of British empiricism such as Hume.

In Scotland the advance of empirical inquiry had a more immediate purpose in view: the formulation of a critique of institutions. Scotland was taking stock of itself: its history, its traditions, its statutes. It is no accident that beginning with Hume, who briefly studied law in Edinburgh and later became Librarian of the Faculty of Advocates, a high proportion of Scotland's intelligentsia trained as lawyers: William Hamilton, Walter Scott, even (at his father's insistence) Frazer himself.[16] Law provided the perfect professional plinth for a gentleman; it was also an absorbing pursuit in its own right. Hamilton took time off from his metaphysical preoccupations to defend his baronetcy before the Sheriff of Edinburgh.[17] The Law of Inheritance, complicated by the Scottish clan system, was one intriguing branch of a legal system then as now distinct from the English, and drawing much of its cogency from a close attention to jurisprudence and the traditions of Roman law. An ample bridgehead thus lay open from legal studies to ancient history, and increasingly, as a comparative view of institutions took hold, to anthropology. Foremost of those who crossed this bridge was the Edinburgh advocate and amateur sociologist John Ferguson M'Lennan (1827–81), whose brilliant but eccentric intelligence was to cast a deep spell over Frazer.

M'Lennan's early speculations as to the origins of human law appeared in the eighth edition of the *Encyclopaedia Britannica*, that monument to Scottish erudition founded by the firm of Bell and Macfarquhar in 1771. The encyclopaedia's first edition, compiled by the Edinburgh printer and polymath William Smellie, had itself contained a lengthy article on law dealing exclusively with the Scottish legal system, of which it had noted, "the civil or Roman law, though they are not to be deemed perhaps proper parts of our written law, have undoubtedly had the greatest influence in Scotland". By 1864, when M'Lennan came to compose his own article, the received view of the Roman legal system had received a severe jolt from Henry Maine, Professor of Jurisprudence at the Inns of Court and later at Cambridge, who in his book *Ancient Law*[18] of 1861 had grounded his interpretation of the surviving codes on an analysis of the Roman family, and especially of the extended family or *gens*. It was this view, founded, he thought, on too narrow a reading of prehistory, that M'Lennan undertook to counter – first in the *Britannica*; then, more decisively, in his book *Primitive Marriage*[19] of 1865, the fountainhead of a great anthropological tradition.

Maine's view, still a starting-point in jurisprudential discussion,[20] had been that Roman jurists had simply enshrined existing social rights, which, originally implicit in the relative status of citizens, were then reinforced by a system of binding written agreements or contracts. The relative status thus embodied was based on the historical realities of early Italian life, in particular on the veritable supremacy, or *patria potestas*, of the male. No descent ever occurred through the mother, whose position, though modified in the provisions of later periods, especially under the Republic, remained throughout subservient. M'Lennan was not so sure. In particular had his attention been arrested by certain customs travellers in North Africa and the Near East had noted among the Arabs. The Bedouin still occasionally observe a wedding-custom whereby the groom and his closest companions ride over to the bride's encampment and stage a mock elopement, normally on horseback. Originally this act of mock capture may have been performed in deadly earnest: women, whom pre-Islamic infanticide had rendered scarce, were at a premium, and marriage partners could only perhaps be secured by sporadic raids outside the clan. At this stage all marriage must have been exogamous, a term M'Lennan coined for unions outside the kinship group; later they became exogamous by law. "It was as if", wrote M'Lennan in muted horror, "a Fraser might not marry a Fraser, nor a McIntosh a McIntosh." The extreme scarcity of partners may also have induced men to share. The polyandry thus resulting had, M'Lennan thought, been of two kinds, depending on whether the men were or were not brothers. In Tibet they always were, and M'Lennan therefore adopted the term "Tibetan" to describe fraternal polyandry, which Strabo seems to have observed among the early Arabs. Among the Nair of Ceylon, however, the husbands were unrelated. Here M'Lennan noted two different forms. Sometimes the men repaired to the woman's own village and resided with her in her tent, which M'Lennan called "beena" polyandry. Alternatively the woman uprooted herself and settled in the men's encampment, where she installed herself as an exogamous member of their community; this M'Lennan called the "deega" form. It was the institution of "beena" – that is, matrilocal – marriage which Frazer was later to find so suggestive.

Whatever form polyandry took, there was, however, one remarkable recurrent factor. Because the wife was held in common, paternity was uncertain and descent could as a result only be accounted through her. M'Lennan was not the first to observe this frequent characteristic of primitive societies: the palm in this respect must go to the Swiss jurist Jacob Bachofen, who in his work *Das Mutterrecht* of 1861, the year coincidentally of Maine's book, had described mother kin as occurring across a wide spectrum of ancient societies.[21] So preoccupied had Bachofen been with the mythological ramifications of this system that he had, however, completely failed to notice its social rationale. It was left to M'Lennan to point out the connection between matriliny and polyandry. Later, as we shall see, it was to transpire that in many early societies, even those which did not practise polyandry, children were deemed the physical offspring of their mother alone. Of this extraordinary contention, over which controversy was to rage for another seventy years, M'Lennan was the precursor. During his tragically foreshortened career M'Lennan was to feed Frazer with many notions – exogamy, totemism, certain facets of taboo – but none of these concerns proved more fruitful or more beset with thorns than the Theory of Matriliny.

What possible light, a naïve modern commentator might ask, could the abstruse and largely hypothetical customs of the early Arabs shed on the august institutions of the Roman law? In order to understand it, you have to fall back on Tylor's Theory of Survivals. If human history was analogous to a set of geological strata laid on top of one another, and, if customs and traditions were like fossils buried therein, the best way to reconstruct prehistory was to look at the fossils and compare them. It mattered not if the fossils came from Ceylon or from Tibet: at some time or another that particular historical stratum must have bent round and joined on to the land mass of Roman history. There was continuity somewhere, even if the layers were not absolutely adjacent, or, as Hume might have put it, contiguous.

If that was true then you had to rethink an awful lot, not merely the history of the Roman people but all early documents into the bargain, the Bible included. The same stratum must some time or other have swept round and engulfed the Jewish people. The book of Judges describes the sons of Benjamin abducting the daughters of Shiloh in a manner strangely reminiscent of bride capture, and Deuteronomy 20 provides for something that looks uncannily like exogamy.[22] As for polyandry, M'Lennan had rested part of his case on another verse in Deuteronomy:

> If brethren dwell together, and one of them die, and have no child, the wife of the dead shall not marry without unto a stranger: her husband's brother shall go in unto her, and take her to him to wife, and perform the duty of an husband's brother unto her.[23]

Thus the ancient Hebrews honoured the custom of the levirate marriage in death if not in life; the Law had proclaimed it.

The trouble was that, if you started construing Scripture in this way, all sorts of uncomfortable insights were likely to come to light. The Israelites were supposed to be God's chosen people, the custodians of his Covenant, to that extent at least outside history. The five books of Moses were supposed to be the Word of God, his message to his people, not the random product of a course of human evolution that had thrown up equivalent customs in other places. The searchlight of scientific inquiry applied to the history of law could illuminate existing institutions, even Scottish institutions, in a fresh and instructive way. Applied to the text of Holy Scripture it was likely to lead to heterodoxy, if not downright apostasy.

One will never understand the rumpus that such a prospect was to cause in Scotland in the 1870s unless one takes a backward glance at developments which had transformed the religious complexion of the country over the previous quarter-century. The Scottish Reformation was in trouble. Dissent had appeared in the ranks, leading to the first of the multiple schisms which were to rend the fabric of the Scottish Kirk for many a long year. The first rumblings were heard in the late 1830's, and had to do with the vexed question of patronage. The Kirk was proud of its independence, its integrity of principle founded on the Westminster Confession, above all of its self-government under the Assembly and, at local level, the presbyters of each congregation. But, for all that, it was an established church, at the beck and call of the civil power. Most galling of all, its ministers were not elected by the body of presbyters of each parish, but imposed from above by local lairds, often in the teeth of much local misgiving. For the purists, who held the memory of Knox's Church dear, this had long seemed insupportable.

The purists had found a shrewed advocate in Thomas Chalmers, Professor of Moral Philosophy at St Andrews and subsequently of Theology at Edinburgh, at whose prompting the controversy over "non-intrusion" waxed fiercer. Disestablishment seemed an impossibility, compromise unthinkable. In vain were counsels of moderation urged. Like Moses of old, Chalmers would lead his people into the wilderness.

"In leaving the Establishment," wrote William Hamilton sardonically in the fatal year of 1843, "in resigning the secure emoluments and respected rank – in turning from the familiar sanctuaries, from the homes endeared to you by old attachments and casting yourselves, your wives and children, on the inadequate and precarious charities of a new, a

partial, perhaps a temporary enthusiasm – how can you more conspic-
uously manifest the strength of your convictions, and pious confidence
in the justice of your cause?"[24]

Yet renounce all of this they did: 451 ministers out of a total of 1,200,
a third of the whole. And second in that audacious exodus as it filed out
of the Assembly Hall strode Sir James Frazer's paternal great-uncle,
Ninian Bannatyne. Frazer, who learned of these momentous events at
Daniel Frazer's knee, has left us an awestruck account of the moment
when the faith in which he was reared took root:

> The final separation of the two churches took place in the Assembly
> Hall at Edinburgh. When the dissident clergy, resigning their livings
> and casting themselves on Providence and the world, trooped out of
> the hall, the Moderator of the Assembly led the way and he was
> followed by Mr Ninian Bannatyne, for as private chaplain to the
> Marquis of Bute, then the Queen's representative at the Assembly,
> Mr Bannatyne took precedence over all the other clergy. In our
> childhood my elder sister Christina and I paid a visit to the good old
> man at his manse in Old Cummock, where he lived alone, for he never
> married. I remember him vividly as a courteous gentleman of the
> ancient school with ruddy countenance, finely cut features, clean
> shaven, and a most gracious and benign manner. He was the only man
> I ever knew who used to call my father by the familiar name of
> Dan. . . .[25]

It was eleven years before the anthropologist's birth in Brandon Place,
Glasgow, that these convulsions occurred, and yet the tale formed part
of the family mythology, familiar as cups and saucers. Daniel Frazer's
people too were chosen of God. Yet it would be wrong to see the great
Disruption of 1843 as simply a dispute over Church government: there
were hard-fought matters of doctrine at stake. Thomas Chalmers had
been a Calvinist of an obdurate and unyielding temper, severe in his
notions of Election and of Grace. Fundamentalist in their literal reverence
for Holy Writ, frugal in their worldly tastes, the adherents of the Free
Kirk were at odds with the world even as they strove to serve it. The
truth, and only truth must be taught. Seven hundred free manses were
established and maintained out of the collection plate, six hundred Free
Church schools.[26] Nor could the training of ministers be entrusted to
the unregenerate. New College, Edinburgh, was founded to raise pastors
for the flock; the presence of William Hamilton as a professor at the
city's university – Hamilton with his quaint Kantian antinomies that

sounded so like agnosticism – was enough to frighten them into endowing a new philosophical chair for the instruction of the elect. Soon other Free Church colleges sprang up in St Andrews and at Aberdeen.

It is to an erstwhile Professor of Oriental Languages and Old Testament Exegesis at the last of these institutions that *The Golden Bough* is gratefully dedicated.

William Robertson Smith was the single largest influence in Frazer's life, and it behoves us to dwell awhile on the wonderful concatenation of events that brought them together. A fatalist might say that they were made for one another: so alike in upbringing, so different in temperament, so compatible in scholarly taste and in their doggedly honest approach to academic inquiry. But, though slighter in frame, Smith was undoubtedly the bolder personality: effervescent, outgoing – a real bearhug of a man. In an early portrait, painted at Aberdeen but now hanging in the Combination Room of Christ's College, Cambridge, where in his latter years he was Fellow, he stares out at one from his table-side, the eyes direct and challenging, willing one to engage him in argument.[27] Was this how he challenged Frazer? A later photograph, taken in his set of rooms at Christ's, has him tireder, broken by years of conflict with his ecclesiastical superiors. But still the neck is erect and inquisitive, the expression as he peruses the volume before him quizzical. Around him leather-bound books rise ceilingwards. The garb is somehow clerical and yet redolent of the East; oriental rugs drape the desks. The cut of his features has a concentration and yet idiosyncrasy that reminds one of a recondite, possibly heretical rabbi. Any moment, one feels, he will cast the volume aside and dash over to Trinity, where the fledgling Frazer, initially a timid author and difficult to get going, would be struggling to put pen to paper. Without Smith's spirited intervention, it was doubtful in the early years if he ever would.

Like Frazer, Smith was of the orthodox gone astray. Dissent seems to have been built into the Free Church tradition: one is reminded how rebellions foster one another. He was eight years Frazer's senior, a vital age difference, the sort that divides an elder from a younger brother. It was from his younger brother George, who died tragically on the eve of going up to Cambridge, that Smith inherited his own academic mantle. Did he seek a younger brother in Frazer? Certainly he was the sort of man whose deepest alliances tend invariably towards the fraternal.

In the Free Church manse of Keig and Tough in the vale of Alford, where Smith first saw the light, prolific mental growths were engendered. The father, Dr William Pirie Smith, was ambitious for his sons, their minds as well as souls. Smith was set to work to master the Hebrew characters at the age of six. Entering Aberdeen University at the age of fifteen, he had the sceptical hangovers of the Humean tradition drummed out of him by Alexander Bain, Professor of Rhetoric and Logic, who set him to read John Stuart Mill's *Examination of Sir William Hamilton's Philosophy*.[28] Thenceforward, Smith's epistemological opinions, like Frazer's, were strictly empiricist. At twenty he entered New College, Edinburgh, to train for the ministry. The atmosphere of the place seems to have been strenuous though given to digression. The Chair of Hebrew and old Testament Exegesis was held by John Duncan, who taught his students "everything but Hebrew". Instead he dilated on the structure of the sacred books, which, conquering an early tendency to scepticism, he now regarded as masterpieces of organic organisation and divine authorship. For Professor Duncan, the scribes of the Old Testament had been stenographers taking down a perfect text. There were, however, snags: interpolations, repetitions, anomalies of phrase and tone. These Dr Davidson, who was appointed Duncan's assistant when it dawned upon the authorities that the good professor did not actually know much Hebrew, argued away by suggesting that God had changed his mind. It was Davidson who in accounting for the textual scrabble of the book of Job devised the theory of "divine afterthoughts". God was a word-processor; cutting and pasting were his business.

It is exciting and oddly moving to contemplate these Free Church intellects of the late 1860s stirring in their chains. The spirit of criticism was afoot, thought was on the wing, and yet and yet . . . . Davidson tried to reconcile textual exegesis with fidelity to the spirit by speaking of a "believing ciritcism". One problem was that for a budding orientalist Scotland was a backwater. The Mecca was Germany, and it was in Germany that Smith thus spent his summer vacations: not in Tübingen, where he might have got into hot water, but in Bonn, where his Hebrew improved. And then on 28 October 1869 mental fodder of the sort he needed was suddenly on offer at home. The next day Smith wrote back to the paternal manse full of the sort of reverie to which budding intellects are sometimes prone:

> I dined with Tait yesterday, with Crum Brown and M'Lennan, an advocate. There is a new talking club to be set up, of which Tait and these two are to be members . . . the object being to have one man at least well up in every conceivable subject. The selection is to be

somewhat strict, so that I was surprised when it was proposed last night to table my name. It might be very useful to belong to such a thing: the attendance being not compulsory, and the meeting twice a week. The thing could not be burdensome, while the circle of acquaintance opened up would be the very best.[29]

That was it: M'Lennan and Smith had met. Two of the liveliest minds in Scotland: what would one give to have been a fly on the wall of the Edinburgh Talking Club, 90a, George Street, where twice a week these fiery intellects clashed? Each man offered his discipline: M'Lennan's was law and, since the publication of *Primitive Marriage* five years previously, the early history of nations; Smith's was Hebrew and the ancient tongues. And remember M'Lennan was forty-two; Smith a mere twenty-three. Smith could not have known it, but he was to devote his best energies to vindicating M'Lennan's hypotheses in the realm of Semitic studies. In the meantime, M'Lennan was the luminary, Smith a volatile outer planet whose elliptical courses had still some way to run.

But, for all that, they could not agree. For M'Lennan was a freethinker, Smith what, despite all the provocations to which he was later subjected, he was always to remain: a believing evangelical Christian. While M'Lennan turned his attention to the problem of totemism, and Frazer, who had left Larchfield Academy that summer, matriculated at Glasgow University, Smith continued on his dutiful way. A year later, on being appointed to his Chair in Aberdeen, he was ordained into the Free Church ministry, and delivered his inaugural sermon on the theme "What history teaches us to seek in the Bible". Therein, of course, lay the rub: it was not so much what history taught one to seek which was the problem as what, having looked, one might find.

For his part M'Lennan was in little doubt. He had applied his Humean intellect to the sacred text and found precisely what he was looking for: bride capture, totemism and sorcery. Smith was intrigued but torn. One can feel the tension in this man's soul: the Free Church college all day, and on those precious, head-spinning evenings the genuine free-for-all of the Edinburgh Talking Club. There he met George Henry Lewes, George Eliot's lover and the editor of the *Fortnightly Review*. The very month of the Club's founding Lewes had thrown open the columns of the *Fortnightly* to M'Lennan to air his latest fad, totemism.[30] Thus had the foundation stone of one of Frazer's later enthusiams been well and truly laid. In the meantime M'Lennan had applied himself to the question of sorcery, and was fast reducing the mystical practices of the Old Testament to a sort of white magic. For Smith, respectfully, this was too much. He wrote passionately to M'Lennan, wrestling over all these Tylorian survivals his friend had discovered littering the Pentateuch:

> The important thing is that the Israelites once used such things, but that Mosaism killed them, and knew itself opposed to them. . . . Does a nation in the course of nature pass through a revulsion of feeling like this, and that at once as far as the principle goes, tho' not without stages in the application of the principle? Remember I don't deny that traces of nature religion are to be found in the Old Testament, only the Old Testament religion did not, I hold, grow out of, but confronted and destroyed these. That is a question for scientific inquiry which we may attack from our opposite points of view without cursing one another.[31]

Smith could not afford to curse. As his orthodoxy bore professional fruit, in the gaudy workshop of his heart he struggled to sustain the integrity of Scripture. While M'Lennan worried his ideas further, and the twenty-three-year-old James Frazer took the high road to Cambridge, Smith struggled to perfect his Arabic at Göttingen under Professor Lagarde, Wellhausen's predecessor. His course seemed set. A reputation as one of Europe's leading orientalists loomed: daring in intellect, safe within the fold.

He reckoned without the Auld Reekie. In their offices at 6, North Bridge, Edinburgh, Messrs. A. & C. Black were plotting the ninth edition of the *Encyclopaedia Britannica*. Who would cover religion? "There's a wee young man in Aberdeen . . . ." And so the commission came that worked Smith's undoing. Tome by tome, with alphabetical relentlessness, the volumes of the *Britannica* dropped down and crushed him. "A" was for "Angels", "Apostle", "Aramaic Languages", for "Ark of the Covenant" and "Assidaeans". That was enough to be going on with: imagine a man trained in Mill's empiricism jousting with angels. Like soap-bubbles the angels dissolved, and meanwhile, like a villain in the wings, "B" lay in wait: "Baal", "Babel" and, horror of horrors, "Bible".

It was the Bible that finished him. There is no need to rehearse Smith's contentions in the fatal article here: the officials of the Free Church in their own time did that thoroughly enough.[32] All that Smith did in simple unaffected language was to set out the conclusions of the Higher Criticism, which in Germany had been conceded for decades. The books of the Pentateuch were not by Moses but by some later, post-Babylonian hand. Deuteronomy was late stuff, rationalisation after the event. The Epistles were not raised on the platform of the Gospels, but *vice versa*.

The Bible in sum was not the orderly outcome of systematic godly dictation, but a hotchpotch composed over many generations by a people who were gradually, and with many backslidings, blundering their way toward the light.

None of this now seems inconsistent with the most scrupulous faith, but in the mid 1870s, in Scotland, it was news. Smith's article appeared on 7 December 1875. On 15 April a newspaper article appeared in the *Edinburgh Courant* attacking it as apostasy. Smith bided his time. He had plenty to be getting on with, having just been appointed to the supervisory Committee for the Revision of the Authorised Version. The Committee met in London, where Smith spent the evenings pleasantly dining with M'Lennan at the Savile Club and little dreaming of the thunderstorm that was about to break around his ears.

In Aberdeen meanwhile they had been having kittens. The new principal was a man named Dr Brown, who held the Chair of New Testament but had not read a book in years. He read the newspapers though, and soon his eyebrows were as high as his theology low. On 14 February 1878 he summoned the people. Smith was arraigned before the Free Presbytery of Aberdeen on a charge of impugning the purity of Scripture. A modern Luther had nailed his theses to the door.

They met in the hall of the Free West Church to decide his fate under a steel grey sky. The place was packed as Dr Brown rose from his seat and, with the rotundity of a litigious people, read the charge:

That whereas the publishing and promulgating of opinions which contradict or are opposed to the doctrine of the immediate inspiration, infallible truth, and divine authority of the Holy Scriptures, or any part or parts thereof, as set forth in the Scriptures themselves and in the Confession of Faith, and to the doctrines of prophets and angels there set forth; as also, the publishing and promulgating of opinions which are in themselves of a dangerous or unsettling tendency in their bearing on the doctrine of the immediate inspiration, infallible truth, and divine authority of the Holy Scriptures, or any parts thereof . . . .[33]

And so on and so forth, for several pages. Smith's career in Scotland was finished. Three years, two trials and thirty-six tracts later, he was dismissed from his Chair.

To us, with the advantage of hindsight, it is obvious what had happened: the Free Church's insistence on the unvarnished truth had turned in on itself, and the light had gone out. Meanwhile Smith's was a modern predicament: he was a much-published academic without a job. A. & C.

Black came to the rescue by appointing him joint editor of the *Britannica*. Then in October 1882 – *o felix culpa!* – a miracle occurred. The Lord Almoner's Reader in Arabic at Cambridge was assassinated in Sinai – by an Arab. Whether Edward Palmer's pronunciation was at fault we do not know, but he had been on a political mission for Gladstone. Smith was appointed as his replacement and was on his way once more: to Cambridge.[34]

As he took the train south he cannot have known that a momentous encounter awaited him in the Combination Room of Trinity College, where, while waiting for a substantive fellowship to crop up elsewhere, he was to reside as a mere Gentleman Commoner. Three years earlier, on completing a dissertation on the dialogues of Plato, James Frazer had been elected a Research Fellow of Trinity for a probationary period of six years. Almost certainly Smith had not heard of him, and despite the brouhaha in the far north it is highly doubtful if he had ever heard of Smith. The meeting led on Frazer's part to a kind of intellectual infatuation that was to revolutionise his somewhat parochial classical interests and convert him into the most famous, the most notorious anthropologist the world has ever known. *The Golden Bough* was on the tracks.

CHAPTER III

A MEETING OF MINDS

IT WAS a Cambridge whose physical reality had changed little in centuries, but whose academic arrangements few today would recognise. As a young Fellow of Trinity, Frazer occupied a set of rooms overlooking the Great Court on a staircase whose previous residents had included Isaac Newton and Lord Macaulay.[1] It was Macaulay who had set the author of *The Golden Bough* perhaps his most tuneful text when in "The Battle of Lake Regillus" he had described the mustering of the Latins:

> From every warlike city
> That boasts the Latian name,
> Foredoomed to dogs and vultures,
> That gallant army came;
> From Setia's purple vineyards,
> From Norba's ancient wall,
> From the white streets of Tusculum,
> The proudest of them all;
> From where the Witch's fortress
> O'erhangs the dark blue seas,
> From the still glassy lake that sleeps
> Beneath Aricia's trees –
> Those trees in whose grim shadow
> The ghastly priest doth reign,
> The priest who slew the slayer,
> And shall himself be slain –[2]

The King of the Wood was an old Trinity conundrum.

If he was a conundrum at once classical and anthropological, that too was very much in keeping. In the Cambridge of the 1880s our hard-and-fast divisions between disciples would have made little sense. In order to appreciate the ambiance which made Frazer's peculiar combination of interests possible, it is necessary to think oneself back into a setting in which the young man's supervisor, Henry Jackson, Praelector in Ancient Philosophy and later Regius Professor of Greek, could correspond with a friend in such terms as these:

> While I write, a spider is crawling over my table. I may not kill it because, as a member of the Winchester governing body, I am a Wykehamist, and spiders are Wykehamists also. I like these traditions.[3]

Jackson, you see, was a governor of Winchester College, and spiders were a Wykehamist totem. There was nothing odd about a Professor of Greek having one foot planted in ethnology. Reminiscing to his brother about his own undergraduate years in the Trinity of the 1860s Jackson could likewise recall,

> J. F. M'Lennan's book *Primitive Marriage* – an epoch-making book – came out in 1865, but father had it, and I annexed his copy and preached M'Lennan versus Maine (with modifications) to the Apostolic Society.[4]

If your training was in the classics, ethnology and law were well within arm's reach. A mere fifteen years before Jackson's matriculation you could not take the classical Tripos without first graduating in mathematics. Jackson's field, like Frazer's, was human knowledge.

It will be instructive to dwell a little on Jackson, who was Frazer's mentor well before Robertson Smith swept onto the scene. Long before Frazer succumbed to Smith, he had succumbed to philosophy. Jackson's own overriding passion was Plato, his lectures on whom were one of the high points of the college year. So determined was he to communicate his love for those matchless dialogues that in his eighties, and long past official retirement, he had to be carried into the room to lecture upon the *Republic* and the *Timaeus*. Between 1872 and 1882 – between, that is to say, the academic reforms of the Gladstone government and the eventual introduction of the divided Tripos – Jackson had lectured on those beloved texts to every classics student within the University. As a somewhat mature first-year undergraduate of twenty-one James Frazer had sat enthralled by those masterly expositions in the academic year of 1874–5,[5] and it was on the Platonic dialogues, or more narrowly on Jackson's view of those dialogues, that four years later he was to write a dissertation for his fellowship.[6]

If a young don was seeking a role model he did not have to look much further than Jackson, whose florid features still stare down at the reader as he mounts the stairwell towards Trinity's Wren Library. The most clubbable and kindly of men, he also beams at one in reproduction from one of the lower staircases of the Athenaeum. That clubbability, that unpretentious willingness to take all and sundry, including a shy young Glaswegian, under his wing, was of Jackson's essence. In hall after dinner he would make his rounds of the tables and invite the privileged to smoke in his rooms until the small hours. Here, especially on Sundays, astonished undergraduates could observe the great man dispense totem talk and tobacco, or in later years overhear A. E. Housman, Kennedy Professor of Latin, openly insult Charles Villiers Stanford, Professor of Music, whose Irish blarney had once more got the better of him. In this exclusively male preserve, this haphazard and recondite snuggery, the normally reticent Frazer flowered.

Diverse ingredients go into the making of an individual mind, and for Frazer the Cambridge of the 1880s perhaps possessed just the right combination of breadth and narrowness. For, if in certain respects the Cambridge of the 1880s had the advantage over us in catholicity of knowledge, socially it was still a hermitage. At least Jackson was married, and that had not been possible for long. It is a daunting thought that, before the final repeal of the University Test Acts in 1871, neither Frazer nor Smith could have pursued college careers, since they would have been debarred as noncomformists. Not that much earlier, Frazer would have been obliged to take Holy Orders. For centuries universities had been staffed exclusively by men of the cloth who had devoted celibate lives to poring over the profane productions of the classics. In such circumstances it is arguable that something like *The Golden Bough*, cloistered in origin yet courageous in its relativism, had always been in the making. If at the turn of the twentieth century it had not materialised, it would surely have had to have been invented.

What had held such speculations in check in the short term was the approach to classical texts traditional at Cambridge. Broadly speaking this had been palaeographic and philological: the productions of the ancients were looked upon primarily as assemblages of words. In the early eighteenth century Richard Bentley, then Master of Trinity, had expended himself on a painstaking recension of the Roman poet–astronomer Manilius, work which Frazer's friend and colleague A. E. Housman was to continue well into the twentieth. To get a corrupt text right was the thing, and Housman for one considered it the ultimate test of scholarly mettle.

To its later disparagers this Lower Criticism, as it came to be known, was occasionally to seem narrow and sterile, but it was the *sine qua non* of any deeper understanding of an author's intentions. On its foundation the Higher Criticism – the systematic relation of textual variants to the intellectual and social history of the peoples concerned – was later able to erect a superstructure of interpretation that bore fruit in fields far beyond the classics. For years, however, the Higher Criticism was thought to be the preserve of the Germans, and English scholars fought shy of it. It was such German-inspired Higher Criticism, applied to the texts of Holy Writ, which had got Robertson Smith into such trouble in Aberdeen. In Cambridge, even in the calmer waters of Graeco-Roman literature, it had been attempted but patchily.

One of the few to take the plunge had been Jackson. What had induced him to do so was less in this instance his abiding interest in folklore than the peculiar difficulties presented by Plato. Faced with those majestic dialogues it was difficult to be purely philological, for though entirely consistent within themselves they were, it was agreed on all sides, scarcely consistent with one another. There were two ways out of this difficulty. One, favoured by Plato's greatest Victorian translator, Jowett of Balliol, was to regard each dialogue as *sui generis*: "The dialogues of Plato are like poems, isolated and separate works."[7] The other, Jackson's method, was to try to trace a development throught them. When in 1879 Jackson was appointed co-editor of the *Journal of Philology* he undertook two projects: the first was to open the pages of the journal to matters ethnographic; the second was himself to publish a series of articles interpreting the Platonic dialogues as a philosophical sequence.[8] To the orthodox this approach was heresy: when Jowett reissued his *Dialogues of Plato* in 1888 he devoted a large part of his Preface to refuting it. But to Jackson's enthusiastic young pupil Frazer, reared in the Scottish epistemological tradition, the historical method was a lodestar to steer by.

Jackson had taken as his cue for the unravelling of Plato's thought a much-disputed passage in the *Metaphysics* in which Aristotle describes how, brought up on the Pythagoreans and their commitment to the Heraclitan vision of perpetual flux, Socrates had later attempted to transcend this by fixing on certain unchanging categories of knowledge.[9] If all was flux, then the world would be incomprehensible: you needed to classify the universe simply in order to describe it. Thus had come about the Theory of Ideas, which in Socrates was merely a means of sub-dividing experience and, through experience, knowledge. It was Plato's achievement – and arguably his undoing – to take these categories of knowing as existent beings. In Frazer's summary, "the Socratic theory of knowing became the Platonic theory of being".

But, according to Jackson, no sooner was this system formulated than it started to break down. In the first place, the categories of knowledge are arbitrary: what you call a quadruped I call a pest. Secondly, it is difficult to see how ideas of relation – upness; downness – can possess existence save as concepts in the mind. Thus was the confident ontology of the *Republic* forced to yield to the more sceptical inquiry of the *Parmenides* and the *Timaeus*. Plato's early realism gave way to the more feasible idealism of what Jackson termed his Later Theory of Ideas. In Frazer's characteristically more vivid prose, "In the deepening shadows the dreamer awoke, and behold it was a dream."[10]

When Frazer came to write his Fellowship dissertation in 1879 – the year of Jackson's editorship – he followed his teacher's sequential method, yoking it to an epistemology essentially Humean. Epistemologically viewed, Hume and Socrates are on level ground, since both of them view language as an abstraction from experience. One starts by perceiving particulars; one proceeds by generalising from them: "The recognition e.g. of our father and mother, of King's Chapel, or of the fountain in the great court of Trinity, is really the result of rapid generalisation." To that extent at least, says Frazer, Plato's epistemology is irreproachable. But knowledge is also relative, and experiences diverge: "As Hamilton said, no two men ever saw the same sun." Furthermore, if Plato conceived of earthly existence as a reflection of superlative and immutable essences, he had the perverse and refractory nature of experience to contend with. Not only was there Good, there was also Evil; not only was there purity, there was also grime. Plato devoted several passages to wriggling from under the consequences of any such recognition. And, in flushing out the vagaries of his thought, Frazer's famous bittersweet irony makes its first unmistakable appearance:

It is true that later the gate of the Ideal was left so far ajar as to allow gross material objects such as beds and tables (or rather their disembodied spirits) to creep in, as it were, by stealth, but they were always looked at askance by their more ethereal neighbours, and indeed when some of them, such as Hair, Mud, and Dirt, presented themselves for admission, the door shut in their face. Thus if we asked the Socrates of the *Phaedo*, what is it that makes a thing beautiful? he had an answer ready – the Idea of Beauty. But had we proceeded to inquire, what is it that makes a Camel? he would not (at this stage) have been prepared to reply – the Idea of a Camel, though doubtless later the camel would have trodden the upper air with his betters, though it cost him his hump to do it.[11]

Yet Plato persisted in what Frazer calls his "gigantic and yet splendid error" until close to the end, when in the *Laws* it finally collapsed and gave up the ghost. Why did he so persist? For anyone interested in the roots of Frazer's thought, his answer is illuminating. It was because, impatient to present an hypothesis at once so cogent and so compelling, Plato short-cut the inductive method. And why had Plato been so impatient? Once again Frazer's answer is sufficient to open one's eyes to much of what was to follow: it was because, as a Southern European, he preferred inspiration to experiment, intuition to logic:

> The long and patient observation and registration of phenomena, the passive watching of sensations as they flip past, was too tedious and unthinking a process for the fiery intellect of the Greeks; they were too full of mental vigour to submit to being for long the passive recipients of sensations. After receiving a few sensations . . . they leaped to a theory. For that long passivity which must precede the discovery of natural laws a more phlegmatic and less intellectual nature than that of the Greeks was needed, and such a nature is supplied by the northern nations. That patient observation of particulars, continued for years, nay centuries, by men of science as a necessary preliminary to generalisation, was not to be expected in a people whose blood (and therefore brain) was quickened by the more genial suns of the south.[12]

If Plato had lived in Glasgow he would have been a lot colder, but he might have got it right.

Of course the Frazerian wit is at work in such a passage, but it does point to the consistency of his thinking in other respects. In particular does it give the lie to the frequently mooted view that in moving across from classics to anthropology Frazer somehow changed fields. Anthropology to him was ancient philosophy; or, put less dramatically, it was the history of human error. As a philosopher Frazer, like Hume, was interested in how people came to believe things. As an anthropologist his concern was how they came to believe things which were wrong.

In hunting down the sources of their mistakes there is a remarkable consistency in Frazer's thinking. For, whether he is discussing the sublime error of Plato's Ideal Theory, or totemism or the periodic expulsion of evils, the root cause is seen to be the same: a breakdown in the inductive, empirical method. There have been many descriptions of Frazer's speciality: cultural anthropology, mythography, comparative religion. The nearest we shall get to it would probably be to describe his field as the epistemology of misconception. The principal difference between Frazer and a philosopher pure and simple lies in this, that, whereas the theoretical epistemologist is interested in the ways in which we come to understand the world, Frazer is interested in how, across a variety of ages and cultures, we have come to misunderstand it.

It is highly significant that when in the mid 1880s, established as a Fellow and in search of a subject, Frazer was casting around for a classical project on which to unleash his energies, his choice should have alighted on Pausanias. Pausanias is the author of the earliest of all guidebooks to mainland Greece, but he is also among the earliest students of superstition. Frazer's reading in this area was already impressive: as an undergraduate in the late 1870s he had wandered far beyond the confines of the normal undergraduate curriculum in search of authors whose strength was the adumbration of belief: Diodorus Siculus, Lucian, Quintilian, the Ovid of the *Fasti*.[13] Among the most useful proved to be Church Fathers such as Augustine and Tertullian who had railed against the convictions of the heathen. It is partly for this reason that when, in 1889, the idea for *The Golden Bough* first occurred to Frazer, he was able to complete the first two-volume version in under twelve months. Much of the material lay to hand in the course of his habitual classical reading: he did not have to "research" it at all. In the meantime Pausanias gave him much to ponder over, not least the already quoted passage in which this second-century Lydian Greek describes the translation of the resuscitated Hippolytus to Nemi. Περιήγησις τῆς Ἑλλάδος is a veritable collector's gallery of such fables as Pausanias had found littering the minds of the Peloponnesian Greeks quite as thickly as the shrines he describes had littered their terrain.

Frazer was to work at *The Description of Greece* on and off for fifteen years. To start with he planned a translation and exegetical commentary: something along the lines of a scholarly recension as the Lower Criticism practised it. But textual criticism was never Frazer's bent; his much later edition of Ovid's *Fasti* is flawed by minor errors, which were always to some extent to be his bugbear.[14] Where he excelled was in the large-scale analysis of setting and theme. It is therefore not surprising that, after completing the translation of the text in the early 1880s, he laid it aside, only to return to a full-scale commentary once *The Golden Bough* in its first two-volume version was complete. Once he did return, his interest had shifted to the archaeological aspects of the problem. In the meantime history had conspired to help him, since he was able to draw on the results of the widespread excavations which had transpired in the interval. Schliemann's work at Mycenae,

Cavvadias and Staes's work at Epidauros, Curtius's excavations at Olympia all served to flesh out the commentary, which gradually grew from two to five volumes.[15]

Frazer was an avid reader of journals, both ethnographic and archaeological: it is therefore of some interest that in seeking the Golden Fleece of archaeological excellence he should have forsaken the armchair methods of *The Golden Bough* and taken himself off to Greece. No sooner was the manuscript delivered to Macmillan in April 1890 than he spent the £100 advance on the first of these trips.[16] When in May his personal copy was ready, it had to be posted out to him in Athens, where he was using the premises of the British School as the headquarters for a preliminary survey of the sites.[17] Frazer signed the copy briskly inside the front cover, and then set out to climb Mount Helicon. On 24 May he clambered down an ivy-clad slope to drink the "clear, ice-cold" waters of the Hippocrene.[18] Editing Pausanias after all was a sweaty business: the good doctor's title literally implies a guided tour. In the autumn of 1895 and coming up to completion, Frazer then returned on a further, more intensive expedition. The 1890 and 1895 notebooks make fascinating reading, first because of their copiousness, and secondly because they illuminate Frazer's methods in other fields.[19] More especially do they demonstrate just how Frazer could impose himself on subjects of which initially he seems to have known little. The 1890 notebook finds him copying out definitions of Doric capitals from cribs: by 1895, not only has he mastered the technicalities, but, rising at dawn each day, he is out there by seven measuring each site with tape-measure and, most amusingly, stop-watch.

Such diligence, sustained over so long a period, must beg the question of motivation. In later years Frazer came to feel that he had expended too much time on his Pausanias. The fact is, however, that he stuck with it through thick and thin, and with a punctiliousness of detail he applied to no other book. From the point of view of strict scholarship, it is arguably his finest achievement. It is, furthermore, the contention of Peter Levi, a more recent translator of Pausanias, not only that Frazer's edition was the keystone of his life's work, but that Pausanias and Frazer were spurred on by much the same concerns:

> Pausanias was capable of entertaining a sophisticated and philosophical solution to religious difficulties, but his deepest engagement was in the local cults and legends and traditions of provincial Greece. There is no doubt that he was a true believer in the most sacred of these traditions: he accepted the warning of a dream and understood the

punishment of a god. He was perhaps like his greatest editor, Sir James Frazer (whose entire work has its roots in Pausanias), in that all his scholarship and topography and encyclopaedic curiosity were a burden undertaken in the attempt to satisfy a deeper anxiety which had once been apprehended in religious terms. The collapse of ancient religion or some deeper collapse was the unspoken object of his studies.[20]

Such a conclusion, once entertained, has extreme consequences for our view of Frazer. Pausanias's piety is not in question: an initiate into the Eleusinian Mysteries, he refuses to divulge them even when germane to what he has to say. Frazer's own initiation, as we have already seen, was into the austerer mysteries of the Free Church of Scotland. On the question of the truth or non-truth of the Christian religion he never in public came clean, preferring the ironic method of distancing himself from it. In private, as his correspondence shows, he was adamant about his apostasy.[21] Does this divergence between the public and private stance betray an essential hypocrisy, as Robert Graves once infamously suggested,[22] or, more crucially, a variety of insecurity he could never quite resolve?

One clue is furnished by the Introduction to his Pausanias, which he wrote when nearing publication in 1898. Here he portrays Pausanias as a sceptic on minor matters, whose scepticism grew less dogmatic as his peregrination of central and southern Greece progressed. By the end Pausanias was inclined to respect what at the outset he had regarded with uncomplicated derision: the mythology and folklore of a peasant people. Such ambivalence, of course, is not rare – one thinks of the self-contradictions of Socrates – but it undeniably struck a chord in Frazer. When in the manuscript draft of the Introduction he attempts to give these intimations voice, Frazer's habitually fluent prose breaks into what one can only describe as a nervous stammer:

⟨This⟩ Thus the composition of Pausanias's work ⟨seems to have been⟩was spread over a period of at least fourteen years and probably of many more. That he spent a long time over it might be inferred from a passage in which he tells us that when he began his work he looked on certain Greek myths as little better than foolishness, but that when he had got as far as Arcadia he had altered his

opinion of them and had come to believe
that they contained a Kernel of deep
wisdom under a husk of extravagance. Such a ⟨total⟩
revolution in a writer's attitude towards his people's
gods is generally ⟨the result⟩ a
total change ⟨in⟩ of attitude towards the religion of his
people ⟨may very well have⟩ seems to ⟨imply a long
course of reflection and⟩ require for its accomplishment a
long course of study and reflection.
Such a total change of attitude towards the religious
traditions of his country was ^{more} probably an affair ⟨,
not of weeks or months, but of years.⟩ ⟨an affair⟩
of years than of weeks and months

(*Note*. The above transcription follows Frazer's manuscript line
for line. Small deletions are placed in angle brackets, while italic
indicates a block of material eventually rejected altogether by
Frazer.)

Fourteen years was the exact time that Frazer devoted to his Pausanias.
Dare one comment, lo how the man describes himself?
And this is not all. The finest passages both in Frazer's translation –
the best of his renditions, better by far than his Ovid – and of his
commentary are those that speak of the indwelling *numen*, the spirit
immanent in landscape. The most vivid of these scatter his empiricism
to the winds. His account of his excursion to the source of the River
Styx, undertaken on 2 October 1895, is copied direct from the pencilled
entry in his little marbled notebook.[24] Forty-two minutes precisely after
his departure from Solos, the valley closes in on him so that he is forced
to abandon his horse and scramble among rock and fern. "I noticed one
or two places where a fall would have been certain death", says the
notebook. "The last slope up to the cliff – a very long and steep one of
loose gravel which gave way under my feet – was almost too much for
me; my limbs seemed to fail under me." The official version alters the
last sentence to "The last slope . . . is most fatiguing", and then continues,

As I was struggling slowly up with the guides, we heard the furious
barking of dogs away up the mountains on the opposite side of the
glen. The barking came nearer and nearer, and being echoed by the
cliffs had a weird impressive sound that suited well with the scene, as
if hell-hounds were baying at the strangers who dared to approach the

infernal water. . . . At the head of this long slope of loose gravel we reach the foot of the waterfall. The water . . . descends the smooth face of a huge cliff, said to be over 600 feet high. . . . At the foot of the cliff it formed a small stream, flowing down a very steep rocky bed into the bottom of the glen far below. The water was clear, but not excessively cold. . . . Only the lower part of the cliff is visible from the foot of the waterfall, probably because the cliff overhangs somewhat. Certainly the cliffs a little to the right of the waterfall overhang considerably. With these enormous beetling crags of grey rock rising on three sides, the scene is one of sublime, but wild and desolate grandeur. I have seen nothing to equal it anywhere.[25]

Frazer is overawed. He is also scared, but not too scared to consult his fobwatch: it is 11.30 precisely. Read in the context of the printed commentary the effect is of an exercise in the late-eighteenth-century sublime, but the disturbance probably runs deeper. Frazer found that a number of legends still hung around the tributaries of the Styx, including one about the singing fish in the river Aroanius which Pausanias had observed but which all his blandishments could not tempt to burst into song.[26] Frazer, who thought the fish were trout, calls the myth of their singing "absurd", but then he was notoriously tone-deaf.[27] However, it is not only in the vicinity of the Styx that Frazer seems to have been gripped by that which his theories disown: the inexplicable force of a mystery.

But we anticipate. In the early 1880s Frazer was a studious, slightly solitary young don with his way still to make. His existence was transformed by the burgeoning of two friendships, and by a sudden expansion of his intellectual horizons such as must have taken the shy young Glaswegian by surprise.

Nine years older than Frazer, James Ward was a college lecturer at Trinity, a former lay preacher, and a practitioner of the still untried discipline of psychology. The two men had met in 1879, but it was not until the early 1880s that their friendship blossomed. In the spring of 1883 they went walking in Spain together and it was in Ward's company that Frazer studied Dante in the original Italian.[28] It is not difficult to see what drew the two of them together. Like Frazer, Ward had come to Cambridge by a slightly eccentric route, having missed out on the leavening experience of the public schools. Spiritually too they had traversed much the same ground. If, as Levi suggests, Frazer experienced qualms over religion, he would have found a sympathetic ear in Ward. Reared like Frazer in the severest Calvinism, he had been taken away from school at the tender age of thirteen as a result of the collapse of his father's business interests, and then read privately in preparation for a theology degree. He had already been called to minister to the Congregationalist flock in Cambridge, when at thirty, and just short of ordination proper, he threw it all in and entered Trinity College to read Moral Sciences. When Frazer met him the certainties that had sustained his early vocation long lay in ruins, though he refused to take the plunge into full-scale disbelief. As his biographer has it, "He buried the past, he burned his boats, but he remained for all that a native of other shores."[29] In 1883 he was teaching in the Moral Science syllabus and was soon to be appointed the first Professor of Mental Philosophy and Logic. Meanwhile he pursued studies in experimental psychology while striving to reconcile his new-found empiricism with the tenets of a religion which, like Smith, he was never quite to abandon.

In the Cambridge of the 1880s the crux of faith was still very much the issue of the day. How these late Victorians turned on the spit! Along the High Table at Trinity, and five years Ward's senior, Henry Chadwick was busy attempting to uphold the primacy of conscience in the crater of religion's demise. Meanwhile Ward struggled to hold on to the barest theism. The Soul having apparently dissolved, he was at least determined to hang on to Mind. Assailed on the one hand by empiricism, with its tendency to reduce everything to a simple stream of sensations, and on the other hand by practical psychology, with its penchant for seeing us as what Tennyson had called "magnetic mockeries", Ward took his stand on the integrity of self: "Whether seeking to analyse one's own sensations or those of a lobster," he wrote, "whether discussing the association of ideas or the experience of emotions, there is always an individual mind or subject in question."[30] Ward had himself done work on the nervous system of the crayfish, but the ghost in the machine refused to be laid.

What mind was to body, God was to the Universe. In the late 1890s Ward gave the Gifford Lectures on Natural Religion at Aberdeen, and used the platform thus provided to launch a frontal attack on the agnostic naturalism then associated with the names of Thomas Huxley and Herbert Spencer.[31] Both men had seen evolution as a scientific panacea; but evolution, Ward argued, was powerless to explain the increasing momentum and complexity of human achievement, since as a manifestation of physical energy its natural tendency should have been to exhaust itself rather than to proliferate. One needed the postulate of God to underline and guarantee the evolutionary process; only through him could the evolving human mind integrate and diversify. It is clear that Frazer and Ward were ultimately at cross-purposes: Spencer was one of Frazer's passions.[32] But in 1883 Ward rendered his friend one inestimable service; Frazer later said he owed his entire career to it. Some time in 1883, possibly on that walking tour of Spain, he lent his friend Edward Tylor's *Primitive Culture*.

We took a passing glance at Tylor in Chapter I, where we concentrated on his Theory of Survivals. This notion was to be of great use to Frazer when he attempted to get to grips with the cult of the grove, interpreting it as a leftover from a bygone age, "a primeval rock rising from a smooth-shaven lawn."[33] But survivalism cannot have been the first aspect of Tylor's thought to spring to Frazer's attention; this was almost certainly the comparative method. Again Frazer later ascribed his immersion in this method to Smith,[34] but Smith used it sparingly, whereas it is the architectural principle underlying all of Tylor's work. It is of course much older than either of them. In the late eighteenth century the philologist William Jones had tried to plumb the origins of language by collating particles from different European tongues which, comparing them with Sanskrit, he concluded to have stemmed from a proto-language named Indo-European. In the following century Sir Henry Maine applied the method to the study of ancient jurisprudence with results that we have already witnessed. The rationale, however, was the same: the comparative method was a way of delving into origins by comparing different kinds of cultural deposit or bits of historical residue. The rite of Rex Nemorensis was just one such piece of residue. At various times Frazer was to apply the method to totemism, burial rites, and the folklore of the Bible. To begin with it must have been a fascinating hobby. Soon he noticed that it offered him a way of widening his classical interests without renouncing them. Within a few years he was using it as a matter of course in his classical work, and eventually it became the talisman which guided him through all of his variegated interests.

What then can Frazer have meant by attributing his conversion to these working-methods to Smith? What he meant was that Smith gave him the courage to employ them. To see how this came about, we must return to the crucial year of 1884.

Frazer had spent the previous Easter walking round Andalusia with Ward. He had returned with Tylor's book tucked under his arm and his head full of the Arabs. One pellucid spring evening he and Ward had sat and watched the sun disappear behind the red fastness of the Alhambra.[35] In the Court of the Lions he had dipped his hand in the cool, jade-green water of the fountains and thought of Pindar. It was Frazer's first extended trip abroad and it made a deep impression; so, when the following January he found himself sitting after dinner one evening next to a slight, bearded stranger who seemed to know something of the Moors, it is not surprising that the conversation turned to Spain. The stranger of course was Smith, and Frazer has left us an account of the meeting:

> I think that one subject of our talk that evening was the Arabs in Spain and that, though I knew next to nothing about the subject, I attempted some sort of argument with him, but was immediately beaten down, in the kindest and gentlest way, by his learning and yielded myself captive at once. I never afterwards, so far as I can remember, attempted to dispute the mastership which he thenceforth exercised over me by his extraordinary union of genius and learning.[36]

In a word, Frazer was worsted. Shame, however, soon gave way to admiration and then a deepening friendship. That September Ward was set aside as Frazer went climbing in the Highlands with Smith. On their return there was plenty to discuss. Smith had rooms in Whewell's Court, the neo-Gothic folly across Trinity Street. Most usefully he was still co-editor of the *Britannica*, which had now staggered on as far as "P". It was not long before he was signing up his colleagues as contributors. Ward was down for Psychology, Jackson for Parmenides. In the absence of stronger preferences Frazer was handed a list of subjects classical, and for the most part Roman: Praefect, Praeneste, Praetor, Pericles, Priapus, Proserpine and – last but not least – Prytanis.

The last and shortest of these led indirectly to Nemi.[37] A *prytanis* was a Greek town councillor, and the prytaneum the earliest version of a Greek *hôtel de ville*. It was a round structure with a beehive roof, and within it a fire constantly burned. In later years its official functions were largely superseded by the *tholos* or rotunda, which in Athens was down in the marketplace. In the time of Pausanias, however, the original prytaneum still stood on the northern slope of the Acropolis,[38] and in it distinguished senior citizens were entitled to provisions at the public expense. From its position within the citadel, and the fact that every Greek town had one, Frazer argued that the prytaneum was none other than the original palace of the king, and that the *prytanis* had preceded the *basileus* as monarch of a Greek city. What interested Frazer particularly was the fire which burned within the threshold. If the prytaneum was the royal residence, then the fire, which was sacred to

Hestia, must have been the cruicible of the kingdom, the centre of royal power. Rome also had a perpetual fire consecrated to Vesta and tended by Vestal virgins, whom Frazer was inclined to regard as having once been the daughters of the king. Nemi too had such a fire, where Diana was worshipped under her soubriquet of Hestia.

There were just too many coincidences, and the following year Frazer took the opportunity in Jackson's *Journal of Philology* to write them up.[39] Here Frazer launches into a dissertation on the kindling of fires in ancient society which acts as a virtual preview of the chapters on fire festivals in *The Golden Bough*. And what is more, a mere year and a half after his introduction to Tylor, he is already letting the comparative method have full rein, bringing in instances from as far away as Madagascar and Southern Africa to adorn his argument. Five years later, when the facts of the Arician priesthood were to occupy the foreground of Frazer's mind, his discussion of Vestal fires would act as tinder for a conflagration of its own.

The pace indeed was quickening, but, though permitted by the terms of his Fellowship, renewed in 1885, to pursue what line he wished, Frazer still lacked the essential ingredient of audacity. It was this impetus that Smith provided, rushing over from Whewell's Court, across Trinity Street, under the Great Gate, up the staircase next to the Elizabethan chapel to the booklined room, overlooking the Great Court and its fountain, where Frazer, brimful of references but not knowing how to begin, was having difficulty with – perhaps Priapus? Frazer had no lack of materials (Lady Frazer once wrote that when she first visited him in his rooms in the early 1890s the ceiling of the room beneath him was billowing like a sail.[40] What he needed, at least initially, was a push. There were times in the very early days when Frazer did not for the life of him know how to set pen to paper. It was then that Smith could urge him gently but firmly – "Get going, man!" – sometimes even suggesting the first sentence. Many of the Trinity contingent were reluctant authors, including Jackson and Ward, whose great article on psychology was to form the basis of his reputation, but whose offering had to be virtually torn out of him. Smith was capable of drawing from friends and associates strengths and originality they did not know they possessed. He must also have been a superb manager of men.

We left Smith at the end of the last chapter on the eve of his departure for Cambridge, broken in spirit perhaps but not in mind. The foundation of his own life's work had already been laid when he met M'Lennan, and he was to spend the remaining nine years of his life working that seam. M'Lennan had implied that all early societies were both totemic and exogamous. If that were the case, the Arabs must have been as well. In the winters of 1879 and 1880, while still in official disgrace, Smith had travelled extensively in the Near East as far as the Arabian peninsula, where he had adopted Arab dress and the nickname Abdullah Effendi.[41] There, in the heartland of the oldest Semitic cultures, he had sought evidence to flesh out M'Lennan's theories. And what had he found? Like M'Lennan he had a wonderful capacity for discovering just what he had been looking for: totem names on every side. The seal was set, and when Smith felt comfortably settled in Cambridge he got to work writing up his conclusions in a set of lectures, eventually published as *Kinship and Marriage in Early Arabia*.[42] The lectures were delivered at Cambridge in the Easter Term of 1885, and Frazer attended every one.

Like God, totemism was a subject very much in the air. M'Lennan cannot conceivably have guessed what he had set going when back in 1869 he had first sprung the idea. Not only did Smith take it up with almost indecent alacrity, but it soon kindled a light in Frazer's eyes. For by now it was 1886, Smith had moved on to Christ's, and the *Britannica*, most importantly, had soldiered on to its next set of letters: S to T.

To us it seems most bizarre that an encyclopaedia should orchestrate an entire enthnographic movement. But in the 1880s the *Britannica* possessed enormous prestige. As late as 1906, when Jackson was putting up for the Regius Chair, he cited his articles in the ninth edition as prime evidence of his scholarship.[43] To us such things are normally potboilers, but the dons of the period thought otherwise. It is arguable that, without the ninth edition of the *Britannica*, *The Golden Bough* would never have been written. Certainly the shape it assumed owed much to entries Smith and Frazer wrote at this time, virtually its building-blocks. That the concerns these two Scots were obliged to address in those ephemeral pieces chimed in so beautifully with their evolving preoccupations is one of the beautiful accidents which occasionally grace intellectual history.

The building-blocks were three. For volume XXI (ROT–SIA) Smith wrote on sacrifice, a subject perfectly in tune both with his religious interests and with the view of totemism he had inherited from M'Lennan. For volume XXIII (T–UPS) Frazer was invited to tackle taboo – the implied theme of *The Golden Bough* – and, by happy chance, totem. We shall deal with each of these articles in the following chapters, but in the meantime we must speed on to 1889.

The scene was set, the iron-filings in evidence. All that was needed now was a strong magnetic force. Frazer had known about the excavations at Nemi for four years. They were reported at some length in *The*

Athenaeum by Rodolpho Lanciani, who had taken the cure there.[44] In any case Frazer would have read the reports in the specialist journals.[45] For six years he had been searching for a niche in anthropology he could call his own. In the process he had expanded his article on totemism into a little book,[46] had lectured to the Anthropological Institute on burial customs,[47] had followed the Vestal fires where they led. But the riddle of Nemi still needed solving, and nobody seemed anywhere near it. In 1885, the year of the dig, Ernest Renan, whom Frazer much admired, had written a play on the theme,[48] but Renan was haunted by spectres of his own and in any case the play had little scholarly foundation. Somehow, somewhere, there had to be a ball of thread that led into the labyrinths of the grove.

It was yet another Scot that acted his Ariadne, but before letting this particular cat out of the bag it is as well to remember the accumulation of conditional clauses with which Frazer loads the third paragraph of *The Golden Bough* in its first edition, a paragraph he drafted in the spring of 1889. It reads,

> . . . if we can show that a barbarous custom, like that of the priesthood of Nemi, has existed elsewhere; if we can detect the motives which led to its institution; if we can prove that these motives have operated widely, perhaps universally, in human society, producing in varied circumstances a variety of institutions specifically different but generally alike; if we can show, lastly, that these very motives, with some of their derivative institutions, were actively at work in ancient antiquity; then we may fairly infer that at a remoter age the same motives gave birth to the priesthood of Nemi.[49]

The inferential process thus sketched out is long, and it depends vitally on the existence of a set of parallel instances. In the absence of wide-ranging evidence, at least at the outset, one example would suffice. In the spring of 1889, while poring over a late-nineteenth-century anthology of travel literature, Frazer found it.

CHAPTER IV

THE KING IS DEAD

THE HAMILTONS are an enterprising breed. The ducal crest has a salamander in flames and an oak-tree fructed and penetrated transversely in the main stem by a frame-saw proper – potent enough Frazerian symbols. Over these emblems runs the motto "Jamais Arrière": "Never behind". It was a Hamilton who discovered the science of "quaternions", a higher branch of the calculus,[1] while William Hamilton's *Lectures on Metaphysics and Logic* were, as we have already seen, an integral part of Frazer's epistemological inheritance. Another member of the family went to bed with Nelson, but Frazer's principal debt is to a different Hamilton altogether.

In the Year of Our Lord 1728, James, Fifth Duke of Hamilton, Chatelherault and Brandon, Marquis of Clydesdale, Earl of Arran, Lanark and Cambridge, Lord Avon, Polmount, Machanschyer, and Innerdale, Second Baron of Dutton, Knight of the Most Noble Order of the Thistle, received a dedication from a clansman of whom he cannot have heard. Captain Alexander Hamilton had spent the previous thirty-five years in the East. He had wandered everywhere from the Cape of Good Hope to Japan, but had spent the greater part of that period as a merchant adventurer and privateering sea captain around the coasts of India. Returning to Scotland in 1723, he had settled in Edinburgh, where five years later he published his *New Account of the East Indies*, the "lucubrations of the Nights of two long winters". His adventures had left Alex Hamilton comfortably off but far from rich. "I have", he wrote in his Preface, "got Holy Agur's wish in Proverbs, XXX.8", which verse reads, "Remove me from vanity and lies: give me neither poverty nor riches; feed me with food convenient for me." Hamilton's pabulum had been his thoroughly Celtic wanderlust, but in his declining years he, like Frazer, ate humbler fare at home.

In the year 1695 Hamilton had been travelling down the coast of Malabar on his way to Johore when he heard a volley of shots issuing inland from the mouth of the Ponnani River. On inquiry he discovered the cause of the affray. The planet Jupiter then being in retrograde motion in the sign of the Crab, the Samorin of Calicut was holding a jubilee to celebrate the next twelve-year cycle of his reign. This celebration was greeted with exuberant public rejoicing, but, as he also later discovered, the festival had not always been so civil. The passage is quoted in all editions of *The Golden Bough*, but it is as well to remind oneself of Hamilton's original:

Many strange Customs were observed in this Country in former Times, and some very odd ones are still continued. It was an ancient Custom for the *Samorin* to reign but twelve Years, and no longer. If he died before his Term was expired, it saved him a troublesome Ceremony of cutting his own Throat, on a publick Scaffold erected for that Purpose. He first made a Feast for all his Nobility and Gentry, who are very numerous. After the Feast, he saluted his Guests, and went to the Scaffold, and very decently cut his own Throat in the View of the Assembly, and his Body was, a little While after, burned with great Pomp and Ceremony, and the Grandees elected a new *Samorin*. Whether that custom was a religious or a civil Ceremony I know not, but it is now laid aside.

And a new Custom is followed by the modern *Samorins*, that a Jubilee is proclaimed throughout his Dominions, at the End of twelve Years, and a Tent is pitched for him in a spacious Plain, and a great Feast is celebrated for ten or twelve Days with Mirth and Jollity, Guns firing Night and Day, so at the end of the Feast any four of the Guests that have a Mind to gain a Crown by a desperate Action, in fighting their Way through 30 or 40000 of his Guards, and kill the *Samorin* in his Tent, he that kills him, succeeds him in his Empire.

In Anno 1695, one of those Jubilees happened, and the tent pitched near *Pennany*, a Sea-port of his, about fifteen Leagues to the Southward of *Calecut*. There were but three Men that would venture on that desperate Action, who fell in, with Sword and Target, among the Guards, and, after they had killed and wounded many, were themselves killed. One of the *Desperados* had a Nephew of fifteen or sixteen Years of Age, that kept close by the Uncle in the Attack on the Guards, and, when he saw him fall, the Youth got through the Guards into the Tent, and made a Stroke at His Majesty's Head, and had certainly dispatched him, if a large Brass Lamp which was burning over his Head, had not marred the Blow; but, before he could make another, he was killed by the Guards; and, I believe, the same *Samorin* reigns yet. I chanced to come that Time along the Coast, and heard the Guns for two or three Days and Nights successively.[2]

What the Duke of Hamilton made of this passage we do not know, though since his father the fourth Duke had been killed in a duel sixteen years previously, he must have been glad that the customs of Calicut did not pertain in Lanarkshire.[3] Now, Frazer for his part had not the slightest intention of inheriting Messrs Frazer and Green of Buchanan Street, but in Captain Hamilton's testimony he was very much interested.

Frazer first read Hamilton's reminiscences in the third volume of John Pinkerton's *General Collection of the Best and Most Interesting Voyages and Travels* of 1811. According to his own later account, this was in the spring of 1889.[4] He was at the time at work on what he calls "a general work on superstition and religion", of which we shall have cause to speculate anon. Among the problems which had fallen beneath his scrutiny was the question of kingly taboo. The King of the Wood offered a telling example of this, but one that was hard to fathom. When he read these three paragraphs of Hamilton's, something seems to have cohered. They offered him a side turning, and Frazer, who delighted in what we nowadays call lateral thinking, could never resist a diversion. He cannot have known it, of course, but it was the crossroads that he had reached.

And so it is that on 8 November 1890, some eight months after reading Hamilton, we find him writing to George Macmillan:

> I shall soon have completed a study in the history of primitive religion which I propose to offer to you for publication. The book is an explanation of the legend of the Golden Bough, as that legend is given by Servius in his commentary on Virgil. According to Servius the Golden Bough grew on a certain tree in the sacred grove of Diana at Aricia, and the priesthood of the grove was held by the man who succeeded in breaking off the Golden Bough and then slaying the priest in single combat. By an application of the Comparative Method I believe that I can make it probable that the priest represented the god of the grove – Virbius – and that his slaughter was regarded as the death of the god. This raises the question of a wide-spread custom of killing men and animals regarded as divine. I have collected many examples of this custom and proposed a new explanation of it. The Golden Bough, I believe I can show, was the mistletoe, and the whole legend can, I think, be brought into connexion, on the one hand, with the Druidical reverence for the mistletoe and the human sacrifices which accompanied their worship, and on the other with the Norse legend of the death of Balder. Of the exact way in which I connect the Golden Bough with the Priest of Aricia shall only say that in explaining it I am led to propose a new explanation of the meaning of

totemism. This is a bare outline of the book which, whatever may be thought of its theories, will be found to contain large store of very curious customs, many of which may be new even to professed anthropologists. The resemblance of the savage customs and ideas to the fundamental doctrines of Christianity is striking. But I make no reference to this parallelism, leaving my readers to draw their own conclusions, one way or the other.[5]

The plan was daring, and it was to span out in four great arches: a short chapter (or book; Frazer was yet to settle on his terms) on the riddle of the grove; a chapter on taboos of various kinds; then the heart of the matter: a dissertation 400 pages long on "Killing the God". The work would end with 100 pages relating the Arician legend to the Norse myth of Balder, though these still lay ahead. Frazer was writing at white heat now: "I am anxious to go out to Greece, with a view to Pausanias, as soon as possible. If you decide to take it the printing could begin, I hope, by the beginning of January, and I should hope to leave for Greece in March."[6]

George Macmillan was a man to whom Frazer could write with confidence. Eton-educated, he was the second son of one of two brothers who had walked from Scotland in the 1840s to found the firm, initially in Cambridge (1, Trinity Street), then in London.[7] He and his cousin Frederick Macmillan now presided over their growing enterprise from 29, Bedford Street, Covent Garden. A canny business head combined with the recreations of a man of letters – Macmillan was Honorary Secretary both of the Hellenic Society (1879–1919) and of the British School of Athens (1886–97) – had produced a disposition with which Frazer felt instantly comfortable, and though they were yet to meet the relationship was to be long and cordial, the summit of intimacy being reached in true Victorian style when Frazer dropped the "Mr" and addressed his friend candidly as "Macmillan".

After the acceptance of the book on the advice of John Morley – a former editor of the *Fortnightly* – they corresponded sometimes several times weekly. "I have given the book a certain dramatic feel at the opening and close", wrote Frazer.[8] Its appearance must mirror that flair, that careful sense of drama. There were to be no new-fangled typefaces: the print must match the grandeur of the subject. A Grecian urn on the spine proclaimed the classical theme. Nothing else would do for the front cover but the eponymous Bough itself, to be embossed in gold after a drawing already prepared by J. H. Middleton, Director of the Fitzwilliam and a friend of William Morris.[9] The Morris-inspired mistletoe was promptly accepted, but what should lie beneath? Green and only green would do: the same shade as Middleton's *Rome*. And then Turner's picture: how should they proceed: wood-engraving; heliogravure? Heliogravure it was.

The debate on the niceties of production continued along with his writing: a hectic pace, high days and holidays notwithstanding. In both Frazer was torn between a necessary haste and an infinite desire to take pains. Seldom is his correspondence so breathless. At one stage he fills several pages with observations on methods of picture reproduction, and then laments his inability to check his ideas against existing models since "the libraries are closed at present". No wonder – one looks for the date and there it is: 25 December 1889, Christmas Day, and Frazer has been at it since dawn.[10]

And what manner of book was flowing in so tireless a fashion from Frazer's unresting pen? Some indication is given by his instructions on advertising the book. Macmillan wants a sort of digest of its contests to appear in *The Athenaeum*. The author will have none of it:

> I find it very difficult to state summarily the gist of the book without disclosing what I may call the plot. . . . Hence I do not wish to announce the result beforehand, and for the same reason I have refrained from giving a full table of contents. To have done so would have been a mistake, it seemed to me, like the mistake of a novelist who should prefix a summary of the plot to his novel.[11]

To us such concern for withholding one's conclusion might seem more fitting in a detective writer than a scholar. Not for nothing was the late nineteenth century the great age of mystery-writing. Seen from one point of view *The Golden Bough* is one of the greatest whodunnits ever written. Beginning by describing an *agon*, a struggle for mastery in which the fittest survives, it continues slowly but inexorably to unmask the victor. The book has both a subject and a story. When the story reaches its resolution, so does the argument. Elucidation becomes enlightenment. *The Golden Bough* is a novel of the intellect; suspense is of its essence.

So, to resume the story. The King of the Wood was forced to defend his title in single combat against all comers. If he lost the contest, he forfeited his title and with it his life. But what was the cause of this duel? True to the spirit of the comparative method, Frazer commences with a sideways leap. The King of Calicut had, it seemed, to defend his title on similar conditions. Could Calicut tell him something about Nemi?

There were three elements in Hamilton's account that interested Frazer. The first was the information that in times past the Samorin of Calicut had been forced to abdicate after a set term of twelve years. The second was the original stipulation that at the termination of this period he must commit ritual suicide. The third was the eventual commutation of this sentence to a ritualised combat in which, defended by the legions of his bodyguards, the Samorin like Rex Nemorensis enjoyed a chance of survival.

Two of these observations agreed perfectly with what Frazer could learn elsewhere of southern India. The kingdom of Calicut, where the Portuguese maintained a trading-post, was at the eastern end of a well-worn trade route from Arabia and the Persian Gulf. The Arab presence was well established in Malabar. One of the first to observe it was Magellan's cousin Duarte Barbosa, a Portuguese adventurer in the pay of the Spanish court. In his *Livro de Duarte Barbosa* he left us a graphic description of the Malabar Coast as it was two centuries before Hamilton's excursion.[12] Barbosa got as far as China, but it is his description of the tip of the Indian sub-continent which is of pertinence here. Twenty miles north of Cape Comorin he discovered a small principality he calls Quilicare which appears on no contemporary map. Here a like rule of kingly succession prevailed, for after a reign of twelve years the rajah was obliged to mount a scaffold especially erected for the purpose and there publicly dismember himself, starting with his nose. His successor was obliged to watch the whole performance. Whether he was chosen for his skill in government or his ability to hold his stomach Barbosa does not divulge.

Since Barbosa's account precedes Hamilton's by some two centuries, it is possible that he was writing at a time before the practice of kingly self-immolation in southern India died out. In that case what he has given us may be a description of the stage of political evolution immediately preceding the one that Hamilton describes. But it was neither the old nor the new custom that interested Frazer so much as the transition between them. This interested him because it enabled him to view the contest for the title of Rex Nemonensis in an entirely fresh light. The rule of succession in Nemi, in fact, seems to have been very similar to that pertaining to Malabar, and Frazer makes great play with the comparison:

the terms on which in later times the King of Calicut held office are identical with those attached to the office of King of the Wood, except that whereas the former might be assailed by a candidate at any time, the King of Calicut might only be attacked once every twelve years. But as the leave granted to the King of Calicut to reign so long as he could defend himself against all comers was a mitigation of the old rule which set a fixed term on his life, so we may conjecture that the similar permission granted to the King of the Wood was a mitigation of an older custom of putting him to death at the end of a set period. In both cases the new rule gave to the god-man at least a chance of his life, which under the old rule was denied him; and people probably reconciled themselves to the change by reflecting that so long as the god-man could maintain himself by the sword against all assaults, there was no reason to apprehend that the fatal decay had set in.[13]

A similar mollification of an ancient rule could be observed in Africa, where, however, the realities seemed to be harsher and the rationale hence easier to discern. "Something new always comes out of Africa", remarked the elder Pliny, citing a common Greek belief, but it might be truer to say that Africa offers something very old. Once again our best informant is Strabo. Leaving Italy behind him, this first-century Greek geographer has now turned his attention southwards to the Ethiopians, a term reserved since Herodotos for the inhabitants of the lands below Egypt. Strabo is particularly interested in Meroë, capital of the Nilotic kingdom of Napata in present-day Sudan. The people of Meroë evidently held their kings in the highest regard, but were none the less capable of treating them in a somewhat peremptory fashion:

> Their greatest royal seat is Meroë ... They appoint as kings those who excel in beauty, or in superiority of cattle feeding, or in courage, or in wealth. In Meroë the highest rank was in ancient times held by the priests, who indeed would give orders even to the king, sometimes ordering him through a messenger to die, and would appoint another in his stead; but later one of the kings broke up the custom by marching with armed men against the temple ... and slaughtering all the priests.[14]

Put like this the rule seems a little arbitrary. Little wonder that King Ergamenes, who was related to the Ptolemies and had a Greek education, put a stop to it. But why had it earlier been enforced? To explain it Frazer turns his attention still further south and forward in time to the Portuguese colony of Mozambique. Along the banks of the Sofala River there reigned in the seventeenth century a dynasty of kings known as the Quitevas. When Father João dos Santos visited them in the seventeenth century he discovered that, though the accession of a new Quiteva was often attended with much controversy, the king was permitted a natural death.[15] It had not always been so. If a Quiteva lost so much as a tooth, he was forced to die. This regulation continued in force until one particular gap-toothed monarch decided to outface his people and live. In his best grasshopper manner Frazer interprets the Ethiopian rule by reference to the Mozambican one. Strabo had said that among other things the kings of Meroë were selected for their physical perfection. Might it not be that the priests decided to exercise their veto on the king's life when, and only when, he showed evidence of weakening?

It thus seemed to Frazer that in early society there were three rules of succession.

1. The king was killed when any sign of physical debility became apparent. This had been, and in some cases still was, the rule in Africa.
2. He was killed at the end of a fixed term, which might range from one to twelve years. This had been the rule in Quilicare, and formerly in Calicut. In such cases, Frazer believed kings sometimes chose substitutes to die in their stead. Sometimes the substitute was the king's own son.
3. The king was obliged to prove his fitness against all comers, and if he fended them off he remained on the throne. This is the rule that Hamilton discovered in Calicut, except that, since the challenge could only be mounted at a jubilee, which occurred once in twelve years, the provision here would seem to have incorporated something of the former rule. The definitive form of the challenge could be seen at Nemi.

But why was the decay of the royal frame esteemed so fatal? The dire consequences feared as a result of the monarch's death stemmed from the very nature of kingship. The king was the pivot of the physical universe:

His whole being, body and soul, is so delicately attuned to the harmony of the world that a touch of his hand or a turn of his head may send a thrill of vibration through the whole framework of things; and conversely his divine organism is acutely sensitive to such slight changes of the environment as would leave ordinary mortals unaffected.[16]

Consequently kings often appear to have lived in a state of virtual ritual quarantine, their every breath or action hemmed in by a *cordon sanitaire* of custom, deference and precautions of every kind. So onerous was the burden thus imposed that the functions of kingship were sometimes divided, the ritual imposition being carried by a sacramental king, while the cares of state and any real power devolved upon another. Where the institution of monarchy itself had lapsed, the ritualistic office occasionally survived. Such ritual kings, outliving by centuries the sequestration of their substantive sovereignty, were the *archon* of Athens, and the *rex sacrorum* of Rome.[17]

There is a maze of seeming contradictions here which many of Frazer's readers must have noted. Kings were treated as divine, yet in the end were forced to die in sometimes appalling circumstances. The reason for this, Frazer thought, was that, since they were supposed to be gods, their mortality should not be made plain. Gods were immortal; that is why they should not be permitted to disintegrate. But, unless they were capable of death, the provision was surely unnecessary. Ancient man seems to have wanted to possess his antediluvian cake and to eat it. He wanted a king who was a god, yet killed him just as soon as his all-too-evident humanity peeped through the self-imposed mask. To put it more cryptically, kings had to be killed so that they could live for ever.

But to put the matter thus is to impose Aristotelian categories on what Frazer saw as a process of imperfect inductive reasoning. Like everything else, early man's views on the world around him were controlled by the association of ideas. Gods were anthropomorphic in that they suffered; they were also forces of nature like the fauna and flora with which the forest or scrub was filled. They were, more especially, like trees.

Evidence here came crowding in, not so much from Asia or Africa as from ancient Europe. The Aryan peoples were, it seemed, especially prone to regarding their gods as like trees and trees as like gods. The leading student of tree-worship in Europe at the time was Wilhelm Mannhardt, whose dissertations *Antike Wald-und Feldkulte* and *Der Baumkultus der Germanen und ihrer Nachbarstämme* provided Frazer with a wealth of information about the tree cults of modern Europe, which Mannhardt, like Frazer, considered to be survivals from a preliterate Aryan past.[18] The object of these cults was the veneration of trees in two kinds: the worship of trees as living beings with souls of their own, and the veneration of sacred personages who were held to embody the spirit of the tree. Such a personage was the Rex Nemorensis. It was Frazer's final contention that the King of the Wood was not a king in the usual sense of the word, but a tree spirit who embodied the spirit of the oak round which he kept watch. He was, as Frazer put it, a departmental king of nature,[19] though with which deity of the Roman pantheon this ecological function connected him Frazer, as his reviewers were later to complain,[20] seemed often to be unsure. Sometimes it was Virbius, sometimes Hippolytus, sometimes Jupiter. The King of the Wood was nothing if not versatile.

The parity between the ways that gods were expected to behave and the functioning of the natural world was thus clearly established, and ancient man would seem to have associated one with the other. This relationship was not only comparative; it was also causal: if the king were permitted to wither away, so might the crops. If kings were gods, they were by the same token natural forces which might gather to a greatness or else abate. Magic, and especially the magic of kingly processes, was, Frazer thought, the way that our forefathers ensured that gods did one rather than the other. Like nature too, kings were both formidable and vulnerable, immortal and in another sense defenceless. It is this paradox at the heart of kingship that both puzzled and delighted Frazer, and to it he addressed some of his most searching insights.

At times he speaks of this double characteristic of kings, their overweening strength and pathetic weakness, as being like an alternating current of electricity. Energy flowed out of them and could harm others. But they were also uniquely open to harmful influences from outside. The electrical metaphor must have come easily to hand in the 1890s, but it is simply an analogy for the paradox which Frazer thought lay at the heart of kingship. His more precise and technical word for this paradox is a "taboo".

CHAPTER V

THE SACRED AND THE TABOO

In the third book of the *Aeneid*, Virgil describes how, fleeing his native Troy and hounded by the resentful attentions of the goddess Juno, Aeneas lands with his companions on an island colonised by settlers from Thrace. Establishing his camp and anxious to secure the protection of the gods for his fresh undertaking, he is about to raise a sacrificial pyre on a mound crowned by myrtle bushes when his intercessions are interrupted by the voice of one who lies buried beneath. "Heu! fuge crudelis terras," the voice exclaims, "fuge litus avarum":

> Ah! flee these barbarous lands, this covetous coast.
> For I am Polydorus. Here was I implanted with
> Iron-tipped spears. Now javelins like a
> Harvest cover me.[1]

Aeneas recognises the speaker as a protégé of King Priam, who, entrusted to the tender mercies of the islands during the latter days of the siege, was murdered once the wooden horse got the better of the Trojan defences and the islanders in a fit of opportunism allied themselves to the Greeks. Their opportunism was, it appears, compounded by avarice, since Priam had entrusted considerable treasure to Polydorus for safekeeping. It is this act of mercenary deceit which particularly offends Aeneas. At this point in the poem he is in Carthage relating his fortunes to Dido and her court, and slips in the rhetorical aside "To what depths would you not plunge mortal minds, you cursed hunger for gold!" ("Quid non mortalia pectora cogis, auri sacra fames!").

"Cursed", though, is an approximation. The Latin word employed by Virgil is not, as one might expect, the habitual term for things accursed – *scelesta* – but *sacra*, implying dedication to a particular god. In the mouth of Aeneas, however, this epithet becomes a term of intense vilification, one of the few instances of its use in this sense in classical literature.

So unusual is the usage that, in his fourth-century commentary on the

Aeneid, Servius devotes a whole paragraph to it. Elsewhere, he says, *sacra* means "set aside for worship" (*devota*) or else "blasphemous" (*sacrilega*). He then goes on to explain its provenance:

> The expression originates in a custom of the Gauls. Whenever the inhabitants of Marseilles (Massilia) are afflicted by pestilence, a pauper volunteers to be provisioned from the public purse on choicest sacrosanct food for a period of one year. Afterwards he is rigged out in the foliage of sacred trees and special ceremonial robes, conducted around the city, and laden with curses so the evils of the community may descend on him. He is then thrown out. This is in Petronius.[2]

It is also in Frazer, who finds in the Marseilles rite a prime example of a scapegoat in classical antiquity.[3] The *Satyricon* of Petronius has come down to us in fragments, the allusion to Marseilles being one of the potsherds, but from what Servius says it is easy to reconstruct the custom. The scapegoat was a *pharmakos*, an agent of public cleansing who took on his shoulders the wrongdoings of the multitude. Yet he was chosen with care and during his year of office dined royally. Though Frazer refrains from treating him as a "temporary king", the *pharmakos* enjoyed some of the king's advantages, as well as sharing in his eventual sorrows. As repository of sin he was reprehensible; as sacrifice, sacred beyond measure. A lone attempt to resolve this seeming contradiction lay, as Servius noted, in the arcane sense ascribed to one Latin word.

The paradox went deeper than the Greeks, or their successors the Romans, could perhaps rationally account for. Macrobius says that to the Greeks animals devoted to a god were *sacer*, and for that very reason hounded out of the fields.[4] How is it that creatures held in such profound reverence could simultaneously be treated with such contempt? A well-known instance of such double-thinking occurs in the last of the so-called "servant songs" in Isaiah, in which the servant of Yahweh is both reviled and revered, "a man of sorrows and acquainted with grief". The passage is now viewed as evocative of the adversities of Israel during the Babylonian exile. Until the late nineteenth century it was taken as prophetic of the Messiah, or more narrowly of Christ himself. Christ too was *sacer*, and he too was "despised and rejected of men".[5]

Frazer is well aware of the Christian parallels, but in the First Edition prefers to keep them in reserve. Analogies, though, were not difficult to find. History is full of kingly or semi-sacred beings who have been obliged to suffer for their privileges. Frazer's initial attempt to bring all of these instances under one umbrella was the work he undertook in 1886 for his *Britannica* article on taboo. His definitive and final attempt was *The Golden Bough* itself.

The word "taboo" first occurs in an English sentence in the second volume of Captain Cook's journal, posthumously published in 1784. Inviting the inhabitants of the Tonga Islands to share his frugal repast one evening, Cook had encountered an unexpected reluctance:

> Not one of them would sit down or eat a bit of anything. On expressing my surprise at this, they were all *taboo* as they said; which word has a very comprehensive meaning, but in general signifies a thing that is forbidden.[6]

In fact the word was *tapu*, and the island can be found on any map; it is called Tongatapu. The passage raises far-reaching questions; was it the food or the islanders who were *tapu*? As connoisseurs of exotic customs were quick to realise, such ideas were not confined to Tonga. The Arabs allude to all such prohibitions by the epithet *harām* (cognate with Biblical Hebrew *herem*). Given the vogue for travellers' tales in the nineteenth century it is not surprising that the word was soon applied to societies remote from the East. The word entered common parlance: however close to home, everything murky and unplumbed was soon "taboo".

It was to bring order to this profusion of instances that Frazer wrote his article for the *Britannica*.[7] The commission came from Smith, who was himself well aware of such prohibitions among the Arabs. Frazer was given *carte blanche*. From Tonga to Athens, from Java to Rome, his subjects dance their two-steps of exclusion. The comparative method has a field day while Frazer practises his hand: valuable preparation this for a *Golden Bough*, for it is only against such a panoramic backdrop, as he was later to insist, that the riddle of Nemi could be solved.

After casting his net over a number of ages and cultures, Frazer weighs in on the ambivalence of the term:

> On looking over the various taboos mentioned above we are tempted to divide them into two general classes – taboos of privilege and taboos of disability. Thus the taboo of chiefs, priests and temples might be described as a privilege, while the taboos imposed on the sick and on persons who had come into contact with the dead might be regarded as a disability; and we might say accordingly that the former rendered persons and things sacred or holy, while the latter rendered them unclean or accursed. But that no such distinction ought to be drawn is clear from the fact that the rules to be observed in the one case and

in the other were identical. On the other hand it is true that the opposition of sacred and accursed, clean and unclean, which plays so important a part in the later history of religion, did in fact arise by differentiation from the single root idea of taboo, which includes and reconciles them both and by reference to which alone their history and mutual relation are intelligible.[8]

Already, you notice, we are on the outskirts of the Wood. In dilating on the vexed lot of kings – "sacred and accursed" – Frazer could almost be describing the Rex Nemorensis, a man privileged in his possession of high office yet constantly vulnerable to the loss of it. Only by regarding Diana's priest as tabooed could such opposites perhaps be reconciled.

In this the King of the Wood was far from unique. The Javanese word for taboo is *pamali*. A man who had carried out a successful head-hunt was *pamali* and for days might not eat from his own hand nor enjoy conjugal relations with his wife. Limitations of the latter sort, as Frazer was later to argue,[9] were perhaps to be explained by fear of a vengeful ghost, for similar rules attached to a Javanese house where a body lay unburied. But women were also *pamali* immediately after childbirth, as in many cultures they are during menstruation. Taken together these examples define a domain amenable only to the mythographer or else perhaps psychologist.

The ancient world knew of such restraints and honoured them. The Greek word for pure or chaste is ἁγνός; for unclean it is ἐναγής. But the word ἅγιος, which we associate with Christian saints, was originally applied to both conditions. The Romans (who, as Frazer charmingly puts it, "preserved more traces of primitive barbarism than the Greeks") enshrined such enigmas at the very heart of their religious system. The Flamen Dialis, the High Priest of Jupiter who resided on the Capitol, was a bizarre and in some ways anachronistic figure beset with a wilderness of restrictions such as the later Romans could hardly fathom. In a paragraph in the *Britannica*, a paragraph which three years later he inserted lock, stock and barrel into *The Golden Bough*, Frazer lists them:

He was not allowed to ride or even touch a horse, nor to look at an army under arms, nor to wear a ring which was not broken, nor to have a knot on any part of his garments; no fire, except a sacred fire, could be taken out of his house; he might not touch or even name a goat, a dog, raw meat, beans, and ivy; he might not walk under a vine; the feet of his bed had to be daubed in mud, his hair could be cut only by a freedman, and his hair and nails when cut had to be buried under a lucky tree.[10]

The recital of such self-denying ordinances in later editions of *The Golden Bough* reminded Freud of the morbid, self-imposed restrictions of the neurotic. For Frazer himself they spoke of a set of ideas far older. The Flamen Dialis, as Frazer was later to put it, existed "between heaven and hell". His whole existence was one complex tissue of taboos. It is far from insignificant that in the Third Edition of *The Golden Bough* Frazer was to interpret the King of the Wood as himself a priest of Jupiter. In the meantime he offers us the Flamen Dialis as a figure *par excellence* privileged and disabled; placed high above his fellow mortals, yet prevented from enjoying their simplest pleasures, a being pre-eminently *sacer*. And with that we come back to Virgil, Frazer's *Britannica* article ending precisely where we began. "The Latin *sacer*", runs its closing sentence, "is exactly taboo, for it means either sacred or accursed."

The ubiquitous nature of the idea of taboo is well attested by the catholicity of Frazer's examples. Since all peoples had known taboos, the mentality both of non-Western societies and of our European ancestors was, Frazer argued, incomprehensible without them. It was especially vital to an understanding of the institution of the kingship in its early stages. For all these reasons, in 1890 the idea of taboo became the organising principle behind the cluster of customs and beliefs Frazer describes in *The Golden Bough*.

Within the overall structure of that book the concept of taboo fulfils two purposes. It is first a pattern of instances intended to explain the peculiar aura surrounding the person and fate of the god–king. It is secondly a logical principle, the ramifications of which are far-reaching. We shall begin with the first.

All kings were hedged about with taboos, so many indeed that in 1911 the subject was to take up a whole volume of the Third Edition. But the essentials are there in 1890. The King of Egypt, says Diodorus Siculus, had to survive on an exclusive diet of veal and goose.[11] If the King of Tonga ate, all turned their back.[12] If the King of Louango in the Cameroons mountains was seen eating by any of his subjects, the witness was immediately put to death.[13] Nobody might look upon the King of Tonquin.[14] The blood of the royals of the forest kingdom of Ashanti might never be shed.[15] The Frankish kings could not have their hair cut.[16] The Mikado could not shave or wash his person, and when he sat on his throne of a morning had to keep as still as a statue.[17] So impatient did one Mikado grow of these restraints that he abdicated in favour of his infant son, who was in turn supplanted by that race of upstarts we know as the Tycoons.[18]

What lay behind this maze of restrictions? The crux, Frazer thought, lay in the nature of a king's power, which early man regarded as both omnivorous and involuntary. It was thus conceived of as more like a force of nature than an operation of the will. To elucidate it, Frazer offers the metaphor of magnetism:

> His person is considered, if we may express it so, as the dynamic centre of the universe, from which lines of force radiate to all quarters of the heaven; so that any motion of his – the turning of his head, the lifting of his hand – instantaneously affects and may seriously disturb some part of nature.[19]

That "nature" in this sentence was a peculiarly nineteenth-century abstraction, or that he could be accused of putting late-Victorian notions of blind "natural" force into the minds of primeval man, does not seem to have occurred to Frazer. Power was like electricity, and like electricity much to be feared. The pulsations induced made kings both uniquely strong and uniquely vulnerable. Everything a king handled was suffused with his emanations, as if electrified by contact with his divine person. Nobody might touch the King of Cambodia, or the Queen of Tahiti.[20] Even a monarch's cast-offs were fatal. Thus a Maori who inadvertently finished off the remains of the chief's meal died instantaneously of stomach cramp on being informed of his crime, and others who availed themselves of the chief's tinder box in his absence expired in sheer terror upon being apprised of the identity of its owner.[21]

But, if kings could harm others, they were themselves unusually susceptible to harm. This vulnerability was a source of great anxiety to their subjects, who depended for their welfare on the health of the sacred person, but its sources lay in evils common to all. The principal source was the weakness of the human soul, which was conceived of as a bird which might at any time take flight. Souls were known frequently to leave bodies, often through the mouth. When one of their companions yawned, the Hindus snapped their thumbs to discourage his soul from escaping.

The danger was enhanced during sleep. Tylor had identified this fear with a belief in dreams as the night escapades of the venturing soul, which might at any point be prevented from returning.[22] Thus many peoples refrain from waking a sleeper, lest his soul should be surprised while absent. In Bombay it was esteemed a capital offence to alter the posture of one who lay asleep, since on its return the soul might not recognise him and turn back.[23] The soul of man could also inhere in his shadow. Thus mirrors were turned to the wall after a death in the house, lest the reflections of the inmates, falling on the glass, might be wafted away by the departing spirit.[24] Frazer thought that Narcissus too must have been slain by the sight of his reflection in the water, despite the legend which attributed his death to devastation at the sight of his own beauty.[25]

If the souls of commoners were this fragile, how much more so the soul of a king, upon whom all depended? It was for this reason that kings could not be seen eating, lest their souls be snatched out of their mouths.[26] For much the same reason they seldom addressed their subjects directly, often speaking through interpreters. Kings were like transmitters with instant conductors leading duct-like to the furthest reaches of the universe. All monarchs suffered from this chronic lack of insulation. Commoners had resistances built into their system; kings had none.

Kings also had bald patches where their resistance was absolutely nil. Certain parts of their body must therefore at all costs remain inviolate. Extreme precautions were taken to make sure that nothing passed over the king's head, this part of his person being deemed especially prone to attack. Marquesan women refused to walk over the deck of a ship in case one of their chiefs was standing below.[27] Kings also suffered weird and inexplicable allergies. The Flamen Dialis might not walk under the trellis of a vine, since the ancients believed blood of his slain enemies to be distilled in the juice of the grape, which was thus especially noxious.[28]

The enumeration of these specific taboos is a considerable adornment to Frazer's argument, but the influence of taboo is also pervasive at a deeper structural level. In the texture of the book as a whole it becomes a dialectic by means of which Frazer interprets refractory evidence in a light sympathetic to his case.

For, if anything which is holy is by the same token loathsome, and anything which is unclean worthy of the deepest veneration, the scope for the interpretation of any given custom is manifestly exceptionally wide. Regarded opportunistically, Frazer could have his cake and eat it.

There are several instances of such arguing in *The Golden Bough*. At times it seems to pulse through the whole work like an insistent two-way charge. It is one reason why Frazer's arguments sometimes give the impression of being so slippery. As he was once to complain of a fellow scholar who in different circumstances refused to lie down: "there is no having such a man".

The most piquant instance of all occurs in the section on the corn spirit, and has to do with horses. We have already observed one specific taboo regarding horses: the Flamen Dialis could not touch or even name them. Was it the horse that was taboo or the priest? Probably the priest, but in one place in ancient Rome horses themselves were clearly tabooed. Ovid and Virgil had said that horses were not allowed in the precincts at Nemi, and in this Pausanias concurred.[29] On the reason for this exclusion the classical authors were again unanimous: the shrine was part-dedicated to Hippolytus in his Latin embodiment of Virbius, and Hippolytus, as Pausanias also relates, was dragged to death by horses.[30]

This explanation has much to commend it – directness for one thing – but it is too simple for Frazer, who needs to argue that the horse possesses a special relationship with the Arician cult. He has just been discussing vegetation spirits, and wants to say that the horse was a tree spirit and hence sacred to the grove. If it was sacred, how came it to be excluded?

It is here that ambiguity of taboos comes to the rescue. For in a world governed by the logic of taboo *a* can be *a* and not-*a* at the same time. Frazer's other principal example of a vegetation spirit is the pig. Now Plutarch, our leading classical authority on the Egyptian cults, connects the worship of Osiris with the pig. When Typhon, Osiris's jealous half-brother, wanted to do away with the god, he adopted the form of a boar, in which embodiment he tore Osiris to pieces. That in any case is the standard form of the myth, but Frazer wants to say that it was Osiris who was a pig, or rather that both he and the boar were embodiments of the corn spirit. Was Osiris then killed by himself? The proposition looks highly perverse until you view Egyptian attitudes to swine as corresponding to a variety of taboo, in which case the vileness and at the same time sanctity of swine suddenly become comprehensible.

Thus armed, Frazer returns to Hippolytus. Hippolytus, as we have seen, was killed by horses, but horses were commonly three spirits. On the analogy of Osiris – the whole discussion of Osiris, which looms so large in the Third Edition, begins simply like this, as an analogy – Hippolytus and the horse (look at his name) can be seen as one and the same, and both can be seen as manifestations of the indwelling *numen* of the oak. This makes much sense in an oak-grove, but now urge it in the face of ancient testimony? You do not exclude a god from his own temple. Frazer's way round this, so devious a route it almost takes one's breath away, is to see the exclusion clause as a kind of cipher. The classical authors said that horses were not admitted to the precincts: what they really meant was, not only were they admitted but, as embodiments of the tree to which the shrine was dedicated, they were annually sacrificed within the grounds.

There is of course not the slightest evidence that horses were ever done to death in the precincts at Nemi. True, there were annual sacrifices to Hippolytus in his Greek home of Troezen, but the victims do not seem to have been horses.[31] Certainly when Savile unearthed a portion of the precinct in 1885 a circular stylobate was found which he took to be the base of a sacrificial altar. There were also models of horses in the side chapels, but between these two pieces of evidence there is a crucial step which is quite simply missing. With Frazer the common ploy when evidence is lacking is to make inferences sideways. On at least one occasion in the Roman year horses were certainly sacrificed: after the annual chariot race on 15 October, when the head of the horse to the right of the victorious team was offered up to Mars.[32]

The October horse had recently been subjected to a searching discussion by Wilhelm Mannhardt, who thought the institution part of an ancient corn cult.[33] Mars was originally a god of the sown seed. If a horse was offered to a vegetation god once a year in Rome, why not in Nemi, the spiritual focus of the Latin League? From this point in the argument the non-existent horse-sacrifice is taken as read.

So far, so good. Frazer's reasoning has a certain judicious smoothness until you remember the immense age of the Hippolytus legends and the manner of his death. Was, then, the legend of Phaedra's amorous obsession with her step-son and of Poseidon's jealous rage, just pious camouflage, rationalisation after the event? If this was the case, the legend that Hippolytus was dragged to death by horses could not possibly have been the root cause of the apparent exclusion of these animals from the grove. By a brilliant sleight-of-hand Frazer convinces – or *almost* convinces us – that the Latins contrived the legend to account for the facts:

The myth that he [Hippolytus/Virbius] had been killed by horses was probably invented to explain certain features in his worship, amongst others the custom of excluding horses from his sacred grove. For myth changes while men remain constant; men continue to do what their fathers did before them, though the reasons for which their fathers acted have been long forgotten.[34]

An important sentence this, and one which well accords with a notion held by Frazer at this time with almost religious intensity: the historical priority of custom to myth. It is certainly very consistent with what Frazer had learned from William Robertson Smith, for whom by 1887 the priority of ritual to myth was almost an article of faith: "legend is to be explained from cult and not conversely".[35] The trouble in this case is that the legend is far anterior to the cult. The earliest date Frazer had for the foundation of the shrine at Nemi was the third century BC, and the myth of Hippolytus was memorably presented by Euripides in Athens some two centuries earlier. In the heat of argument Frazer has allowed his taboo-logic to betray him into the appearance of a *non sequitur*.

We can, as it happens, reconstruct Frazer's argument for him. What he means is that the Hippolytus legend existed centuries earlier in Greece, and that Virbius was a separate Italian deity, some form of wood sprite. When the Latins inaugurated the horse-sacrifices at Nemi – if such sacrifices ever took place – they needed a rationale, and borrowed the Hippolytus myth to lend lustre to the cult. By a common process of religious syncretism Virbius then became Hippolytus, while out of deference to the latter gentleman horses were excluded from the grove.

But, whatever way one looks at it, Frazer's interpretation of the Arician cult depends upon an appreciation of taboo. Without the falling of that particular seed, it is doubtful if the corn would ever have stood so high. Certainly he would not have come to understand the institution of kingship in the way that he did, in which case Hamilton's evidence when he came upon it in the spring of 1889 would have passed him by. All of which is tantamount to saying that without "Taboo" *The Golden Bough* would never have been written.

Reading through Frazer's correspondence and jottings from the years 1883–9, it is clear that there are any number of routes his thinking might have taken. Some of these he indeed took later on, and some were cul-de-sacs it will soon be our pleasure to explore. Though it might be truer to state that in Frazer's wonderfully inclusive mind nothing was ever quite an impasse. All roads led to the grove at Nemi, though some of them converged before reaching the outskirts of the wood. Not for nothing was one of Diana's soubriquets "Trivia", "Diana of the crossroads". Her grove bristled with such convergences, at one of which we must now pause.

CHAPTER VI

TOTEMS AND TOTEM FEASTS

THERE is one other way of describing the ambiguous attitude towards the horse exhibited in the shrine at Nemi: in Nemi the horse was a totem. Frazer as a matter of fact never phrases it this crudely, preferring to imply that the ancient Latins retained the remnants of a totemic attitude, and that they focused this attitude on the horse. William Robertson Smith, I think, would not have been so squeamish – but, then, totems were his obsession.

We must return once more to the auspicious year of 1887. You will remember that back in 1869 G. H. Lewes, editor of the *Fortnightly Review*, had commissioned an article on totemism from M'Lennan. The article appeared in instalments under the title "The Worship of Animals and Plants" in the October and November issues of that year and the February issue of the next.[1] Smith was coming up to twenty-four at the time, newly acquainted with M'Lennan's head-spinning theories, and the article set a light in his eyes. For the next twenty-five years he laboured to prove that totems existed in ancient Arabia, and more widely among the Semites. While under a cloud at Aberdeen he had made two trips to the Arabian Peninsula, writing back excitedly of totems lying thick under the soles of his feet. By 1885 he felt able to set out the implications of totemism for Arab society in his Cambridge lectures *Kinship and Marriage in Ancient Arabia*, which Frazer gleefully attended.

So, when in the following year the *Encyclopaedia Britannica* reached "T", Smith was determined to do totemism justice. In the meantime Frazer had already cut his teeth on "Taboo", but it is a measure of the respect in which Smith held him that he entrusted totemism, a subject so dear to his heart, to one whose published books amounted at the time to a school edition of Sallust.[2] "Totem" was a latish submission, but Smith was adamant that space must be made for it. Smith wrote to the publishers – torture though it was, "Torture" must go:

I hope that Messrs Black clearly understand that Totemism is a subject of growing importance daily mentioned in magazines and newspapers, but of which there is no good account anywhere – precisely one of those cases where we have an opportunity of being ahead of everyone and getting some reputation. There is no article in the volume for which I am more solicitous. I have taken much personal pains with it, guiding Frazer carefully in his treatment; and he has put about seven months' hard work on it to make it the standard article on the subject. We must make room for it, whatever else goes.[3]

As Smith neatly puts it, torture was of "decaying" interest. Frazer, however, was far from decaying; in fact he was writing like mad. Nothing illustrates so well as his work on totemism that precocious burgeoning of ideas to which Frazer was always prone. Smith's letter implies that at the outset his protégé needed a helping hand, but soon there was no stopping him. By the time volume XXIII of the Britannica was set in type Frazer had already published a book on the subject, the tiny *Totemism* of 1887. Already he was corresponding with many of the leading authorities in the field. By 1910 he was to have enough material for the four volumes of *Totemism and Exogamy*, to which in 1937 he added the supplement called *Totemica*. Taboos might come and taboos might go, but Frazer sprouted totems to the end.

The term "totem" is North American, first employed in an English text in 1791 by the traveller and interpreter James Long, who requisitioned it from the language of the Ojebway Indians.[4] As such totemism enjoys, *pace* Freud, no local connection with taboo. In Frazerspeak, however, the two Ts are twins, and Siamese twins at that. The reason lies in their moment of conception. "The researches I made for these articles", wrote Frazer in 1935, "were the beginning of a systematic application to anthropology."[5] The concepts behind the articles became columns by which *The Golden Bough* with all its manifold ramifications was to be supported.

Totemism was in any case a profoundly fashionable subject at the time, though one which seemed to generate more heat than light. Following the great totemism debate of the 1880s and 1890s a century after the event is rather like attempting to follow an especially acrimonious football commentary shared between several commentators none of whom can see the pitch. Much useful investigative field-work was done during these decades, especially in Australia, but the controversy itself raged exclusively between metropolitan scholars of early society none of whom had any real intention of visiting the Antipodes. (Frazer once solemnly intended to visit New Guinea with A. C. Haddon, but his Pausanias got the better of him, and so did his wife.) Dispatches were for ever arriving from the outback, only to be pounced upon by armchair ethnologists eager to snatch the palm from rivals whose grasp of the technicalities was as theoretical as their own. No sooner was Frazer's *Totemism* out in 1887 than missives started arriving from Andrew Lang, who had already had something to say on the subject in his *Custom and Myth*, published earlier in the very same year. Lady Frazer once said that she had to take one of Lang's indecipherable twelve-page letters on totemism in to Jimmy with the breakfast every day of the week. The letters contained a lot of chat interspersed between the totems. "I'm at work on a novel, more diverting than one's heavy performances. No doubt we should try to write (more) rarely, but the flesh is weak."[6] Lang's weak flesh eventually betrayed him into open hostility, the casus belli in this instance being the Arunta of central Australia, over whom he and Frazer failed to agree.[7] Frazer remained forgiving; indeed, in the face of such provocations as Lang's *The Secret of the Totem*[8] his tolerance was nothing less than heroic.

The controversy was made no easier by Frazer's inability to make up his mind. By the time *Totemism and Exogamy* appeared in 1910 he had already exhausted three theories of totemism, though to do him justice he stuck to the third. He was in fact to abide by the last, the so-called "conceptional" theory of totemism, to the very end, but it is the first two theories which are significant in the genesis of *The Golden Bough*. We must take them in order.

To begin with Frazer was inclined to see totems as boxes in which early man kept his soul for safekeeping when separated from his body. I shall call this Frazer's Depository Theory. The totem was a sort of soul-safe. An integral part of it was the notion of souls being detachable; in *The Golden Bough* Frazer calls the supersition thus invoked the belief in the "external soul". This theory Frazer had initially acquired not from Australia but from the Dutch ethnographer George Wilken, with whom he had actively corresponded since 1885. The ultimate source of the theory, which was far from original, was a moot point. When Edward Tylor – more by oversight than anything else – implicitly accused Frazer of not acknowledging *all* his sources, Frazer wrote him a tart letter saying that their relationship, valuable as it had been to both of them, was now at an end.[9] In time Frazer came round, but there must have been occasions when he asked himself whether the totems were worth it.

Frazer also got a little help from Suffolk, or rather from Edward Clodd, banker, amateur folklorist, Edward Fitzgerald groupie, militant rationalist and onetime President of the Folk Lore Society. A city man during the week, Clodd spent his weekends at his Aldeburgh retreat writing popular studies of folktales. One he published in the *Folk-lore Journal* in 1884 was entitled "The Philosophy of Punchkin".[10] It was based on an Indian folktale about a prince who seeks to emancipate his mother from the control of a wicked sorcerer called Punchkin, a feat he eventually contrives by systematically dismembering a parrot which contains the magician's soul. As he tears the bird limb from limb the magician's body falls to pieces until there is nothing left but a disembodied head which promptly expires with a groan.

This story, and the philosophy of mind behind it, meant a lot to Frazer. If John Stuart Mill valued Pushkin more highly than pushpin, Frazer preferred Punchkin to either. The story delighted him because he came to see Punchkin's parrot as a prototype of the totem. In 1889, when he was preparing the First Edition of *The Golden Bough*, the whole theory of the external soul also had a deep effect on the way Frazer came to think about the oak, whose external soul was, he argued, the mistletoe. By this reading the mistletoe itself was a totem of sorts.

But to start with Frazer was interested in the external soul for the quite different reason that he thought it could help him solve M'Lennan's riddle of the origins of matrimony. There is nothing odd about this. Smith's lectures of 1885 had also sought to interpret Arab marriage customs through an application of totemic ideas: the link in any case was very apparent in M'Lennan. Along with totemism, marriage in 1887 was very much a subject *à la mode*. The general impression seemed to be that marriage had passed through various stages from a possible early sexual communism. One of the most important, and at the same time puzzling of these stages was that which M'Lennan had dubbed "exogamy".

It had long been known that among certain pre-industrial peoples marriage within the clan was not merely discouraged but hedged around with the severest penalties. So substantial was this evidence that in *Primitive Marriage* M'Lennan had suggested that all societies had at one time or other passed through a stage when marriage within the kinship group was outlawed; this he termed "exogamy". The most impressive evidence came from Australia, where, it seemed, aboriginal society was organised according to a complex, interweaving set of clans, not all of which were confined to a given geographical area. These clans possessed the characteristic that, not merely did they share the same totem, but marriage between members was strictly taboo. In Australia, it seemed, totem-allegiance was the acid test of kinship. So impressive was this evidence that Frazer had spent a considerable period in 1887 classifying all known aboriginal societies into clan groupings, which to distinguish from localised tribes he termed "phatries". Much of *Totemism* is devoted to this classification.

But whence had the fear of marriage within the clan arisen? It was rational on eugenic grounds, but early man knew nothing of eugenics. Marriage within clans might be considered a variety of incest, and incest was the one crime which all peoples seem to regard with the utmost horror. Perhaps a clue could be extracted from that other persistent feature of pre-industrial societies, rites of passage. Birth, puberty, death were all marked by ceremonies more or less awesome, but none were more so than those which attended the onset of adolescence. At this vital turning-point of a young person's life many societies stage a kind of symbolic death and resurrection whereby the inititiate lies down in a charade of death and is then ceremonially resuscitated.[11] What was the purpose of a custom apparently so w\idepread, and what had it to tell us about mankind's other social arrangements?

Again we must return to 1887. Frazer had just published *Totemism*, and was newly enthralled by his Depository Theory. Among the Ojebway Indians, in Fiji and in the Lower Congo he had noted this custom of adolescents lying down in a masquerade of death and then being dramatically raised. Might this not be the moment at which the soul was deposited in the totem? If so, much about the mentality of prehistoric man might be explained: his phobias, his rituals, his notions of life and death. If the soul of the adult male was laid aside for perpetual safekeeping, the probable motive could only be the evasion of some danger recognised by every member of the clan. If the act of stowing away the soul did not occur until puberty, then this danger must pertain to adult life alone: must in fact be sexual.

Was sex then so dangerous? In the 1880s, for bachelor dons, it may well have been, but the reasons for so thinking were older, in fact classical. Many civilisations seem to have thought at least one form of sexual intercourse to be attended by considerable peril: namely, the deflowering of virgins. This belief was commonly regarded as the origin of sacred prostitution in the ancient world. Herodotos says that the Babylonians used to prostitute their unmarried daughters:[12] he says the same for Cyprus and Lydia (in what is now Turkey), in both of which the *jus primae noctis* went to a total stranger. By the time of Herodotos the system had become institutionalised, but it would appear to have originated in a series of *ad hoc* arrangements by which an outsider took upon himself the onerous task of relieving a young woman of her maidenhood. Once the danger was past, she could safely be bestowed in matrimony.

So much was conventional wisdom, but as Frazer was to point out, the matter was not that simple. Prostitution implies that the man pays for the young girl's favours, whereas in a number of recorded instances – in Malabar, the Philippines and Central Africa – it was the deflowerer who was paid.[13] The motive cannot therefore have been pleasure, but the removal of some dire hazard. In the case of widows, danger was to be apprehended from the jealous spirit of the deceased husband. The Koryaks of the Kamchatka Peninsula in north-west Russia used to pay strangers to brave the wrath of such unappeased spouses before any widow could remarry. This posthumous connubial jealousy was supposedly so extreme that only a foreigner could risk it. When the second Bering expedition arrived in Kamchatka in 1729 there was a serious backlog of widows, and the problem resolved itself to everybody's satisfaction within a matter of hours: which was just as well since Bering had run out of funds.[14] But this reasoning only applied to widows. With unmarried girls, or women not otherwise claimed by zealous ghosts, the cause of the apprehended peril had to be different.

For several weeks in the autumn of 1887, immediately after completing his *Totemism*, Frazer seems to have thought that he had the answer: the danger inhered in the woman's blood, which was viewed as frankly diabolic. This would certainly account for the fear of deflowering virgins. But women were also known to be subjected to fierce taboos during their monthly periods, where the menses were similarly shunned.[15] The controversy came to a head in October 1887, and can be followed in a remarkable run of letters, now in the Wren Library at Trinity College, Cambridge.[16] The correspondence, which lasted a fortnight, passed between Frazer and his erstwhile supervisor Henry Jackson. They had clearly been writing for some time. The bone of contention seems to have been this: Frazer thought all sexual intercourse dangerous, Jackson only intercourse with a virgin (to be sure, he had more to go on). One blushes rather at the naïveté of the tone.

> Trinity College
> Cambridge.
> 25th October, 1887.

My Dear Jackson,

 Many thanks for your criticisms which greatly help to clear and sharpen one's ideas. I reply:

(1) I do not think it necessary to draw the line so sharply as you do

between consummation and subsequent intercourse. The effusion of blood proves that there is a demon in the woman wounding her, but this demon is not permanently (if at all) driven out at consummation; *menstruation* is a proof of his continued presence in the woman. Thence as women are always possessed by a devil, there must *at any time* be a danger in sexual intercourse, because it is then that the demon visibly stabs. But he may be there with his knife always; hence the need of abstinence on special occasions (war etc.) which are dangerous enough in themselves. . . .

(2) As to the *limitation* of the effusion of the blood, the answer too seems simple. The slighter the wound, the weaker the hand that inflicted it. By fasting you have thenceforth weakened the devil and so far made him less dangerous; he can still strike, but not so deep. Surely treatment of the patient aimed, not at the man or woman himself or herself, but at the devil in his or her inside, is thoroughly in accord with savage ideas. Gubernatis (*Msi Nuziali*, 2nd Ed, p. 214) quotes an ancient Indian as saying "tempo opportuno per la copula è il momento in cui alla sposa che si trova nel mese è appessa cessato il sangue". Exactly: the devil has exhausted himself and the husband seizes the opportunity before he (the devil) can recruit his strength.

As to the "effusion of blood *desired*", it is of course common, but in all cases, I believe, so far as my memory goes, the object professed or rather flaunted openly is the proof of virginity. But virginity only gets a value late in the social development; the idea of virginity in itself having value is one, I would venture to swear, which a savage is unable to grasp. Therefore all customs based on the value of virginity must be late and may be entirely omitted in discussing the origin of marriage laws.

As to your explanation (from your point of view) of the desire for a husband to have the blood shed by someone else, the fact that in both the examples the substitute must be a *stranger* (this point being particularly insisted upon) tells against you as I said. But two cases are not enough; more evidence is wanted.

Your explanation of "effusion of blood not desired", if I understand it rightly, seems to involve the contradiction of both desiring the effusion of blood and not desiring it – desiring it as a proof of virginity (which by that time, you say, must have been valued) and not desiring it because the absence of blood would be the "form of the form" of capture.

I think that I have parried your objections to my view or rather conjecture; but if you see an opening, pray strike and spare not. This discussion is to me very stimulating.

Jackson was Frazer's sounding-board, a friend and former teacher who could contribute the odd telling caveat while retaining the secrecy so essential in a rapidly evolving field. A psychoanalysis of this letter might prove a rewarding exercise, but had better be resisted. The interpretation of the rhythm method is especially piquant. Meanwhile the dovecotes were still fluttering – two days later, we have this:

> Trinity College,
> Cambridge.
> 27th October, 1887.

My dear Jackson,

There is abundance of evidence that women at menstruation are regarded as most dangerous; they are secluded at these times amongst all the lower races and all contact with them carefully avoided. Whatever they touch contracts pollution. There is another class of facts which must be looked sharply after – the use of the *blood* of victims to expiate sins of unchastity. Examples are rare, but they occur.

I am inclined to put aside all other work in order to devote myself exclusively to following up this line, & I might have a volume out in a year. Pausanias, I fear, must stand aside.

You will use your discretion in speaking about these facts and ideas? Having got, as I think, on the track, I should like to follow it out for myself.

Three years later the accumulated evidence concerning menstruation appeared in *The Golden Bough*, but what was this volume of which Frazer had such lavish hopes? Not *Totemism*, which was already in the press. It was clearly a work on the origins of marriage, and more especially on sexual taboos. It was for this then, rather than *The Golden Bough*, that the work on Pausanias was laid aside. For a time it had Frazer breathless with excitement. Two weeks later, with the publication of the slender monograph on *Totemism*, Jackson is still sworn to secrecy, but the grounds of investigation have shifted. Frazer has been digging into the causes of exogamy, and has happened upon what he takes for the root. Strangers are preferable as marriage partners because in the eyes of the community they are exempt from taboo, and magic cannot touch them. This at least was certainly the case in New Zealand. Was this what lay beneath M'Lennan's old chestnut of bride capture?

> Trinity College,
> Cambridge.
> 9th November, 1887.

My dear Jackson,

Please accept a copy of *Totemism*. I should be extremely glad to hear any criticisms you may have to make on it and to discuss them with you.

May I also ask you to read, mark and inwardly digest the following:

"The interest taken by spirits of the dead in mundane affairs seldom extends beyond the limits of the tribe to which they belong. Hence, persons taken in war and carried away as slaves by another tribe cease from that moment to be under the care of any *Atua* [a Maori tutelary spirit]. The *Atua* of their own tribe trouble themselves not to follow them among a hostile tribe and hostile spirits; while the *Atua* of the tribe whose slaves they are never give them a thought. They are therefore independent of the law of *tapu*, as far as they are individually concerned – a fortunate circumstance for the comfort of the female portion of the community; for it is owing to this belief that male slaves are able to assist them in a variety of menial offices connected with carrying and cooking food, which they could not in their free state have meddled in without incurring the anger of the *Atua*, and its consequences – sickness, and perhaps death." (Shortland, *Tradition & Superstitions of the New Zealanders*, p. 82 sq.)

Nothing more is wanted for the explanation of exogamy. You will keep it dark.

But then the clock in the Great Court booms midday, and with the last chime Frazer's illusions flee:

> Trinity College,
> Cambridge,
> 9th November, 1887.

A mare's nest I fear it was after all. A few minutes, or rather half a minute's conversation with R. Smith burst my bubble [*sic*] exogamy. I wrote hastily – having seen the passage, and being in the act of sending you a copy of *Totemism*, I put it in a letter, but I don't think it amounts to much.

In my book which takes shape more and more I do not mean to propound a theory of exogamy, perhaps, not even to refer to the subject. I will deal only with special points, not with a broad theory of society.

With that rather crestfallen little note, the correspondence ceases. It is interesting that even now Smith commands an absolute veto, but what is this book which is falling into place? It cannot concern totemism, for about that Frazer has just written. It cannot concern exogamy, because he says that he is willing to exclude the subject altogether. Nor, from the sense that pervades this correspondence of a very specific discovery can it have been a treatise on general anthropology, something along the lines of Tylor's *Primitive Culture*. In his recent biography of Frazer, Robert Ackerman suggests that *The Golden Bough* grew out of such a book, but there is no evidence that such a work ever existed. Had it done so, it would have flown in the face of Frazer's whole working-practice, which was to work from small matters towards larger ones. It is true that in a letter to George Macmillan at this time Frazer speaks of a general work on primitive superstition and religion, as he does also in the Preface to *The Golden Bough* three years later. But the tone and direction of his letters to academic colleagues, who are the only ones likely at this stage to have been party to the actual content of the work, suggest that, having disposed of totemism, Frazer was busy extending his article on taboo into another monograph. As this project proceeded, sexual taboos seem to have fallen into the background (though they are there in *The Golden Bough* in abundance) and Frazer was drawn more and more to taboos surrounding priestly kings. It was out of that background, once he had noticed the catalytic passage in Hamilton, that *The Golden Bough* eventually emerged.

There remains a *postscriptum*. Frazer abandoned his attempts to explain the origins of human marriage, and M'Lennan's problem remains even now unsolved. The Depository Theory, however, is written large and clear in *The Golden Bough* – in all editions of that work, even those written long after the theory itself had been abandoned. As for Frazer's darker speculations concerning mankind's fear of menstrual blood and its implications for totemic exogamy, there exists one memorial, a passage tentatively phrased but crucially positioned in the architecture of the book. It occurs in the chapter on the external soul immediately after the discussion of "Death and Resurrection at Initiation Rites" (running head). For those who know the background it is one of the more telling passages in the work, a lone monolith halfway down a trail which led nowhere:

> Thus, if I am right, whenever totemism is found, and wherever a pretence is made of killing and bringing to life again the novice at initiation, there may exist or have existed not only a belief in permanently depositing the soul in some external object – animal, plant or what not – but an actual intention of so doing. If the question is put, why do men desire to deposit their life outside their bodies, the answer can only be that, like the giant in the fairy tale, they think it safer than to carry it about with them, just as people deposit their money with a banker rather than carry it on their persons. We have seen that at critical periods the life or soul is sometimes temporarily stowed away in a safe place till the danger is past. But institutions like totemism are not resorted to merely on special occasions of danger; they are systems into which everyone, or at least every male, is obliged to be initiated at a certain period of life. Now the period of life at which initiation regularly takes place is puberty; and this fact suggests that the special danger which totemism and systems like it are designed to obviate is supposed not to arise till maturity has been attained, in fact that the danger apprehended is believed to attend the relation of the sexes to each another. It would be easy to prove by a long array of facts that the sexual relation is associated in the primitive mind with many supernatural perils; but the exact nature of the danger apprehended is still obscure. We may hope that a more exact acquaintance with savage modes of thought will in time disclose this central mystery of primitive society, and will therefore furnish the clue, not only to the social aspect of totemism (the prohibition of sexual union between persons of the same totem) but to the origin of the marriage system.[17]

This is how things stood in 1890 when the first *Golden Bough* appeared, but Frazer's interest in totemism was far from played out, nor did his attempts to plumb the origins of the totemic system stand still. The Depository Theory held steady for twelve years until the spring of 1899, when fresh evidence arrived from an unexpected quarter.

Baldwin Spencer was a zoologist of a Darwinian turn of mind who had attended Tylor's lectures at Merton while reading for a natural-science degree at Exeter College, Oxford, in the 1870s. When a young Fellow of Lincoln, his work on the pineal eye of the lizard won him widespread recognition in the scientific community, and he was elected to a Chair in Zoology at the University of Melbourne at the tender age of twenty-seven. There he remained for the rest of his life. But the experience which more than any other transformed his existence was his attachment as scientific adviser to an expedition mounted by W. A. Horn to the area surrounding Alice Springs in 1881. For the rest of his long life he remained, like the investigator of the Torres Straits, Frazer's friend A. C. Haddon, torn between natural science and ethnology.

It was on the Horn expedition that Spencer made the acqaintance of Francis James Gillen, Sub-Protector of the Aborigines, and established with him a working-relationship which was to form the basis of a lifetime's ethnographic work. Gillen supplied the local know-how while Spencer brought his incisive analytical intellect to bear on the material of their researches, and incidentally wrote the books which appeared under both their names. It was a series of investigations into the society of the Arunta, a people inhabiting the far interior of the Northern Territory in the vicinity of Ayer's Rock, that led to a series of discoveries regarding aborigine social structure which were to shake the totemic debate to its foundations.

The opening gambit was a letter from Frazer to the Methodist missionary and amateur ethnologist Lorimer Fison, whom he had met when Fison visited England in 1894.[18] Already Frazer had got wind of Spencer and Gillen's investigations, and, when he wrote to Fison asking for further particulars, the letter was handed on to Spencer, who then undertook to keep Frazer abreast of his researches. It thus fell to Spencer to shatter at one blow one of the mainstays of Frazer's earlier book on totemism. One of the principal conclusions both of the *Britannica* article and of the monograph of 1887 had been that there existed, at all times and throughout the known world, an absolute taboo on eating the totem, whom the totem-holder was pledged by all means to protect. This was totally consonant with the view of totems expressed in the Depository Theory, according to which to eat the totem would be a form of cannibalistic suicide. It was this tenet of the totemic philosophy which in his first letter Spencer was to scatter to the winds in one brief sentence:

There are plenty of restrictions as to eating various types of food, but in no case are the restrictions concerned with totems. A Kangaroo man eats and kills a kangaroo, an Emu man kills and eats an emu and so on.[19]

"Such traditions", Frazer was later to write, "fly straight in the face of all our old notions of totemism."[20] None the less the revelations energised Frazer, who had just completed his Pausanias and was thinking of getting down to work on a revision of *The Golden Bough*. A hectic correspondence with Spencer followed, leading to Frazer's promise to find a publisher for *Tribes of Central Australasia*, the manuscript of which Spencer had sent him. The publisher he found was, naturally enough, Macmillan.[21] (Eventually Frazer was to exhaust this stock of good-will. The long-suffering Macmillan systematically took on all of Frazer's protégés until 1919, when he put his foot down over Malinowski – not a wise sticking-point.) Frazer subsequently guided Spencer's book through the press, making the occasional stylistic change and overseeing the proofs. Already he had taken full cognisance of the implications of Spencer's discoveries for his own work. The Depository Theory, and everything which emanated from it, would have to be rethought. The approach Frazer adopted was typical of the absolute candour and moral courage he demonstrated on all such occasions. In the spring of 1900, while engaged on the Second Edition of *The Golden Bough*, he announced in the pages of the *Fortnightly* – the very same forum as M'Lennan had chosen for his pioneering discussions on totemism – that concerning this most vital link in the chain of comparative ethnology he had quite simply been wrong.[22]

What in Spencer had proved so disarming? From much of the new work Frazer took nothing, his attention having been alerted by one thing alone: a set of disclosures concerning an aspect of aboriginal life of which no one had so far written. The aboriginal economy was, it appeared, much affected by violent changes which engulfed the outback at the commencement of the rainy season. Suddenly what had been to all appearances a barren waste burgeoned into exultant life, whereupon with almost biblical profusion there sprang up in the wilderness witchetty grubs, yams, vegetable life of all kinds. To this abrupt transformation in the face of nature the aborigines were far from indifferent. Throughout the tract of Central Australia where Spencer and Gillen carried out their investigations there occurred at this time of year a series of *intichiuma* ceremonies, spring festivals at which members of the clan mounted foraging expeditions for their own totemic animal or plant. What then occurred is described by Spencer in one of his letters:

After the short season of plenty . . . all the collected store is taken to the men's camp. Here in the first place the men who are not of the totem place their stores before the head man (he is the head of the totem of that locality). The head man takes one pitcher full and with the help of the other members of the totem grinds its contents between stones, and after he and the other men of the totem have taken and eaten a little he hands all back to the other men. Then he takes another pitcher full – this time from his own store, and after grinding it up he and the men of the other totem eat a little and pass the greater part of what has been collected on to the other men. After this, the individuals of the totem eat sparingly of the grub; if they eat too much then the effect of the ceremony would be injured and there would be fewer grubs.[23]

For Frazer the *intichiuma* ceremonies were the heart of Spencer's book. When the manuscript was submitted to Edward Tylor for his comments he suggested that the whole tedious section be cut out, thus provoking a furious letter from Frazer to Macmillan.[24] Whatever else went, the *intichiuma* ceremonies must stay. What had so moved him? It is hard to resist the impression that Frazer had been influenced by Spencer's wording: "After he and the other men of the totem have taken and eaten a little . . . ." One could comment on this at length – Frazer did – but the most timely response would seem to be another, infinitely more familiar quotation:

Who, in the same night that he was betrayed, took Bread; and, when he had given thanks, he brake it, and gave it to his disciples, saying, "Take, eat; this is my Body which is given for you: Do this in remembrance of me."

For centuries men had quarrelled over the import of the Christian Communion service. It had once been a prime *casus belli* in the German, English and the Scottish Reformations. The Catholic view was that the Communion was a privileged participation in a divine meal (if Christ were regarded as totem, the Australian rite would indeed provide a parallel here). The Protestant view, as expressed in the Prayer of Consecration just quoted, and which Spencer seems to echo in his letter, was that it was simply a feast of remembrance.

As a son of the Free Church of Scotland Frazer would have been reared in the Protestant doctrine. There existed, however, in those *fin-de-siècle* times a strong tendency among Protestant-educated ethnologists of an agnostic persuasion to embrace the Catholic interpretation, since it enabled them to write off the Mass as magical and hence subtly to undermine it. The object was not so much to demythologise the Mass, as, precisely, to mythologise it and hence write it off as spurious. Tylor for one was a Quaker, and took this line most strongly.[25] So it is not difficult to see why Frazer should have welcomed Spencer's revelations so warmly. Indeed, one can almost hear him clapping his hands in delight. Already by the December of that year he is gibbering on to Mary Kingsley about the Mass as sorcery and mumbo-jumbo. Miss Kingsley wrote back that, if Frazer took this line, he would have the clergy to contend with: "Of course I have no objection to you taking the view that the Mass is magic, but I want to know how you are going to get on with bishops if you do?"[26]

Miss Kingsley and Frazer clearly got on well together; despite wide differences of temperament and training, they had this bantering vein in common. But beneath the raillery Frazer had a serious point. Ten years previously, when Frazer was just getting under way on *The Golden Bough*, William Robertson Smith had floated certain ruminations on the practice of what he termed totemic sacrament, but, despite his classical and Semitic instances, had failed to come up with a single modern example of it. Now Spencer had described a set of rituals which looked very much like totemic sacrament, and in so doing had brought Smith's whole notion of sacrifice once more into the limelight.

Smith's ideas on human sacrifice had been hanging in the air for some time. They had first been articulated in his *Britannica* article on sacrifice, which appeared in a volume prior to Frazer's piece on totems. Smith had then sat down and expanded the article into a series of lectures entitled *The Religion of the Semites*, delivered in 1889 at the University of Aberdeen, where the atmosphere was more beneficent than it had been in the Free Church college.[27] It was Smith's single greatest contribution to human knowledge, and remains the single most important text underlying *The Golden Bough*. At the innermost sanctum of this book had stood a theory about the sacrificial intentions of the oldest Semites, the ancestors of both Arab and Jew – ideas which had proved influential and applicable way beyond the area of Smith's immediate concern.

Frazer had read Smith's lectures on Semitic religion avidly on their first appearance in 1889, at the very time he was working on the manuscript of his own great work. The effect had been devastating – perhaps a little too devastating – and in the Preface he records the impact:

My interest in the early history of mankind was first excited by the works of Dr E. B. Tylor, which opened up to me a mental vista undreamed of before. But it is a long step from a lively interest in a subject to a systematic study of it, and that I took this step is due to the influence of my friend W. Robertson Smith. The debt which I owe to the vast stores of his knowledge, the abundance and fertility of his ideas and his unwearying kindness, can scarcely be overestimated. Those who know his writings may form some, though a very inadequate, conception of the extent to which I have been influenced by him. The views on sacrifice set forth in his article "Sacrifice" in the *Encyclopaedia Britannica* and further developed by him in his recent book *The Religion of the Semites* mark a new development in the historical study of religion, and ample traces of them will be found in this book. Indeed the central idea of my essay – the conception of the slain god is derived directly, I believe, from my friend. But it is due to him to add that he is in no way responsible for the general explanation which I have to offer of the custom of slaying the god.

Despite the equivocal language of this acknowledgement – Smith is responsible for the "conception" though not the "explanation" of the dying god – the gesture is such as to invite the closest possible comparison. Frazer was to spend the rest of his life recoiling from the implications of these statements, but it is obvious that in 1889 when Smith's book appeared, *The Religion of the Semites* provoked in him a state of temporary intellectual infatuation akin to his admiration for the man. *The Religion of the Semites* was a mountain range that loomed large on Frazer's intellectual horizon – particularly so in 1889, when his own ideas were in the formative stage and when, as never afterwards, he was still so prone to be led.

But, if Frazer finally departed from Smith's arguments, they were undeniably his starting-point. We shall thus never appreciate the significance of *The Religion of the Semites* for Frazer unless we pay it the compliment of dealing with its arguments in detail. Before proceeding any further we must therefore dwell for a while on the work of the inscrutable, learned and lovable man to whom *The Golden Bough* "in gratitude and admiration" is dedicated.

CHAPTER VII

SACRIFICE AS EUCHARIST

BY THE TIME of Spencer and Gillen's revelations concerning totemic sacrifice in the Australian outback, Smith had been dead for five years, but the new ideas would not have surprised him, nor would Frazer's talk of the Mass. Nobody could deny that the notion of a sacrificial victim, and of the privileged participation in his death of a circle of worshippers, was anything but unique. The crucial question was how far the atavistic, and far from palatable, ideas of pagan peoples – the Canaanites of Palestine, for example, or their near-neighbours the Phoenicians – had invaded and infected Hebrew sacrifice. Christ was "the firstfruits of them that slept", but in what sense was it appropriate to envisage his person being devoured, and how far did an understanding of his "full, perfect and sufficient sacrifice" involve an appreciation of, even a direct drawing-upon, the slaughter of lambs, oxen and pigs?

Nobody suggested that the question was straightforward. There were to begin with many different types of sacrifice: human, animal, vegetable. What was the relationship between these various kinds? The issue was comparatively straightforward when, as in the case of oxen or sheep, the animal itself was revered. It was far more complicated when the beast was regarded with revulsion. Pigs, for example, were abhorrent to all the Semites, as they are to this day – whether to Arab or to Jew. They were also deeply distasteful to the ancient Egyptians. Both Smith and Frazer discuss this matter, though their term is not "abhorrent", but the two-edged sword "taboo".

Listen to Frazer in *The Golden Bough* of 1890 dilating on the annual Egyptian pig-sacrifice to Osiris:

> In ancient Egypt, within historical times, the pig occupied the same dubious position as in Syria and Palestine, though at first sight its uncleanness is more prominent than its sanctity. The Egyptians are generally said by the Greek writers to have abhorred the pig as a foul and loathsome animal. If a man so much as touched a pig in passing, he stepped into the river with all his clothes on, to wash off the taint.

86

To drink pig's milk was believed to cause leprosy to the drinker. Swineherds, though natives of Egypt, were forbidden to enter any temple, and they were the only men who were thus excluded. No one would give his daughter in marriage to a swineherd, or marry a swineherd's daughter; the swineherds married amongst themselves. Yet once a year the Egyptians sacrificed pigs to the moon and to Osiris, and not only sacrificed them but ate of their flesh, though on any other day of the year they would neither sacrifice them nor taste of their flesh. Those who were too poor to offer a pig on this day baked cakes of dough, and offered them instead. This can hardly be explained except by the supposition that the pig was a sacred animal which was eaten sacramentally by his worshippers once a year.[1]

When one considers the terms of this description – a "foul and loathsome animal" who is none the less "sacred" – it is clear that Frazer is calling our attention to a contradiction of much the same sort as we aired in an earlier chapter. In such terms as Frazer's Greek sources (Plutarch, Strabo, Diodorus Siculus) employ, this contradiction is difficult to resolve. But, if the pig could be regarded as an Egyptian totem (the approach favoured by Smith) and if the habitual prohibition against eating the animal, lifted once a year only, came to be regarded as a variety of taboo, then the paradox was much more easily understood.

In the First Edition of *The Golden Bough* Frazer had laid his hands on a number of examples in which a sacrificial victim was simultaneously revered and reviled, the pig being only the most obvious. The *intichiuma* ceremonies of the Australian aborigines had now come to strengthen this limb of the argument. Here too was a ban more honoured in the breach than in the observance. Here too were a people enjoined to abstain from certain forms of nourishment and yet, under periodic conditions of great sanctity, partaking with relish of just this forbidden food. Smith's term for such an exemplary mystery was a "totemic sacrament", and it now looked very much as if in the First Edition of *The Golden Bough* Frazer had described just such a rite.

The impression that, when it came to sacrificial rites, Smith and Frazer stood on the same ground was one shared by many, if not most, of the readers of Frazer's book on its first appearance in 1890. Smith's *The Religion of the Semites* had appeared a few months previously, and the two authors had turned to many of the same sources: Herodotos, Plutarch, Strabo. The trouble was that, while Frazer was prepared to concede the existence of totemic sacraments, and after Spencer's intervention was ever more inclined to concede it, when it came to Nemi he demurred. For, let there be no mistake, when it came to the Roman rite Frazer laboured under no illusion that he was dealing with totemism proper. The Latins never regarded the horse on the sacrificial altar as a totem *per se*; it was merely *like* a totem. Nor was the King of the Wood in the least totemic: both he and the horse were arboreal vegetation spirits. Frazer's argument was essentially developmental. The Latin peoples were not totemic folk, but they had long memories, and their ancestors must, he thought, at one stage have raised themselves from a state of social existence in which totems were a recognisable ingredient. This in essence is what Smith had said about the Hebrews. The disagreement, therefore, was not so much about totemism as about what a sacrament was, and what – more fundamentally – a sacrifice was.

The crux of the problem is set forth in Scripture:

> I will not reprove thee because of thy sacrifices, or for thy burnt offerings: because they were not alway before me.
> I will take no bullock out of thine house: nor he-goat out of thy folds.
> For all the beasts of the forest are mine: and so are the cattle upon a thousand hills.
> I know all the fowls upon the mountains: and the wild beasts of the field are in my sight.
> If I be hungry, I will not tell thee: for the whole world is mine, and all that is therein.
> Thinkest thou that I will eat bull's flesh: and drink the blood of goats?

So speaks the poet of Psalm 50 (in Coverdale's rendering), assuming the indignant voice of Yahweh, while simultaneously giving vent to a disquiet common among authors of the later books of the Old Testament concerning the seemliness and efficacy of blood-offering.

Two and a half millennia later similar misgivings were to surface in an England where the Oxford Movement had seemed to undermine the traditional Protestant squeamishness in ritualistic matters, and to replant notions belonging to another time and place:

> The daily sacrifice, more awful really than the sacrifices of the antique world, stirred him as much by its superb rejection of the evidence of

the senses as by the primitive simplicity of its elements and the eternal pathos of the human tragedy which it sought to symbolize. He loved to kneel down on the cold marble pavement, and watch the priest, in his stiff flowered vestment, slowly and with white hands moving aside the veil of the tabernacle, or raising aloft the jewelled lantern-shaped monstrance with that pallid wafer that at times, one would fain think, is indeed the "panis caelestis", the bread of the angels, or, robed in the garments of the Passion of Christ, breaking the Host into the chalice, and smiting his breast for his sins.[2]

So Dorian Gray, in a scene first published the very same month as *The Golden Bough*, watches the Catholic sacrament from a side chapel and with a hushed, unholy dread simultaneously drinks in the chilled sanctity of the celebration and the intoxicated corruption of his own senses.

The corruption and the sanctity were facets of an anxiety deep-set in the late-Victorian mind. Nor was this anxiety unique to those, such as Wilde, of a High Church inclination. Scottish Presbyterians too had agonised, and none more so than Frazer's friend and mentor William Robertson Smith. From the time of Knox, religious controversy in Scotland had fastened on the difficult significance of the central act of Christian worship, variously styled the Lord's Supper, the Communion or the Mass. For Protestants it was a Eucharist, an act of thanksgiving; for Catholics, and increasingly for episcopalians of an Anglo-Catholic persuasion, the literal enactment of a death. But, whichever way you chose to view it, the celebration enshrined a sacrifice of sorts. Sacrifice was, moreover, a central ingredient in the religious tradition of the Jews, of whom there were increasing numbers in Scotland at the time. Along with the need to evangelise came the need to understand: both a common Judaeo-Christian legacy and, more broadly, that pool of ritual and belief which, Smith believed, the ancient Hebrews held in common with other Semitic peoples. For, as with his move to Cambridge the focus of his research had shifted from the Lower Criticism of texts to the Higher Criticism of societies, so it had grown ever clearer to Smith that the ritualistic provisions of the Old Testament derived from a prehistoric past in which Hebrew and Arab coexisted as members of a common Semitic stock.

As a guide in these matters the text of Holy Writ was something of a mixed bag. The attitudes evinced by the various authors of the Old Testament towards animal sacrifice are passionate but contradictory. "For thou desirest no sacrifice, else would I give it thee", sighs the author of Psalm 51 to his recalcitrant creator; yet sacrificial rites of diverse kinds are not merely observable in the regime of the Hebrews, but crucial to its interpretation. When in Genesis 15 Yahweh sets his seal on his covenant with Abraham and his kindred, the patriarch is bidden to take a goat, a ram and a pigeon, and, dividing each animal, to set the bleeding halves at a distance so that the spirit of God may pass between them in the likeness of a lamp.[3] That such rituals had their roots in rites still more grisly is strongly suggested by the story in Genesis 22 of Abraham's willingness to sacrifice his son Isaac, only to be told that a ram is just as acceptable.[4] Like the Greek legend of Iphigenia, this incident would seem to record the commuting of human to animal sacrifice. The Ammonites, another Semitic people, regularly immolated their children to Molech, and, while the stipulations of Genesis turn their back on any such carnal proceeding, they lend their blessing to the animal rites which supplanted it. Yet, when we turn to the books of Isaiah and Jeremiah, which are arguably not much later than Genesis, we meet outspoken invective directed against the animal sacrifices of a subsequent generation. What sort of a God was it that generously acknowledged the tribute of sacrifice, then promptly berated his people for perpetuating rites that he himself had sanctioned?

For scholars of Smith's time, influenced as they were by the Tübingen school of biblical scholarship, an answer to this question seemed to present itself in the shape of a developmental view of Scripture. If, as men such as Wellhausen had come to believe, the text of the Bible, rather than descending out of heaven in a curtain of cloud, had been painstakingly collated by post-Babylonian scribes who availed themselves of the opportunity to modify the wording to suit their immediate requirements, it might be possible to observe the fastidious spirituality of the later Jews refining itself out of the grosser practices of their forefathers.

To such an undertaking, while a professor in Aberdeen, had the young Smith dedicated himself. The upshot had been such as might have burned the fingers of less courageous men. But official misunderstanding did not daunt Smith's zeal; nor did it cause him to revise his faith. To the end of his days he remained a practising Christian – one, what is more, who retained in full measure the wholesome, abiding convictions of his youth. Henceforth, to justify the ways of God to man, and more especially to reconcile the tenets of a revealed religion with what might be ascertained of the religious consciousness underlying the oldest scriptures, was the whole object of his endeavour. Indeed, the deeper he went, the more convinced he grew that the convictions of the founding fathers of Semitic religion foreshadowed the robust dogmas in which he himself had been raised.

What, we might well ask, was a biblical scholar such as Smith doing meddling in matters that we now regard as more properly the concern of the anthropologist or else ancient historian? The answer lies in his view of the biblical text. If, as the German scholars who had trained him had come to believe, the received order of the scriptural canon bore no closer relation to the order of its composition than the received order of the Shakespearean canon does to the order of composition of Shakespeare's plays – if, for instance, the provisions of the Levitical Law as expounded in the books ascribed to Moses represent a fabrication intended to justify much later practice – then the text of the Old Testament is a very poor guide to its own exegesis. Internal evidence is simply not enough. We must look beyond the highly literate society that slowly emerged between the first settlements, the establishment and fragmentation of the kingdom, the exile and its aftermath, beyond the highly stylised, codified temple-based religion as it existed in the time of Judas Maccabaeus. All of these represented stages in the evolution of the faith, but the post-exilic scribes who codified the Law, and later the Pharisees and Sadducees against whom Christ railed, were apprised of notions of the truth by the standard of which the crude rituals of the earliest Semites appeared not simply wanting, but often noxious. In order to recover what had existed in the first place there was nothing for it but to clear away the layers of subsequent accretion and peer unsteadily at what lay beneath.

The hardest stage to view unhindered was the age of the patriarchs. Not a word of the Pentateuch was, Smith believed, contemporary with the events described. Through the sandbanks of later elaboration occasional glimpses could be caught of a society of nomadic pastoralists whose doings the later Hebrews regarded with a mixture of nostalgia and mistrust. What kind of a world did Abraham and Isaac inhabit? One clearly very unlike nineteenth-century Palestine, unlike even the urban society against which Isaiah directed his scorn, or the settled agricultural communities among which Jesus of Nazareth grew up. It was a society in some ways closer to that of the Canaanites: a closely knit society of peripatetic herdsmen, intermittently gathering around their hill-top shrines, the *asherim* or sacred poles whose persistence into later ages caused the prophets so much disquiet.[5] It was a society to which the nearest modern equivalent seemed to be the Bedouin of the Arabian Peninsula and Sinai. Suspended from his duties at Aberdeen, it was therefore to Arabia that Smith went during the course of two long winters, those of 1878–9 and 1879–80. A photograph of him in Arab dress[6] – "Abdullah Effendi" he called himself – is still extant; this time he looks less like a heretical rabbi than a silver-tongued tribal elder. (In his own book on the Old Testament, Frazer once compared Samson to Rob Roy:[7] looking at Smith's photograph, one can perhaps understand why.)

Like many scholarly travellers before him and since, Smith set out on his journey predisposed to vindicate theories he was already inclined to believe. In Smith's case these theories were M'Lennan's: exogamy, bride capture, totemism. With the bride capture he could hardly fail. M'Lennan's evidence had itself been Arabian (as had Strabo's for polyandry). T. E. Lawrence observed a form of mock bride capture shortly before the First World War, and a highly ritualistic form of the same custom is a feature of Bedouin weddings to this very day. With the totems, however, Smith was on more contentious ground. M'Lennan had taught that all societies, of whatever age or clime, had passed through a totemic stage. If this was true of all societies, it must apply equally to the Arabs. The task which Smith set himself during these two visits to the Arabian Peninsula had therefore been to prove that in the institutions of the nineteenth-century Bedouin we had a dim reflection of a much earlier society in which the touchstone of the totem had been absolute. Excitedly he wrote back to Scotland of "totem facts" lying round on every side "crying out" to be explained.[8] Five years later, in the opening lecture of *Kinship and Marriage in Ancient Arabia*, he announced his theme:

It is, I think, possible to show that the Arabs once had a system which M'Lennan has expounded under the name totemism and if, as among other early nations, totemism and female kinship were combined with a law of exogamy, it is also possible to construct, on the lines laid down in *Primitive Marriage*, a hypothetical picture of the development of the social system, consistent with the Arabian facts, and involving only . . . the action of such forces as can be seen to have operated in other societies in the very way in which the hypothesis requires . . . .[9]

One can see now whence Frazer's preoccupation with totemism and exogamy arose. If you supplement M'Lennan with a selective reading of Arabian ethnology, you get Smith. If to that you then add generous lashings of the comparative method laced with a good dash of classics, you get Frazer. The recipe for all of these concoctions, however, was written out by M'Lennan, whose theories – shafts of light trained on a prehistoric age of which we still know very little – possessed a kind of fragmentary, chaotic brilliance and a sort of audacious conceptual originality that the Victorians found irresistible. Perhaps his single most lasting contribution was his notion of the totemic clan, which in *Kinship and Marriage* Smith paraphrases thus:

A totem tribe . . . is one in which the belief that all members of the tribe are of one blood is associated with the conviction, more or less religious in character, that life is in some mystical way derived from an animal, a plant, or more rarely from some natural object.[10]

Elsewhere Smith speaks as if the life of the clan literally inhered in the totem, as if the clansmen and the totem were in a sense synonymous. The deity to whom each clan owed fealty was conceived of as an overlord, a *ba'al* or territorial grandee with whom all members of the clan shared bonds of kinship. Tribesmen and god were literally of one blood, kindred. The earliest sacrifices – gifts of corn or wine, or in pastoral societies of the firstlings of the flock – were in the nature of a communal meal signifying a pact. It is in this sense that the covenant between God and Abraham was to be understood: an accord by means of which a local deity bound a people to himself, a blood bond. Such enactments were both expressions of thanksgiving for the fruits of the earth and celebrations of the communal life. They were thus, in the literal Greek sense of the word, eucharistic. The Protestant theology of sacrifice thus implicitly preceded the Catholic.

But there was a catch: anything might be offered except that in which the life of the clan inhered – in other words, the totem. The food taboos of the Jews and Arabs were thus to be understood in the light of totemic rules forbidding the consumption of animals deemed too sacred to touch. It was from this idea that Frazer derived his early axiom of the totem as a forbidden food: forbidden, that is, for all clan members. We recall Frazer's interpretation of the pig taboo in Egypt: in Smith's reading (though not, as we shall discover, in Frazer's) the pig, then, was an ancient Semitic totem.

This notion of totemic exclusiveness, which Frazer at first was inclined to take almost too seriously, was based in the first instance on classical evidence. The goat was by all accounts sacred to Pallas Athene, whose statue in the Parthenon was wrapped in an *aegis*, or goatskin.[11] Now Apollo Lycius, the Wolf Apollo, had a famous shrine in Argos. Around the shrine prowled wolves who fed on the offerings.[12] But wolf meat itself might never be offered. Instead, the sacred meat of rival cults was laid out for the scavengers to devour. All this fitted in rather neatly with a totemic view of sacrifice – provided, that is, that you could convince yourself that the Greeks had passed through a totemic stage (a possibility about which Frazer was to entertain some doubts).

As with most rules, it was the exceptions that made this one really interesting. On rare occasions, it would seem, at times of especial peril or else at certain fixed periodic intervals, the clan did indeed dine off the flesh of the totemic animal. These infringements of a time-honoured rule were invariably marked by a solemn, awe-inspiring gravity and accompanied by every expression of heart-felt regret, as if one of the initiates were himself being slain – inevitably so if, as Smith himself strongly implies, the god and the totem were regarded as synonymous. It was this exception to a habitual totemic rule that Smith termed the "totemic sacrament".

As in *The Golden Bough*, much of the discussion centres around the pig-sacrifice to Osiris. But Smith had two additional classical examples on which Frazer was also to draw. The first of these was the annual slaying of a steer during the Diipolia at Athens, at the conclusion of which, according to Pausanias, the officiating priest was compelled to flee in shame.[13] The second and more significant was the annual slaughter of the Apis bull in Egypt as described by Herodotos in the second book of his *Histories*. Since this example is so central to Frazer's own argument, it will be as well to quote it in full.

The Apis bull was carefully selected: he must have a white triangle on his forehead, a vulture with wings extended on his forehead, a crescent on his right flank and a scarab on his tongue. If these conditions were met he was held to be a reincarnation of the god Ptah and was worshipped under the title "The Renewal of Ptah's Life" at Ptah's own city of Memphis. The custom so amused the Persian invader Cambyses that he had the bull lamed in the thigh and whipped through the town, to be left to die slowly in the temple to demonstrate his mortality. But, despite all the veneration, once a year Apis was sacrificed in the most public manner:

> The method of sacrifice is as follows: they take the beast (one of those marked with a seal) to the appropriate altar and light the fire. Then, after pouring a libation of wine and invoking the god by name, they slaughter it, cut off its head and flay its carcase. The head is loaded with curses and taken away – if there happen to be Greek traders in the market it is sold to them; if not it is thrown in the river. The curses they pronounce take the form of a prayer that any disaster which threatens either themselves or their country maybe diverted, and fall upon the severed head of the beast. Both the libation and the practice

of cutting off the heads of the sacrificial beasts are common to all Egyptians in their sacrifices, and the latter explains why it is that no Egyptian will use the head of any sort of animal for food.

The methods of disembowelling are various, and I will describe the one which is followed in the worship of the goddess whom they consider the greatest and honour with the most important festival. In this case, when they have flayed the bull, they first pray and then take its paunch out whole, leaving the intestines and fat inside the body; next they cut off the legs, shoulders, neck and rump, and stuff the carcase with loaves of bread, honey, raisins, figs, frankincense, myrrh and other aromatic substances; finally they pour a quantity of oil over the carcase and while the fire is consuming it they beat their breasts. That part of the ceremony done, they serve a meal out of the portions left over.[14]

From whatever angle the rite is viewed, it is incomprehensible without a recognition that to the Egyptians Apis was intensely holy. There is no getting away from this. The rapt attitude of the worshippers, the universal expression of regret amounting to ecstatic sorrow: all this leads one to the inescapable conclusion that the circle of initiates is sacrificing the most precious thing they know. Smith's view was that the Apis bull was a sort of prototype of the totem. But the totem, as he has already told us, could not be killed except under the most exceptional circumstances. Why then was the normal rule suspended? Smith has two explanations, which we shall take in turn.

The first was that the immolation of the totemic creature represented a variety of expiation, whereby in satisfaction for unassuaged blood-guilt the god sought reparation from the circle of kin. By the most scrupulous logic such satisfaction might only be achieved through the relinquishing of one of the kindred: it was thus that Ammonite babes were forfeited to Molech and Iphigenia laid out to secure fair winds. But, where human victims were not forthcoming, the act of penance might be commuted through a process of substitution. The customary form was that of an animal standing in for the human victim. In the case of totemic cults, who more fitting, more literally an equivalent of the injured party, than the totemic animal itself? The god as beast died for his people.

This interpretation had much to be said for it, including its compatibility with the Christian doctrine of Atonement. The difficulty was that it could only be applied to societies habituated to the idea of guilt, which Smith thought a late stage in human development. In the case of the Semites it was his contention that the idea of sin was quite foreign to early nomadic wanderers such as the patriarchs. They could offend their tutelary deity, and did: in which case a communal celebration of the eucharistic kind was quite sufficient to make up for it. But an abstract sense of wrongdoing – as opposed to a purely personal affront – was something that did not enter the Hebrew mentality until Assyria destroyed the northern Kingdom of Israel and nearly did the same to Judah. This provoked a pained search after causes and a consequent desire to make penance. Later on, when local sacrifices to a tribal god were supplanted by a hieratic system of blood-offering executed centrally in the precincts of the temple, a theological justification had to be provided in terms of an expiation for personal or national wrongdoing. Thenceforth the sacrificial animal was "made over" to the temple authorities in reparation for an alleged transgression. There are passages in *The Religion of the Semites* where Smith speaks of the inception of remorse as a response to organisational needs, as if mankind were incapable of feeling guilty unless required by the priests to do so.[15] At times this insistence on the artificiality of the emotion of guilt reaches ludicrous heights. Frazer, who thought it far-fetched, said that over this issue Smith was misled by his own happy, guilt-free temperament. The deeper explanation probably lies in Smith's inherited Protestantism and his consequent desire to rid the institution of sacrifice, whether primitive or Christian, of any element of fear-stricken propitiation.

Expiation, then, could not be the rationale behind the oldest totemic sacraments. Had it been so, the cultic relapses of the later Jews would not have inspired the prophets with quite so much horror. The sacrifices which so appalled Jeremiah and others during the lead up to the conquest must have possessed a motive other than contrition. Beneath the sophisticated religion of Jeremiah's day we seem to catch a glimpse of a different world altogether, a world dominated by furtive re-enactments of rituals and strange forms of abandonment such as the prophets regarded as proof positive of the depravity of the people. Bizarre practices lurked behind the elegant façade of sixth-century Jerusalem: Ezekiel visualised "every form of creeping thing, and abominable beasts" emblazoned upon the walls of the temple.[16] These practices proved resilient. The author of Isaiah 65 inveighs against those "who eat swine's flesh, and broth of abominable things is in their vessels". Peering into this broth, Smith found not merely swine but dogs, even mice.

But these creatures cannot always have been reviled: such indulgences were throwbacks to a distant past in which these animals were regarded as holy: "The evidence of these examples is unambiguous", writes Smith. "When an unclean animal is sacrificed it is also a sacred animal."[17] Such beasts, then, were originally totems, and in partaking of their reviled flesh the inhabitants of Judah must have been harking back to a murky past when such rites were commonplace. With Babylon knocking at the gates, sheer funk had driven the people back on the pieties of their forefathers.

Smith's term for such atavistic rites is "Mysteries":

Here therefore we have a clear case of the re-emergence into the light of day of a cult of the most primitive totem type which had been banished for centuries from public religion, but must have been kept alive in obscure circles of private or local superstition, and sprang up again on the ruins of the national faith, like some noxious weed in the courts of a deserted temple.[18]

With these rites Smith felt that we were entering a different terrain altogether, that occupied by the brand of ritualistic performance that the Greeks dignified by the title μυστήριον. We are on the boundary of those Near Eastern cults which swept across the Aegean in the sixth century: the cult of Dionysus, the rites of Adonis, the self-lacerating rituals of Attis.

For it was not only the consumption of forbidden meat that offended the prophets. Other importations flourished. Isaiah 17 has this:

Because thou has forgotten the God of thy salvation, and hast not been mindful of the rock of thy strength, therefore shalt thou plant pleasant plants, and shalt set it with strange slips . . . .[19]

For Smith, the Authorised Version is hedging its bets here: those "pleasant plants" and those "strange slips" were actually gardens of Adonis. About the same time Ezekiel observed a group of women in the gateway of Jerusalem bewailing the dying Tammuz. The Phoenician cult of Tammuz and Astarte therefore had its adherents in Jerusalem. The Jews called Astarte the horned or mooned Ashtaroth and depicted her in one of her many manifestations as a calf: hence the anger of Moses at the golden calf his followers had erected at the foot of Mount Sinai. The Hebrews were somewhat prone to backsliding; they also loved to flirt with the superstitions of their neighbours: "And they forsook the Lord, and served Baal and Ashtaroth . . . ."[20] Baal was an omnivorous title implying a lord or master, but the Baal of Phoenicia (the Zidon or Sidon of the Old Testament) was Tammuz, whom the Greeks called

Adonis. Adonis-worship, then, was a feature of Old Testament life, and with it Smith enters a completely new phase of his argument.

Smith sometimes speaks of the mystery religions as being a peculiar intensification of eucharistic rites, as if in his desire to forge the strongest possible bond of mutual dependence between himself and his people the god was prepared to vouchsafe everything, even himself. In certain passages in *The Religion of the Semites*, however, his argument is more complicated and more interesting. Smith always believed ritual to precede myth; the myth of Adonis he therefore views as a gloss on a sacrificial rite – in this case the slaughter of pigs, which were Adonis's totem. In the best-known version of the myth Adonis was slain by a boar, just as Hippolytus was slain by horses. If horses were sacred to Hippolytus, then swine must be sacred to Adonis. Osiris was dismembered by his brother Set, who was out hunting wild boar; and swine, as we have seen, were sacred to Osiris. In all these cases, it would seem, the adherents of the cult argued backwards from the sacrifice of the totemic animal to a putative theological origin. If swine were slain at certain sacred festivals, then on these occasions the god too must be dying:

> Originally the death of the god was nothing else than the death of the theanthropic victim; but when this ceased to be understood, it was thought that the piacular sacrifice represented an historical tragedy in which the god was killed. Thus at Laodicea the animal sacrifice of a stag that stood for a maiden, and was offered to the goddess of the city, stands side by side with a legend that the goddess was a maiden who had been sacrificed to consecrate the foundation of the town, and was therefore worshipped as its Fortune like Dido at Carthage; it was therefore the death of the goddess herself which was annually renewed in the piacular rite.[21]

These early identifications of god with sacrificial victim were not to be confused with the expiatory rites of which we spoke earlier. The earliest men were not, in Smith's view, possessed of the sort of moral consciousness that would make such an equation possible. Why then did the god die? Because gods were facets of the natural world in which death and renewal were a commonplace. The sacrifice was not performed to perpetuate the god's life, nor was it performed to shorten it. But the orchestration of the seasons – the annual fall of leaves, the decay of nature followed by the glorious resurrection in the spring – was part of an underlying rhythm of which both the god and his embodiment, the sacrificial victim, partook. The identification of the god with his circle of kindred, to be found in the earliest eucharistic rites, was here extended to the whole natural creation, which expired and rose as one:

> The annual mourning for the death of Adonis, which supplies the closest parallel in point of form to the fasting and humiliation of the Hebrew Day of Atonement, is simply a sincere commemoration of the death of the god, in which his worshippers take part with appropriate wailing and lamentation, but without any thought corresponding to the Christian idea that the death of the God-man is a death for the sins of the people. On the contrary, if, as in the Adonis myth, an attempt is made to give some further account of the annual rite than is supplied by the story that the god had once been killed and rose again, the explanation offered is derived from the decay and regeneration of nature. The Canaanite Adonis or Tammuz was a form of local Baal, who, as we have already learned, was regarded by his worshippers as the source of natural growth and fertility. His death therefore meant a temporary suspension of the life of nature, and was held to be annually repeated not merely in ritual symbol in his sanctuary, but in the annual withering and decay of vegetative life. And this death of the life of nature the worshippers lament out of natural sympathy, without any moral idea, just as modern man is touched with natural melancholy by the falling of Autumn leaves.[22]

"The significance of the death of the god in Semitic religion is a subject which I must not enter in this connection", Smith states tantalisingly at the conclusion of his discussion of the mysteries in Lecture X of *The Religion of the Semites*. It was a subject to which he hoped to return in the second series of lectures, which he never lived to deliver, yet he had already opened up a path which others were to explore to great effect, not least his protégé Frazer. To superficial readers of *The Golden Bough*, especially in its later editions, Smith's account of the death of a god as a reflection of natural processes looks uncannily like much that they find there, especially perhaps in the volumes *Adonis, Attis, Osiris*. To infer that the theories are identical is, however, to jump the gun in more than one respect. It was a mistake which many of Frazer's readers made from the beginning, and it had a tendency to anger him.

The temptation is strong, and one can see why. *The Religion of the Semites* was published by A. & C. Black in 1889, in which year Frazer was wrestling with the underlying tenets of the book that was to emerge the following year as *The Golden Bough*. At Frazer's insistence, his book even looked like Smith's.[23] Frazer had read Smith's work in proof, and, even if he had not, his close connection with his mentor at this time would have ensured that its guiding intimations flowed through his bloodstream.

In reality the whole tenor of Frazer's mind was different. As in the years 1887–9 his confidence in his own powers grew, he was more and more inclined to disown Smith's thinking on major subjects while retaining a fundamental respect for the originator's wisdom. The result was a theory of sacrifice which appeared to resemble Smith's, but which at root was utterly opposed to it. In order to chart the depth of the eventual divide, we need to take a further look at the genesis of Frazer's own thinking.

CHAPTER VIII

SACRIFICE AS MAGIC

FRAZER'S most explicit disclaimer of Smith's theory of sacrifice occurs in the Preface to the Second Edition of *The Golden Bough*, written six years after Smith's death:

> In an elaborate and learned essay on sacrifice Messrs H. Hubert and M. Mauss have represented my theory of the slain god as intended to supplement and complete Robertson Smith's theory of the derivation of animal sacrifice in general from a totem sacrament. On this I have to say that the two theories are quite independent of one another. I never assented to my friend's theory, and so far as I can remember he never gave me a hint that he assented to mine.[1]

One can sense the note of irritation in Frazer's voice here: in 1900 his theory was all the more likely to be confused with Smith's because in the interval Spencer and Gillen had brought the whole subject of totemic sacrament to the fore, and Frazer was determined to draw on their material. The Australian evidence was indubitably important. "But from the practice of the rite by a single set of tribes it is a long step to the universal practice of it by all totem tribes, and from that again it is a still longer stride to the deduction therefore of animal sacrifice in general. These two steps I am not yet prepared to take."[2]

It has to be asked whether Frazer's reluctance to embark on the road set out by Robertson Smith was due to lack of evidence alone. Frazer was more than willing to lean on unsubstantiated hypotheses when they suited him; some of the most startling conjectures in *The Golden Bough* hang by a single thread, and a very slender thread at that. By far the more likely reason for his reluctance is temperamental, or – less subjectively – the result of a deep-seated philosophical disagreement as to the nature and justification of this sort of anthropological inquiry.

The trouble with Smith's approach was that, whether he was dealing with eucharistic celebration, with expiatory rites or with the mysteries, his invariable starting-point was the emotional response of the worshippers. If such states of mind were in any way amenable to empirical investigation, Frazer would possibly have had no quarrel with this approach. As matters stood, however, no such empirical method existed. Nor could Frazer quite rid himself of the suspicion that Smith's treatment of such states of feeling represented a sort of back-projection of his own devout, questing disposition.[3] Allegiance, ecstatic identification, dread, joy: all these were purely subjective attributes for which the scientist in Frazer had no room. If one wanted to understand the nature of early man's ritualistic performances, one was better off investigating not what he felt on such occasions, but the actions he observably performed and the principles of knowledge or perception on which these seemed to be based.

To clarify this difference of approach it might prove instructive to contrast Frazer's disquisition on the pig-sacrifice to Osiris quoted at the beginning of the last chapter with Smith's verdict on the Apis bull.[4] Both rites are Egyptian, but it will immediately be observed that Frazer's line of approach, in stark contrast to Smith's, answers to what in our own day we might classify as a variety of social behaviourism. Frazer is not interested in what the ancient Egyptians said or even implied about their attitudes, beliefs and motivations; nor does he call his sources – Herodotos and Plutarch – in evidence over matters of interpretation. It was as if he had systematically trained himself to ignore the explanations such have to offer for the customs they describe. His one area of concern is what the Egyptians *did*. As with Nemi, if there was any implied conflict between performance and declared doctrine, then it was the former that had to be called in evidence against the latter, rather than the other way round.

The priorities thus set out, it must be stressed, were procedural rather than historic. Later, when he was working on the Third Edition, Frazer crossed swords with R. R. Marett, recently appointed to a Readership in Social Anthropology at Oxford, who had claimed Smith's posthumous support for his own theory that, *en masse*, "ritual is historically prior to dogma".[5] If anybody claimed this it was Frazer. In fact, neither man did, Smith claiming that doctrine was *logically* prior to ritual in the sense that you could observe men's convictions working themselves out through their rituals; and Frazer claiming that you looked at the rituals first and then, disregarding the explanations offered by the participants, worked out your own explanation based on a reconstruction of some sort of elementary epistemology which you proceeded to ascribe to the people concerned. In reality, it is best to distinguish three stages or processes, which did not have to occur in chronological order. There were the perceptual principles – Kantian postulates if you like – on which primitive man based his view of himself in relation to the world around him; there were rituals which to a certain extent enshrined these; and there was the ecstatic response, which often led to a set of stories – myths – lending significance to the whole. Smith thought that the last gave you an insight into what had occurred, though they often came afterwards, and were sometimes even a distortion. Frazer claimed that all doctrines were distortions more or less, since they were justifications after the event. What you therefore did was to examine the ritual carefully in an attempt to discern the logical or pseudo-logical premises on which it was based. You could then account for the myths and doctrines as ways of making the resulting rituals palatable.

Another way of describing Smith's approach to these matters is as a religious one. Now, the term "religious" was to be much bandied about during the 1880s and 1890s, with only a gradually crystallising sense of what, in very precise terms, it might mean. The terminology of *The Golden Bough* illustrates this perfectly. The sub-title of the First Edition is 'A Study in Comparative Religion', though at this stage Frazer was using the term in the most elastic sense possible. He was later to refine it, as we shall see, but even in 1890 there existed in Frazer's mind a profound mistrust of religious explanations of religious – or, as he would later have put it, of magical – events. What he wanted from the outset was a pragmatic explanation of these procedures befitting his empiricist background. The question of spiritual awareness he could, and would, leave in abeyance.

Frazer began by introducing into the discussion a distinction between "sacrament" and "sacrifice" which in Smith is blurred. Indeed, where the term "sacrament" occurs in Smith it is often in the Catechismal sense of "an outward and visible sign of an inward and spiritual grace", and thus implicitly includes sacrifice.[6] Frazer, however, thought that these words represented stages of a process. Though this is nowhere stated explicitly in his work, his understanding of the two terms has much in common with the sense ascribed to them in the liturgy of the Lord's Supper. In the Free Church of Scotland as in other Protestant churches this consisted of an act of offering or oblation ("The Offertory") followed by a feast in which the communicants were invited to share. Of these the Offertory was arguably the more ancient. Indeed, it had always been the contention of the Reformers that everything else had been grafted onto this simple act of eucharistic thanksgiving, the taking of the bread and the wine being a historic afterthought.

There is thus throughout the First Edition of *The Golden Bough*, and especially its great third chapter, a fundamental distinction, retained in later versions, between what Frazer calls the "sacrifice" and what he terms the "sacramental meal". The sacrament was in effect a way of participating in the sacrifice at one remove; hence the *maniae*, or man-shaped loaves, baked at Aricia were, he felt, the means by which the populace shared in the human sacrifices which he believed had at one time taken place there, and in the armed combats which he thought had later supplanted them.[7] Hence the two actions served one another. It will be helpful to take them in order, commencing with the sacrifice.

Sacrifice can be viewed in two lights: as offering and – as in English parlance – as renunciation. Both of these concepts presented the scientific thinker in Frazer with difficulties. An offering assumes a recipient, which in turn entails a religious frame of reference such as Frazer is from the outset inclined to reject. Renunciation entails the voluntary forgoing of material advantages, and, for an evolutionist such as Frazer, to suggest this without proposing a compensatory practical motive would be nonsense. Somehow the voluntary relinquishment of material advantages had to be reconciled with the struggle for survival, no easy task in an area in which men's declared motives were a poor guide to the reasons which lay, often obscurely, behind their conduct.

Back to Smith, who in a revealing passage in his eleventh lecture had spoken of the death of the god in Semitic religion as "corresponding to the annual withering up of nature".[8] Might this be something to do with it? Perhaps so, but Smith's reference is the merest hint: the details had still to be worked out. Sacrifices occur everywhere, among all sorts and conditions of men, from hunter–gatherers to nomadic pastoralists to farming folk. These were unlikely all to view "the annual withering up of nature" in the same light. Whatever proposals Frazer came up with, they had to be trenchant enough to suit the very special circumstances at Nemi, flexible enough to embrace diverse customs from many different times and places, and in congruence with Frazer's evolutionary model, so as to suggest stages of development.

Once again, his ideas are most fully worked out in the case of Egypt. The Egyptians had enjoyed a long history during which they had, Frazer believed, passed through three distinct evolutionary stages. The earliest Egyptians, he thought, had been totemic hunters devoted to a motley crew of local, tribal deities, some of whose cults had even survived in an enhanced form into the Ptolemaic period. Next had come a pastoral stage in which the people venerated the animals they herded: the cow, the bull, the ram. Lastly, in the Nile basin they had evolved an agricultural system with its attendant needs, its fluctuations of fortune, its seasonal rhythms. At this stage, like many another agricultural community before them, they had inaugurated annual harvest festivals during which the corn spirit had to be placated to ensure a fair yield. In the case of the Egyptians, that corn spirit, Frazer argued, was Osiris.

Now Herodotos, as we have already heard, tells us that a pig was annually sacrificed on the eve of the Feast of Osiris. The fullest information on the cult, however, is supplied by Plutarch, who also gives us the local legend purporting to explain it.[9] Son of earth and sky, the god Osiris brought to mankind the benefits of agriculture. He taught men to plant the seed and train the vine round the trellis; he taught them the arts of peace. So consumed was he with zeal for his task that he left the kingdom in the charge of his sister–wife Isis and roamed the land to spread the glad tidings, a one-man mobile educational unit. But his success provoked the envy of his brother Set, whom Plutarch calls Typhon. With seventy-two companions Set plotted Osiris's undoing, luring him into a coffin under the pretence of seeing whether it would fit him, then slamming down the lid. The conspirators then launched the coffin on the Nile, whence, followed by the weeping Isis, it floated out to sea and on to the Phoenician city of Byblos. Here it was built into a pillar supporting the great roof of the palace, but Isis begged for and procured it. With great joy she returned to the lands of the Nile, but when she was away one day Set found it while he was out hunting for wild boar, and, opening the lid, rent the carcase in pieces and scattered the limbs of Osiris to the winds.

Now this was just the sort of baroque, prettified fairy-tale behind whose comely façade Frazer always suspected the satisfaction of some quite straightforward practical need. Nor was he alone in this. Even Plutarch, to do him justice, thought the tale a little far-fetched:

They [the Egyptians] consider the pig to be an unclean animal, for it seems to copulate when the moon is on the wane, and the bodies of those who drink its milk comes out with rashes and scabrous scores. When they sacrifice a pig once every year in the full moon and devour it, they narrate the story of Typhon, who, as he was pursuing a pig in the full moon, found the wooden coffin in which Osiris lay and tore it up; but they do not all accept the tale, believing rather that it is a misunderstanding, like many other notions.[10]

Among those who would not accept the tale was Plutarch, who thought that it had something to do with the honouring of a supreme being or *logos* (Plutarch was a Platonist, and gets high marks for sublimity). Another was Frazer, though his explanation was more down-to-earth, and I think he would have fought shy of the word "misunderstanding". For him it was more like a code. Osiris was clearly a god of agriculture, the scattering of whose members spoke loudly of the scattering of the seed. The tears of his sister Isis foreshadowed the inundation of the Nile basin, on which the fertilisation of the fields depended. At the time of the scattering Set was hunting a boar, but this was just the sort of thought-transference that covered up something much starker: Set was really hunting Osiris, who on this argument *was* a boar. Plutarch says that his sacrifice took place at full moon (the moon being Isis), but more crucially it took place in November, when the flood was beginning to subside and the seed was sown in the freshly irrigated fields. Later, in March or April, the corn – wheat, barley and sorghum – was reaped. Amongst the scavengers known to disturb the corn at this season were pigs.

Frazer was later to overlay his interpretation with the lineaments of a religious theory, but in 1890 his view (though at this stage he was not using the word) was frankly magical. The view, so simple that it is almost alarming, stated in the first *Golden Bough*, is that by a process of erratic induction the Egyptians took as the embodiment of the spirit of the crops the very pigs who ravaged them. Only a god, it was argued, would lay waste his own property in so peremptory a fashion.[11] Osiris was annually done away with in the person of the corn spirit. As the Nile shrivelled in its course and the seed was placed in the ground, he died to be reborn at the harvest. The annual inundation in late summer was the weeping of Isis at his demise.

This theory looks very like Smith's until you realise that at no point has Frazer mentioned the *celebration* of the god. God and people were not of one flesh, nor was the habit of mind on which such a scenario depended necessarily totemic. Celebration there was, but for Frazer it was a form of embellishment: a way of lending majesty and dignity to a conjuring-trick. To begin with Frazer had difficulty sorting these two processes out – the trick and the elaboration – but of one thing he was always sure: you did not take the religious content of the cult as a clue to its purpose. The cult of Osiris, with its temples, its priests and its liturgies, was a cover-up.

Equivalent customs pertained wherever the agricultural revolution had turned nomadic peoples into settlers. The Greeks too had corn spirits, whom they likewise sacrificed annually. At the autumn womens' festival of the Thesmophoria the Athenians threw live pigs down a ravine, the remains being collected the following season and mixed with seed corn to be laid out on the altar of the goddess Demeter, in whose honour the festival was held.[12] To credulous minds the fall of pigs into the chasm suggested the descent of Persephone into Hades, which likewise occurred in the autumn. Here was another gorgeously redundant fairy-tale, and to it the Greeks had added a telling incident. They said that at the time of Persephone's first descent a swineherd called Eubuleus was tending his flock when he was caught up in the subsidence. Officially the sacrifice enacted not the demise of Persephone, but this fortuitous accompanying cascade.

For Frazer this fable bore all the signs of a camouflage. There were too many tell-tale elements: the cult bore the marks of its origin. A Θεσμος is a law; Dracon's laws were *thesmoi*. During the festival Demeter was honoured with the title Demeter Thesmophoros, Demeter the Lawgiver. All of which pointed to the establishment in the distant past of a settled agricultural system with its necessary discipline and accompanying advantages. Nor was this all. The pigs were thrown into the very ground whence the corn sprang up, and as at Eleusis there was something strongly chthonic about the whole cult. The refined worship of the goddess and her fugitive daughter were not the underlying point. Behind this religious adornment, as with Osiris and Set, Frazer discerned a cruder corn cult, with Persephone as pig paying the penalty for a propitious seedtime, to rise again in the spring like fresh ears on the stem. Not for nothing was Demeter known to the Romans as Ceres.

If Frazer's interpretation of the Thesmophoria smacks of conjecture, with the Bouphonia harvest festival he is on surer ground.[13] The Bouphonia took place on the Acropolis in July at the conclusion of threshing. It was one of the very few occasions on which an ox was sacrificed. Its distinguishing element, as commentators saw it, was the procedure enacted to evade blood-guilt in the aftermath of the slaughter. Briefly discussed by Pausanias, its fullest description occurs in the *De Abstinentia* (Περὶ ἀποχῆς ἐμψύχων) of Porphyry, a third-century adherent of the beliefs of Plotinus, and a strong advocate of vegetarianism. In the *De Abstinentia* he is arguing that the eating of meat represents a falling-away from an earlier period of perfection when only vegetables were consumed. As grist to his vegetarian mill, he takes up the origins of the Bouphonia. Two aspects of the festival attract his special attention. The first is the method of selecting the sacrificial beast, a form of trial by ordeal: "Placing oat-cakes on a brass table, they drive oxen round it,

and the ox that tastes of them is slain."[14] Later, after the sacrifice, the
knife which had been plunged into the ox's steaming side was subjected
to trial by jury, found guilty and flung into the Aegean. Pausanias also
mentions this,[15] but Porphyry's contribution is to ascribe the origin of
the feast to an apocryphal crime, the legend of which he relates at length:

> Formerly men only sacrificed fruit, not meat, of which they never
> partook. The story goes that one day, when a sacrifice was taking place
> at Athens, a foreigner called Domius (or Sopater), a farmer from
> Attica, became so worked up that he seized an axe and slew an ox
> who was approaching the altar at the end of its day's work. Later,
> when Sopater was found guilty, he argued his way round it by insisting
> that in future the crime should be committed in common, and that an
> ox should be regularly slaughtered in the city, just as it is at present.
>   They selected maidens to draw the water with which the knife was
> to be sharpened. Then a certain individual presented the axe, a second
> struck the ox, and a third cut its throat. Then everyone partook of its
> flesh. Afterwards they stuffed the skin with straw, and lifting it upright,
> placed it at the head of a plough as if it was about to till the fields.
> The case then went to law, and everybody involved was called on to
> account for his actions. And the drawer of water blamed him who
> sharpened the axe, and he blamed the man who handed it over, and
> he blamed the one who struck the blow, who in turn blamed the knife.
> As the knife could not defend itself, it was condemned.[16]

This is all very fascinating, and certainly points to a pervasive guilt
springing from some sense of affinity with the beast. Porphyry's argument
was that the means of tempting the ox to the altar identified the festival
as in origin a vegetable sacrifice, but this is to read history back to front.
Agriculture succeeded the herding of cattle and not *vice versa*, and
presumably the various types of sacrifice followed suit. This at least is
Frazer's view, since he regards the ox as a corn spirit. Just as the pigs
which ravaged the Egyptian corn represented its indwelling spirit, so the
ox that approached the altar on the Acropolis was attracted by cakes
baked from corn which was rightfully its property. In both cases the
attraction, the devastation, sprang from ownership. An alternative story
of the origin of the festival had it that it was instituted at a time of
drought, when presumably the harvest was retarded. The title of the
festival, literally the "ox-murder", reiterated the sense of guilt, as did the
trial. By killing the spirit of corn, so Frazer argued, the ancients hoped

magically to influence the course of the seasons and hence the agricultural
yield on which their lives depended.

The similarity between various facets of the Bouphonia as described by
Porphyry and the Apis sacrifice described by Herodotos – the expressions
of regret by everybody concerned, the stuffing and setting-up of the
hide – is very obvious. Bearing this in mind, and the open provocation
provided by Smith, we might expect Frazer to interpret the Apis bull
too as a corn spirit. But, he does not, and with Frazer's treatment of the
Apis evidence we come to an entirely fresh aspect of his argument.[17]
Apis, whom later tradition yoked insecurely with Osiris to form Apis–
Osiris, or, as he is more usually known, Serapis, made more sense, Frazer
thought, as a god of the herds. His worship had no particular connection
with agriculture. His later embodiments, in which he attained an
importance undreamed of in earlier days, were the result of syncretism or
religious accretion. Originally he was a reincarnation of Ptah worshipped
exclusively at Memphis. His Mediterranean renown came later when the
older cults of a nomadic, cattle-rearing people, such as in prehistory the
Egyptians must once have been, met the newer cults of the agriculturalists.
Then, when the religious imagination of the Mediterranean peoples –
Greek as well as Egyptian – stepped out to embrace novel and lavish
forms, he blossomed out as Serapis, in whose worship the distinction
between cattle and corn god fades.

    If Apis had not been a corn spirit, why then had the Egyptians
slaughtered him? It is here that Frazer steps into the breach with some
classical information that Smith had overlooked. Taking his information
exclusively from Herodotos, Smith had assumed that the killing of Apis
was annual. But in *Isis and Osiris* Plutarch gives a very different
impression. As so often with Plutarch, the information comes out
sideways, during a digression on arithmetic. The Egyptians counted not
decimally but by fives, employing the fingers of each hand:

In the Egyptian language the word for παντα [all] has the same root
as the word for πεντε [five] and their expression for calculating is "to
compute by fives". The number five can also be squared making
twenty-five, which is the exact number of letters in the Egyptian
alphabet, and the number of years Apis is permitted to live.[18]

To Smith's account of the Apis cult Frazer is therefore able to add two facts: the information, gleaned from Plutarch, that the sacred bull was never allowed to live for more than twenty-five years, and the fact, evident even from Herodotos, that his cult was national rather than local. If it was national, then, like the Osiris cult that later came to be associated with it, it was probably not totemic, since totems were confined at their broadest to an extended clan. By the time of the cult's inception, Frazer believed, the Egyptians had already passed beyond the totem stage: sacred animals were not always totems.

In addition Frazer rejected the idea, essential to Smith's interpretation, that the worshippers in any direct sense identified with the victim, since such identification implied community of consciousness, an idea to which Frazer was never friendly. For Frazer all thought was individual thought, and, though individuals might share ideas, such sharing was the result of diffusion within the kinship group, or rather of the inspired leadership of chiefs. The whole idea of a spontaneous eruption of subliminal feeling, manna to men such as Marett and highly suggestive to Freud, was to Frazer anathema. The whole axis of Smith's thought depended on the implied existence of emotions which Frazer the scientist regarded with the most profound distrust. If there was such a thing as a definitive explanation for animal sacrifice, it had to be pragmatic. It had to minister to man's material rather than his religious needs.

That in the closing months of 1889 Frazer believed himself to be in possession of such a portmanteau theory there can be little doubt. Writing to Macmillan on 8 November, he sketches out his key ideas, one of which is a solution to "the question of the meaning of a wide-spread custom of killing men and animals regarded as divine".[19] The meaning was not that which Smith ascribed to it. In order to clarify the difference still further, we have to turn back to Plutarch.

Plutarch had said that the sacred bull had to be disposed of after twenty-five years. Herodotos had stated, and Plutarch confirmed, that Apis had to be in peak condition, free from all physical blemishes, which his priests were expressly bidden seek out. The logical inference is that the Egyptians believed that any impairment of Apis's prowess and vitality through aging would lead to a corresponding impairment of his divinity. Twenty-five years is a fair span of adult vigour for a bull. Frazer then remembered the sacred buzzard of Mexico, which was also executed after an ordained period.[20] Then, again in Egypt, Ammon was annually killed and his head was draped in a ram's skin, or so states Herodotos, who Hellenized him as Zeus ("for", he says, "*Amun* is the Egyptian name for Zeus"[21]). Could not all of these sacrifices be of the same kind: not propitiatory acts for wrongdoing (an explanation even Smith had rejected), nor totemic communions or thanksgiving for blessings received, but a convenient and dignified method of disposing with one manifestation of the divine, and a means of letting its energy flow into the next and younger manifestation?

That in essence is what Frazer came to believe. The process was a magical one which can best be characterised as a law for the conservation of energy. When a divine animal sickened, its energy declined; this could best be restored by killing the animal and letting the power thus released flow through other channels: in other words, through another animal of the same species on whose head the prerogatives of the god could be supposed to have devolved. Put another way, it was a method of perpetuating nature by cropping it. This theory had several advantages over Smith's. It was much closer to common sense, and could be understood by reference to an analogy with natural processes which was both self-evident and universal. It had no need of an elaborately hypothetical reconstruction of primitive psychology, nor did it depend upon a system of thought and social organisation as uncertain and remote as totemism. It fitted the bill.

But there was a corollary. The energy of the declining embodiment of the god's powers was never completely spent. It could therefore conveniently be siphoned off by devouring his body in a sacred meal. This was possible whether the god was a corn spirit or a divine animal, and was thus applicable to all stages of human development. It was also a means of cementing society, and retaining a vital connection with the source of the community's strength. It was this process of sharing out the god's vitality through vicarious participation in his sacrifice that Frazer termed the sacrament.

Thus at the conclusion of the Thesmophoria the women of Athens feasted themselves on pork and by so doing implicitly took nourishment from the declining Persephone, the dying corn. "The meal", says Frazer, "must have been a solemn sacrament or communion, the worshippers partaking of the body of the god".[22] Likewise, after the sacrificial ox had been felled during the Bouphonia festival up on the Acropolis, those present ate of the flesh of the victim – less, it might be thought, to diffuse the guilt of the proceedings than to draw strength from the remains.[23] Similarly, it was Frazer's contention that on certain awestruck occasions the worshippers of Attis and Adonis may have dined off the flesh of the pig and thus of the god himself.[24] And the Ainu of Japan annually selected a young bear for honoured treatment before slaying it, finishing again by glutting themselves on its flesh.[25]

Where the god was a corn spirit, and no sacrificial animal provided, the cereal itself might be eaten as a substitute. Thus Lithuanian peasants baked a loaf from the fruit of the field and ate it ceremonially with beer brewed from the barley. Thus Brahmin priests offered up rice cakes on the altar; thus the Chief Priest of Onitsha in Igboland initiated the agricultural year by partaking of a piece of the new yam.[26] Should he refuse, or the harvest be delayed, great distress might follow. Sometimes the first fruits were prepared so as to resemble the body of the god. So Swedish peasants prepared a loaf in the shape of a little girl; so the farmers of La Pélisse in France suspended a doughman from a fir-tree during the harvest, to be broken and distributed by the mayor when the crop was safely in. So the Aztecs of Mexico created an immense figurine in dough in the likeness of the god Huitzilopochtli, and after a ceremonial period of fasting, ate him. "This is my body which is given for you . . .".

The examples are replete, and were to grow more so. The custom of eating the god seemed to be almost universal. The examples, of course, were not the whole point: what was important was their contribution to the total argument. The sacramental theory has two ramifications, one an express one, the other implicit. Implicitly, there was the analogy with Christianity. For, if the sacrifice proper was the equivalent of the Offertory, the sacrament was the equivalent of the Communion. Later editions were to speak of "transubstantiation" in Mexico,[27] but in 1890 the parallelism is nowhere spelled out. It drifts rather in the wind as a gentle sighing breeze, or perhaps a sinister undercurrent.

That, of course, is how Frazer intended it. Whatever his subjective feelings, which were complicated enough, he did not mean to undermine men's faith, but he wished to open their eyes. Had he laid bare the essence of his argument in 1890, he would perhaps have offended a substantial section of his general readership, and that he especially did not wish. It may, however, be as well to linger for a moment on the tendency of the implied argument which runs through the text like a constant subterranean stream. What had Frazer asserted, really; or, to put it another way, what had he denied? If he was right, there was an element in the Mass, the Communion, the Lord's Supper, call it what you will, which was – as he was still crowing to Mary Kingsley in 1899 – purely magical. That in itself might not have caused offence: what else is substantiation except a particularly inspired variety of magic? What was more damaging was his implied undermining of the moral foundations of eucharistic theology. There is nothing moral about the procedure of drawing strength from a god: it is simply natural in the sense that cropping a beast is natural, or even eating it is – a form of biological perpetuation. If Frazer was claiming that the rite of Holy Communion was magical not simply in the mode of its operation but in its quintessential significance, Miss Kingsley was right, and he would have the bishops to contend with.

There are times in the next few years when one can observe Frazer looking nervously over his shoulder at the Christians coming up behind him, armed with brickbats presumably and with harsh reviews in the ecclesiastical press: let him that is without doubt cast the first stone. As it transpired, before 1900, when in the Second Edition Frazer came clean about his view of the Crucifixion, the Christians were very kind to him. On the surface, this is quite surprising. Frazer had implied much that might give offence to Catholic and Protestant alike. His construing of sacrifice was, of course, much closer to Catholic dogma than Protestant. When Frazer rejected Smith's norm of eucharistic thanksgiving, he threw out with it any possibility of regarding Communion as a cosy get-together between God and man. That could not have looked well to Protestants, but it also was unlikely to find favour with Catholics, who thought of transubstantiation as a much more dignified process than the crude forms of magical rite Frazer had described. No wonder that in his letter to Macmillan in November 1899 Frazer signalled both excitement and caution. "The resemblance of many of these savage ideas and customs to the fundamental doctrines of Christianity is striking. But I make no reference to this parallelism, leaving my readers to draw their own conclusions, one way or the other."

For the Christian faithful there was and is, of course, a way out: the language of eucharistic theology is itself saturated with parallels, in fact derives much of its meaning from them. "O . . . Lamb of God . . . that takest away the sins of the world" does not imply that Christ was the *only* lamb; indeed, if he was, the statement would be meaningless. If Christ was indeed the "full, perfect and sufficient sacrifice", as Frazer left it open for his readers to believe, he was in no sense required to be the unique sacrifical victim. Indeed, the whole tradition of Atonement theology implies that there had been dozens before him. Christ was the point at which the sacrificial process was transcended; he was the fulfilment of the Law.

So much is speculation and personal preference. Frazer's more immediate concern was to explain certain facets of the cult at Nemi. It was known that the inhabitants of Aricia excelled in the baking of a particular variety of loaf made in the shape of a man and called *mania*. Now Mania, which to us means madness, to Romans was the grandmother of wraiths. For her benefit at the Compitalia, the feast of *lares* or household gods, woollen figures were hung outside the houses to dispel prowling ghosts. Thus at least says Macrobius, who imputes the custom to a commutation of what were earlier human sacrifices.[28] Might not the *maniae* baked at Aricia have been sacramental objects: loaves baked in the likeness of the slain god and then eaten so as draw sustenance from his vital, though cruelly sapped, forces? If so, then the slaying of Rex Nemorensis, which originally occurred at some set period, and which by the time of the Antonines had converted itself into a duel between rival contestants to the kingly title, was both a sacrifice and a sacrament: sacrifice in that the king was killed, yielding place to younger and stronger man; sacrament in that, through the consumption of the *maniae* loaves, the celebrants shared at one removal in his divine person. With this final contention in 1890 Frazer closed his great third chapter on the killing of the god, and with it his case as far as sacrificial practice is concerned.[29]

It may be as well, however, to cast a backward glance at the distance Frazer had travelled from Smith. There were important points of convergence, and important points of divergence. On one thing they were agreed: however you viewed the sacrificial rites of the earliest men, they were not expiatory: they were, to use Smith's term *"pre-moral"*. The roots of this idea lie in the Protestant tradition. Smith's researches had partly been motivated by a desire to place on a proper historical footing the idea of sacrifice as an act of participation rather than to penance. For Smith, the sacrifices of the earliest Semites had been inspired by a desire to share the fruits of the earth and to confirm an allegiance to a *ba'al* or spiritual overlord. Fear, a sense of culpability, a longing for propitiation – itself the child of dread: these came later. Throughout *The Religion of the Semites* Smith argues that the evolution of a sense of sin was the result of, rather than the justification for, changing sacrificial practice. Propitiation was not the solution to sin; was a way of giving substance to the institution of expiation, which had arisen independently, as a response to other, largely organisational, factors.

On the amorality of sacrifice Frazer was only too willing to concur, but for reasons Smith would have found strange if not repellant. Certainly Frazer did not regard sacrifice as in essence propitiatory. If Frazer and Smith, the cautious agnostic and the renegade minister, had one thing in common, it was the desire to emancipate the concept of sacrifice from its overtones of furtive dread. Their motives for so desiring, however, were of a completely different order. For Smith, fear in the face of

Providence implied a lack of trust in God's unsearchable wisdom. For Frazer it implied reverence, or at least concession in the face of divine displeasure. These had their place, but in a later scheme of things which in the Second Edition, once his terminology had sorted itself out, he came to call "religious". Though religious justifications could be adduced for sacrifice, they had nothing to do with its origins, which were magical.

And what was this magic? The difficulty in the First Edition is that the term shifts, and its instability does nothing to clarify the argument. Realising this, Frazer devoted much of the process of revision in 1900 to a refinement of the term, producing a hefty chapter entitled "Magic and Religion" which was later to expand itself into two whole volumes.[30] Thus was his early embarrassment assuaged. Yet the notion is there in the First Edition clearly enough, if intermittently explained. Magic was an application, or perhaps misapplication, of the Association of Ideas, operating in this instance as a primitive law of the conservation of energy. When a crop threatens to wither, you prune it as you do roses. When a species threatens extinction, you cut back its numbers selectively. Early man seems to have realised some of this, and to have embodied the precepts of a primitive technology or human husbandry. The god was not so much immolated as cropped, or perhaps culled. His energy would then flow into another manifestation, since gods were always breaking out miscellaneously, anywhere. If the successor was the god's son, so much the better, because the line literally renewed itself. In any case, gods could appear promiscuously, and sometimes simultaneously in a variety of poses: one thinks of the many facets of Apollo or of Zeus. Kings were similarly versatile, and it would not have unduly worried the intelligence of early man that the same god-force should erupt in successive forms in other respects quite unlike one another. Success would out, and the Survival of the Fittest prevail. The pulse of life, the *élan vital* – one thinks again of electricity, and of Herbert Spencer's versions of Darwinian survivalism – was in any case maintained.

These principles are cogent if limited, and, though Frazer was to surround them with much additional explanation and set them in a wider context of man's intellectual development, in essence he did not change them. Nor would he perhaps have been inclined to expatiate further had he been understood better, or had not fresh, and sometimes unsettling, information come to light to complicate and in some cases challenge his propositions. The Second and Third Editions of *The Golden Bough* overlay the basic theories with occasionally rococo encrustations of gold, the configurations of which are sometimes pleasing and sometimes gauche. They do not necessarily alter the basic assertions, though Frazer's hope was that they refined them. The debate would carry on in Frazer's head for a further twenty-five years. The First Edition had been completed in a little under twelve months. Warts, solecisms and all, the two-volume work of 1890 is in its own way a masterpiece, perfectly in period, enshrining in all its gaudy, captious splendour the genius of the time. He would not inevitably do better.

CHAPTER IX

THE PROGRESS OF THE MIND

YET misunderstood he had been, and it was only human to wish to put matters to rights. From 1890 to 1898 he was temporarily pulled aside from anthropology by the need to complete work on Pausanias, but he bitterly resented the intrusion, seeing his great edition of the *Description of Greece* increasingly as a curb upon his energies. By 1898 *The Golden Bough* had already become a way of life: his reputation, for better or for worse, depended upon it. No sooner was Pausanias off to the printers than he was itching to get back to the riddle of the grove. He wrote to Macmillan, asking for an interleaved copy of the First Edition, then spent several weeks copying in his amendments. The writing was to be nearly as swift as before, Frazer supplying the printers with manuscript chapters as and when he completed them. By July 1899 they were ready to go:

I am glad to tell you that I have the first chapter of *The Golden Bough* ready for the printers and will send it off when I hear from you. It is to be printed by my old friends R. and R. Clark, is it not?

The additions to the first chapter are very considerable, and though I do not anticipate the additions to the later chapters will be in the same proportion, I think it will be desirable to adopt a smaller type than in the first edition.

I feel pretty sure of making a greater impression with the new than with the old edition. The matter is certainly increased, and I hope that with practice my style has gained in freedom and ease. The good opinion of some competent judges of style has at least encouraged me to write with more confidence than before. So while I am doing all that I can to improve the substance of the book, I shall be glad that the printer and binder should do their parts towards making it outwardly as comely as may be.[1]

Eventually, with the help of the smaller typeface, the enlarged matter was squeezed into three volumes, though the grand sweep of four chapters was maintained. Frazer's concern for outer comeliness was understandable: there had been the odd flaw in the First Edition. Apart from the occasion misprint – "prao" for "proa" throughout – J. H. Middleton's mistletoe had been cramped into one corner, not emblazoned between the title and the author's name as the artist had intended. Also it had lost its surrounding gold band. The result was not unpleasing, but, as Frazer wrote to Macmillan, "His [Middleton's] friend William Morris commented on it unfavourably, and no wonder."[2] In 1899 it was a bold man who braved the wrath of Morris. Aestheticism had taken its toll during the 1890s, even in the austere courts of Trinity. As Frazer wrote to Bedford Street with his habitual pungency, "I wish the book to be beautiful as well as good."[3]

"Good" was another fulcrum word in the 1890s: Wilde's Lady Windermere was to have been a "Good Woman", just as Hardy's Tess had been a "Pure" one. Dissent was in the air, and Frazer had done his bit. But the heady days were over: the decade was drawing to a close, and along with it the century. Once the writing was over, the Frazers travelled to Rome, he to recuperate, she for her health. As production of the new edition raced to a finish he wrote from the Hôtel Printemps, Via Veneto, urging more speed, for "my wish is that the book should be published in the century in which it was written".[4] Product of the nineteenth century it might well have been, but it would help lay the century to rest.

There was talk of haste in all of his letters now, less from pressure of other projects than from a desire to make up for lost time. Plenty had happened since 1890, and Frazer had been out of the swim. Matters mythographic and anthropological had seldom been more vigorously debated than in the years since the First Edition burst upon the world. England was rife with ethnology and folklore: compendia such as Jevon's *History of Religion* (1896), Lang's *The Making of Religion* (1898), even a book entitled *Religion and Myth* (1893) from Frazer's missionary friend James Macdonald of the Free Manse, Reay. In *The Myth of Perseus* (1894–5) Sidney Hartland had attempted Frazer's approach of extruding the totality of folklore from one single, legendary strand, as on a less recondite level had Grant Allen in his *Attis* (1892). The ethnographic literature from the colonies – Mary Kingsley's *Travels in West Africa* (1897) Sir Alfred Lyall's *Asiatic Studies* (1899) – had likewise grown apace.

From Frazer's point of view the decade had been dominated by two tendencies, on neither of which could he look with any favour: a growth in the occult, and some confusion as to his own meaning. By dint of an irony to which he cannot have been blind, the second had sometimes been employed to abet the first, the sturdy rationalism of the First Edition taken as underpinning a range of modish phenomena – from Theosophy to spiritualism to worse – none of which could he look upon in any other light than as a species of historical relapse. Man's progress lay towards science, not the dark backward and abysm of time: one needed to understand magic simply in order to conquer it.

It had been a decade of bitter feelings too, and the Folk Lore Society had been the arena for many of them. Rationalist and irrationalist faced one another across a widening gulf. It was in November 1894 that Edward Clodd as President had stood up and attacked the activities of the Society for Psychical Research as "the old animism under . . . vague and high-sounding phrases", only to be reprimanded the following summer by Lang: "I see nothing wrong in a glass ball, but if I give my friends the lie, then I act as the dreamless Irish king would have done had he called all liars who averred they could dream."[5] The membership had naturally enlisted – more on Clodd's side than on Lang's. Meanwhile back in Cambridge Frazer, a corresponding member, bided his time. The tilt of his feelings can of course be guessed. When, in the month of the publication of the Second Edition, William James moved into the Hôtel Printemps and tried to interest him in the paranormal, he got short shrift.[6] As Frazer himself would have added, "and no wonder". The 1890s had witnessed a frightening increase in credulity: Madame Blavatski, the Theosophical Society, the Golden Dawn. It was the age of the psychic groupie, and Frazer was determined to be seen not to join them. Still less did he wish to be cited in support. All the more reason, in this bewildering atmosphere, to make it plain what precisely he had meant by "magic".

To begin with, the sub-title would have to be changed. The First Edition had been "A Study in Comparative Religion", but in 1890 he had been quite content to construe magic as religion's handmaid. With all that had happened in the meantime, this simply would not do. He instructed Macmillan:

By the way I intend to alter the sub-title to "a study in *magic and religion*" instead of "in *comparative religion*". I find that in fact there is almost more of magic than of religion in my book, and as in the new edition I draw a sharp distinction between magic and religion, it seems only right that magic as well as religion should appear in the title. I don't think that the change will be any disadvantage from the advertising point of view. So please in your notices of the forthcoming book describe it as "The Golden Bough: A Study in Magic and Religion."[7]

And so it was to remain. The "sharp distinction" between magic and religion was the principal reason for the enlarged first chapter, and has since been hailed as a breakthrough. In fact by 1900 it was verging on an anthropological commonplace. Frazer's contribution was not to be the demarcation of these terms but his placing them in chronological order and marshalling them next to science in one luminous evolutionary trinity.

Valuable spadework had already been done by one Frank Byron Jevons, "Classical Tutor in the University of Durham", whose *History of Religion*, largely forgotten now, had appeared in 1896. A textbook for students and other interested parties, this was for the most part a blend of Smith and Frazer, but it also had much that was original to offer, including a theory that the priest–king had been killed not because he was ailing but because he had committed sacrilege by slaying the sacred animal – a view closer to Smith than it was to Frazer. More importantly, Jevons had divided the ingredients of early man's world into the natural, defined as that which he could control, and the supernatural, defined as that which he could not. The former was the domain of magic, the latter of religion. Magic in its turn had much in common with science. Both assumed a consistency in nature, together with some form of natural law which could be manipulated to beneficial effect (for oneself) and to detrimental effect (for one's enemies). One could even divide up magic, just as one could divide up science, along clear inductive lines:

> There is no fundamental difference between savage and scientific logic. On the contrary, they are fundamentally identical. The uniformity of nature, the principle of induction, the theory of causation, the inductive method, from the common framework of both logics: the savage would probably be able to give his assent to all the principles of Mill's logic.[8]

In *A System of Logic* (1843) John Stuart Mill had drawn up the boundaries between four so-called "Methods" or varieties of induction, three of which Jevons now sought to apply to magic. The first was the Method of Agreement, where a single cause gave rise to a single effect; the second, the Method of Disagreement, where an additional element in a causal mix led to an unpredicted effect which could therefore be ascribed to it; the third, the Method of Concomitant Variation, where clusters of cause and effect altered in unison, giving rise to a belief in the identity of the clusters. Each of these, Jevons claimed, possessed its magical equivalent. There is a hazy overlap between these divisions and Frazer's, but the absolute parity of types is much less important than the recognition, common to both men, that the erratic practices of our remote ancestors possessed a kernel of empiricism akin to that possessed by science.

The trouble was that the topography was vague and drifting. It was all very well to take up where Mill had left off, but his Methods fitted magic but awkwardly. A better start had been made by Frazer in 1890 when he had spoken of "sympathetic magic", but one needed to go further and define it. In 1896, in his *Myth of Perseus*, Sidney Hartland had taken one more step when he had attempted to portray sympathetic magic as a sort of logical synecdoche in which part stood for the whole: a hair for a man, a shoe for its owner.[9] Hartland has a number of examples of such synecdoche – hair, blood, sweat, teeth, footprints, the refuse from food, discarded clothes, and finally names – most of which were to recur in Frazer.

It was at least a start, and, taken together with Jevons, possibly irresistible. Now, when Jevons's book appeared in 1896, it received a warm though anonymous review in the pages of the *Folk-lore Journal*. The author was no less than Sidney Harland, who went for the nub:

One term that he has not disentangled is "Sympathetic Magic". It has lately been the custom to label all magic "sympathetic magic". This is to confuse at least three kinds of magic. First we have Incantations, in which the object is attained by the use of certain verbal formularies. Next, we have Mimetic Magic. When the savage flaps a blanket to cause the wind to blow "as the sailor still whistles to bring a whistling gale"; when before going on the warpath or the chase he executes a "dance in which the quarry or the foe are represented as falling before his weapon"; when water is sprinkled to produce rain, and so forth, all of this is not "Sympathetic" but "Mimetic Magic". It is to this kind of magic that the maxim "like produces like" is specially applicable. We should confine the term "Sympathetic Magic" to practices, whether of injury or benefit, upon substances identified with, though in effect detached from, the person (or thing) we intend to reach, practices which are believed directly to affect the person (or thing) aimed at by means of sympathy between him (or it) and the substances actually acted upon.[10]

It was at this stage, late in the day and understandably a bit out of breath, that Frazer embarked upon his second edition. Since setting out in 1890 he had seen the hares outstrip him. But Fraser was a tortoise; the day would at length be his.

In the First Edition sympathetic magic had been portrayed in four pages as the nimbus surrounding the god–king.[11] This certainly was no longer enough. First, what manner of thing *was* magic? One way of looking at it was at a technique of explanation; another, as a technique of influence. Theoretical magic was a kind of rudimentary pure science, hooking up connections through a loose variety of induction, a sort of pragmatic guessing-game. Practical magic was a kind of improvised technology based on these guesses, but how more meaningfully to divide it? We have already spoken of the Scottish epistemological tradition stemming from David Hume and relayed to Frazer via men such as Hamilton and Veitch. This tradition now came to Frazer's rescue: he would replace Mill's divisions with Hume's.

The two crucial branches of Hume's Association of Ideas had been "similarity" and "contiguity in space and time". Applied to magic, and adapting Hartland's terminology, these now yielded "imitative" and "sympathetic" magic. An example of each will suffice. In the ancient kingdom of Ashanti in time of war, the wives of soldiers absent at the front staged a mock fight in which they stabbed at pawpaws with knives, just as their embattled menfolk were slicing at the heads of their enemies.[12] The first method of attack, on the principle of imitation, aided the second. Theocritus in his second idyll tells us of a witch who cast a fibre of her lover's clothing into the fire so that he would melt with love for her. The fibre had been in contact with the lover, so he would melt also.[13] As in Hartland, part stood for the whole.

Some confusion was caused by the fact that in 1900 Frazer still employed "sympathetic magic" as a generic title for the class, within which he distinguished between "imitative magic" and magic by contact, which he also called "sympathetic". This clearly would not do, so in the Third Edition he revised his terms. Imitative magic now became "homoeopathic magic", and magic by contact "contagious magic", with "sympathetic magic" reserved as a generic title for all kinds. Following through from Jevons, we thus have

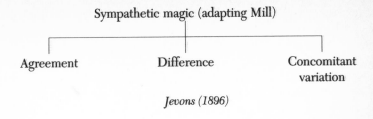

Sympathetic magic (adapting Mill)

Agreement   Difference   Concomitant
                                       variation

Jevons (1896)

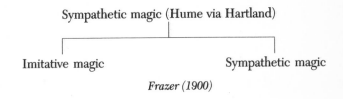

Sympathetic magic (Hume via Hartland)

Imitative magic   Sympathetic magic

Frazer (1900)

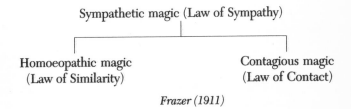

Sympathetic magic (Law of Sympathy)

Homoeopathic magic   Contagious magic
(Law of Similarity)   (Law of Contact)

Frazer (1911)

The mould was now set, and into it Frazer could pour his ever-growing store of examples.

But the real controversy had not been over how to divide magic, but whence and how it had arisen. Was magic a primitive stage of intellectual development out of which men had eventually emerged into the dim temple of religion, or had it evolved gradually as, painstakingly and with many a false turning, mankind learned to control his environment? Opinions diverged, but there was one branch of received opinion according to which religion had broken out of the warm cocoon of magic, like a butterfly from its chrysalis. Jevons, though, thought magic and religion different in kind; when they coincided, as they often did within any given society, it was because both principles were at work, and one half of the community clung to magic, while the religiously minded, whom he took as the more advanced, pledged themselves to the priests. By 1900 most commentators favoured the magic – religion dichotomy and accepted the affinity of magic with science; the disagreement was over how, and in what order, they had developed.

For Frazer one principle was sacrosanct: magic, religion and science were all products of the individual human mind, not, as Robert Marett was later to claim, of some act of communal osmosis. Great changes were brought about by great men. Fundamental to Frazer's reconstruction of prehistory, then, was an attempt to force himself under the skin of the originator. Understanding implied empathy. Nor again was he unique in this. Writing in 1899, the Indian administrator Sir Alfred Lyall had tried to define the relationship between magic and religion. Why did Indian Brahmins, like priests everywhere, so hound and harry the witch? Was this persecution based on envy, a recognition of superior power, or was the magician simply a sitting target whenever the priest's blandishments failed? To work this out you had to understand the principles according to which the magician operated. Lyall portrays him as a sort of prototypical scientist, and imagines his moment of discovery, an individual experiment performed in an open laboratory:

> Witchcraft is thus supposed to begin when a savage stumbles upon a few natural effects out of the common run of things, which he finds himself able to work by unvarying rule of thumb. He thence infers that he has in some wonderful way imbibed extra-natural power, while he has only picked up accidentally one or two of the roughest keys which open the outer lid of the physical world. He has hit upon a rudimentary materialism; and, while he fancies himself to be entering upon a mysterious department in which he can do without the popular fetish, he in fact becomes a Fetish unto himself (which is partly true), not in the essential conditions of the things which he sees and handles. His characteristic must always have been this, that he has some real knowledge, or faint tincture of it – and that, while the vulgar crowd round him ascribe all strange coincidences to the spite or favour of idols or demons, the witch makes bold to dispense with divine intervention, and to rely on his own arbitrary tricks.[14]

For Lyall, then, the inception of magic was the inauguration of a form of what we might today term an intermediate technology. It was that anyway for the more audacious minds, the cautious continuing to hedge their bets, putting their money both on witchcraft and, just in case the magic failed, on religion. But this was to shut their eyes to real possibilities and turn backwards to unreason. There was nothing to be gained from such a retreat. The magician had at least stumbled upon something indubitably clever, if far from infallible. In order of intellectual resource, it was the magician who was the revolutionary, not the priest. Lyall does not commit himself on the question of historical priority – a practical administrator, he is interested in ruling a territory, not in plotting its past. But, logically, there was no denying the fact that religion appeared to come first.

There was a great deal to be said for this point of view. That magic should have issued in an age of scientific inquiry which, haphazard at first, at length led to surer practical procedures, hypothesis succeeding hypothesis until the truth was reached, was an entirely credible scheme. Alchemy led, by a very few intermediate steps, to chemistry; the guesswork of the medieval physicians, fixated as they were on Galen, led via an erratic and winding path to the medical science of the age of Harvey. The belief in the power of thermal waters was arguably both magical and scientific. Frazer too noted these facts, and could only account for the suggested continuity by a temporary revival of magic immediately following the demise of religion and before the onset of science proper. But the idea that magic, lock, stock and barrel, had succeeded religion simply would not do. Early ritual had to be magical ritual. To have conceded anything else would have been not simply to revise *The Golden Bough* but to recant it.

Frazer saw no need to recant, finding support for his version of events in two arguments, both of which we should today reject. The first was the universality of magic: its drawing on axioms deep-seated in the human mind and unvarying from civilisation to civilisation. Magic was the bedrock of the psyche; like the earth's crust it was of one kind, while religion, being a later deposit, varied as flamboyantly as did the upper geological strata. To find the essence of things you had to dig down. And downwards, through a reconstruction of recorded and unrecorded history, Frazer dug, finding magic at the bottom of each successive shaft.

But, since evolution proceeded at an uneven pace, you could also dig sideways. The other supportive limb of Frazer's argument was a claim that the oldest civilisations extant seemed to be without any trace of religion. It was mandatory that of all surviving primitive societies the simplest and least developed was that of the aborigines of Australia. The aborigines, it appeared, possessed totems but they did not possess gods. They emphatically possessed magic; *ergo* magic was older.

How had the transition from one to the other come about? Lyall appeared to explain the inception of magic by a recognition of the inefficacy of prayer. Frazer reversed the order, but he kept the logic. Religion succeeded magic when men recognised the inefficacy of witchcraft. When they saw that their ruses did not work, metaphorically or literally speaking they fell down on their knees:

> By religion, then, I understand a propitiation or conciliation of powers superior to man who are believed to direct and control the course of human nature and human life. In this sense it will readily be perceived that religion is opposed in principle both to magic and to science. For all conciliation implies that the being conciliated is a conscious or personal agent, that his conduct is in some measure uncertain, and that he can be prevailed upon to vary it in the desired direction by a judicious appeal to his appetites and emotions.[15]

This was the turning-point in mankind's spiritual and mental advance. Marett later called it the Birth of Humility, but in Frazerian terms it was more like the Birth of Supplication. Viewed another way, it was the Birth of the Gods, for gods would not exist if they were not needed. Now, Jevons had thought the concept of the supernatural must be primary. You do not propitiate gods unless you previously believe in their existence. Would any man invent a god in order to conciliate him? For Frazer, however, mankind evolved the concept of divinity when magic failed him. Necessity, the Mother of Invention, was also the Father of the Gods.

The mixed brood thus engendered were not brothers or even half-brothers, but in most human communities they lived *en famille*. Distinct in origin, religion and magic were often difficult if not impossible to sort out. Jevons again:

> no religion is free from the danger of relapse on the part of some of its believers, and the recrudescence of a belief in magic. Hence it is that we find religion and magic acting and reacting upon one another. Even a religion so comparatively developed as that of ancient Rome, sanctioned the resort in times of stress, such as an exceptional drought, to magic, and fell back on the *lapis manalis* as a rain-making charm. Sometimes religion will have a fixed *modus vivendi* with sorcery, and take magic into its own organization, as in Chaldaea. On the other hand magic, even when its relation to religion is one of avowed hostility, will implicitly recognize the superiority of its rival by borrowing from or travestying its ritual; the superstitious mind, incapable of understanding prayer, will recite the Lord's Prayer backwards as a spell more powerful than any of its own; and the Irish peasant uses

holy water where the simple water would have been considered as sufficiently efficacious.[16]

Frazer produces a striking example of such peaceful coexistence in the first chapter of the Second Edition. The Egyptians, at least from the time of Akhenaten, deified the sun. Their faith in the omnipotence of this deity did not, however, go as far as taking his rising and setting for granted. Day by day, in the temple of Ra, they sought to aid his comings and goings with the charms of imitative magic. Having personified the forces of darkness in the demon Apepi, they formed an effigy of this devil in the likeness of a hideous crocodile or else multi-coiled serpent, housed in a case on which they inscribed his hated name in green ink. Then every night as the sun reached the rim of the western horizon the effigy was bound with twine, spat upon, then lunged at with a knife and trampled underfoot. The procedure was repeated whenever a sandstorm threatened to dim the sun's brightness, or when there was a sudden squall of rain. "The fiends of darkness, clouds, and rain felt the injuries inflicted on their images as if they had been done to themselves", writes Frazer. "They passed away, at least for a time, and the beneficent sun-god shone out triumphant once more."[17]

But, if magic and religion were successive stages, how was such coexistence tolerable? Jevons had interpreted the resilience of magic within a religious context as a sort of Tylorian survival, but for Frazer it was something more complicated and more interesting. Religion had not emerged out of the cocoon of religion, nor was either strictly parasitic on the other. Though of distinct provenance, they were related by a process akin to symbiosis. Religion may have taken over from magic; it may in all times and places have persecuted it; but it could never dispense with it entirely. Often it grew around the extant core of magic which remained within it like a kernel inside a fruit. For this very reason it was very often invisible until the peel was taken off to reveal the zest, the flesh, the seed lurking within. It was thus that the rituals of Adonis had grown up around a set of simple water charms intended to fertilise the fields, and the rites of Osiris around a need to secure the annual inundation of the Nile, the fostering of the seed. For this reason theology was very often useless as an explanation of religion, or indeed of magic. For the very same reason – a corollary that was to grow more and explicit in Frazer's work – magical explanations could never entirely account for religion. Where the two coincided, magic, though a necessary condition of the combination, was decidedly not a sufficient one.

Who controlled these processes? The answer in the case of magic was the magicians, in the case of religion the priests. Frazer's individualistic psychology ensured that his reading of history was cognate with his theory of power, potentially even with his politics. If kings were gods, they were also magicians, and even priests. Pre-eminently they were men who were able to use privileged skills to hoodwink or, more helpfully, advance a whole population. Such men, Frazer argued, gained the support of their fellows because they were able to manipulate the conditions of life itself: the rain, the sunshine, the wind. The divine right of kings, then, was a sort of sublime bluff. That at least was how kings operated under a magical regime, but, when religion became the order of the day, what then?

Five years after the publication of the Second Edition, Frazer was given a chance to answer this question when in the Lent Term of 1905 he was invited to deliver a course of lectures at Trinity College on the theme "The Evolution of the Kingship in Early Society". He was fifty-one at the time, and it was only the second time that he had lectured. It threatened to hold up the Third Edition, so on 5 May we find him writing to Macmillan,

> My book has been delayed for about three months by lecturing this term [in fact it was the term before], a sin with which I have not often had to reproach myself, having indeed perpetrated it only once before in my life. On this occasion I was led to commit the crime by the thirst for gold, which more than ever I perceive to be the root of all evil.[18]

The *radix malorum* in this case led to Macmillan's promise to publish the lectures as work in progress towards the Third Edition, into which they were eventually integrated in 1911 as part of *The Magic Art and the Evolution of Kings*. In the meantime Frazer uses them to discuss the whole question of kings and their manipulation of power in contexts both magical and religious.

The manuscript of the lectures still exists in several fluent folios, with Frazer's nervousness about lecturing all too obvious from the pause and emphasis marks added in red ink. The argument is strongly reductive. In it he distinguishes between two sets of political conditions under which early man – or by extension, it would seem, any man – organised himself. The first of these he calls oligarchy, or sometimes democracy. The concatenation of these two terms might surprise some later readers – it would sound especially odd in the ears of modern Greeks – but it has

to be recognised that what he has in mind is less the political line-up of
the modern world than the state of affairs in much earlier societies,
particularly those of the classical world. Fifth-century Athens was arguably
both a democracy and an oligarchy. The other system is what he
describes as despotism, dictatorship or, more worryingly, civilisation. The
identification between the last two terms comes out especially clearly
towards the end of the lecture series and flows relatively undiluted into
The Magic Art. Frazer's original wording from the lecture manuscript is
as follows. He is describing the supplanting of the democratic by the
despotic form:

> The political revolution is now complete. The democracy of savage
> society has been exchanged for the despotism of a more developed
> civilisation. The constitutional change has actively contributed to the
> great advance which the community has simultaneously made not only
> in material wealth, but in knowledge and refinement. The crudities of
> savagery have been in a large measure purged away, sentiments have
> become more polished, manners more polished. Old symptoms of
> superstition are fallen into disrepute: the foundations of the sciences
> are being laid. . . . But it seems to be a law of nature that all things
> should revolve in cycles, or perhaps we ought rather to say in spirals,
> since even when the course of history seems to turn back on itself, it
> nevertheless pursues a different and upward path. Political mutations
> are not exempt from this law: they too follow the same tortuous line
> of progress. Hardly has monarchy touched its highest point in a
> despotic or theocratic government than the political pendulum begins
> to swing back in the direction of oligarchy and democracy. To change
> the metaphor, despotism sooner or later breeds within itself the seeds
> of its own decay.[19]

"And not one day too soon", late-twentieth-century readers might add.
Frazer always held at best a jaundiced view of the virtues of democracy:
his comments in 1918 on hearing that Lloyd George intended to call a
general election *in advance of* demobilisation are most revealing.[20] Yet
almost twenty years later, with Europe spiralling towards another
disastrous war, he published an essay called *Condorcet and the Progress
of the Mind* in which he plighted his faith once more in the light of
reason as the one beacon which might save mankind from the yawning
abyss, though significantly not this time seeing it as the exclusive preserve
of leaders.[21] His faith in the leadership of the unencumbered great is
therefore best viewed in the light of a commitment to the unfettered

human intelligence. People make decisions best singly; too many cooks spoil the broth. There is none of us without a sneaking respect for this point of view. (Have you ever known a committee take a *right* decision? Committees are contrivances for making mistakes.) It is certainly congruent with Frazer's individualistic psychology. If great thoughts could only occur in great minds, then a single leader, unembarrassed by a need to compromise with others less gifted that himself, could work wonders. Leadership was in measure the art of invention, and what inventions were ever made by a crowd?

Frazer is very precise about the stages through which this social control was supposed to pass. To begin with you had the Age of Magic, when the magicians – rainmakers, conjurers of sun and wind – were accorded the respect due to kings. These notables had their wicked and sometimes enlightened way with the people until the more critical among their adherents began to notice that not all of their tricks were working, and began to demand some say in the matter. But the magicians were one step in front of them, and just before the secret was out converted themselves into priests. This was the dawning of religion, but, before the worship of supernatural deities became properly established, there was an intervening period during which the magician–kings took advantage of their vestigial kudos to pass themselves off as human gods. It was to this period that the phenomenon of divine kings properly belonged. Among them were the kings of Latium:

> The Kings of Alba Longa, the predecessors of the Roman kings, appear also to have aped Jupiter; for Virgil describes them as wearing the crowns of oak, the god's special emblem, and one of them is recorded as having set up as a god in his own person, the equal or superior of Jupiter. To support his pretension and overawe his subjects, he constructed machines whereby his mimicked the peal of thunder and the flash of lightning. Like the similar story of Salmoneus, this legend may preserve a reminder of a real custom observed by the early Kings of Greece and Italy, who like their followers in Africa down to modern times have been expected to produce rain and thunder for the good of the crops.[22]

These magico-religious patriarchs held sway until the strain of popular discontent or scepticism grew too much. There then occurred a sort of primordial *coup d'état* and democracy reassumed its erratic, unguided path. Most political theorists would view this as an advance. The unsettling fact is that Frazer, invariably and unequivocally, viewed it as a decline.

Truth, then, was dependent upon power, which in turn was dependent upon magic. There is a glaring paradox here. Frazer was strongly committed to a form of evolutionary meliorism. His version of this meliorism involves the placing of religion of a higher point of evolutionary advance than magic. Yet, because of the affinity of magic with science, it often looks as if, when it comes to allocating points for utility, he gives magic the edge.

Indeed, it is hard to escape the impression that in a roundabout sort of way Frazer had a lot of respect for magic: for the real McCoy that is, not for its modish nineteenth-century revivals. In 1909, four years after the kingship lectures, he was lured into lecturing again, this time to the Royal Institution. His subject on this occasion was "the influence of superstition on the growth of institutions" (the Royal Institution, one assumes, included). Perhaps he was feeling out of sorts with the modern world; he had just beaten a hasty retreat from Liverpool, where he had spent all of five months as Professor of Social Anthropology.[23] The commercial abrasiveness of the place seems to have bruised something in him; he retained the Chair, but at ruinous expense fled back to Cambridge. Be that as it may, he was in nostalgic mood, and chose for his theme an impassioned defence of credulity. Nineteen years later this would become "A Plea for Superstition", and be reissued under the title *The Devil's Advocate*. The *advocatus diaboli* was Frazer himself. The props of civilised society, he said, were embedded in the mire of magic. Marriage would have been impossible without exogamy; property without the idea of an external soul; kingship without sorcerers; respect for human life without the fear of ghosts.

But, for all that, Frazer could not reconcile himself to the abyss. Having devoted the hour to a defence of magic, he closes by passing judgement upon it. The following passage is about the most even-handed he ever delivered on the subject of superstition, and is well worth quoting at length:

As a body of false opinions, therefore, superstition is indeed a most dangerous guide in practice, and the evils which it has wrought are incalculable. But vast as are these evils, they ought not to blind us to the benefits which superstition has conferred on society by furnishing the ignorant, the weak, and the foolish with a motive, bad that it be, for good conduct. It is a reed, a broken reed, which has yet supported the steps of many a poor erring brother, who but for it might have stumbled and fallen. It is a light, a dim and wavering light, which, if it has lured many a mariner on the breakers, has yet guided some wanderers on life's troubled sea into a haven of rest and peace. Once the harbour lights are passed and the ship is in port it matters little if he steered by Jack o' Lantern or the stars.

That, ladies and gentlemen, is my plea for superstition. Perhaps it might be urged in mitigation of the sentence which will be passed on the hoary-headed offender when he stands at the judgement bar. Yet the sentence, do not doubt it, is death. But it will not be executed in our time. There will be a long, long reprieve. It is as his advocate not his executioner that I have appeared before you tonight. At Athens cases of murder were tried before the Areopagus at night, and it is by night that I have spoken in defence of this power of darkness. But it grows late, and with my sinister client I must vanish before the cocks crow and the morning breaks gray in the East.[24]

When it came to publishing the lecture, Macmillan wanted him to do away with this peroration. Was it not too sententious, too rhetorical? Frazer demurred: "I prefer to retain the dramatic ending, not only because it is dramatic, and from the literary point of view perhaps effective, but because after having said a good deal in excuse of superstition I wish my last words to be of condemnation."[25] It is thus that in its closing moments Frazer deserts his role as counsel for the defence and, passing sentence, stoops down like a venerable Areopagite to inscribe his *theta* in the sand. *Thanatos* (death) it is: superstition must die.

This is of course the other side of Frazer's temperament, the side represented by that passage in the Second Edition in which he speaks of superstition as a seething cauldron into which man may even now disastrously, if not always wittingly, fall. His words are more ominous here, less tinged with whimsy or wistful regret. One remembers the irrational manias of the 1890s. May this passage have been intended as a stern reproof aimed at those who in that giddy decade had taken his talk of magic too seriously and sought to misapply it?

It is not our business here to consider what bearing the permanent existence of such a solid layer of savagery beneath the surface of society, and unaffected by superficial changes of religion and culture, has upon the future of humanity. The dispassionate observer, whose studies have led him to plumb these depths, can hardly regard it otherwise than as a standing menace to civilisation. We seem to move on a thin crust which may at any moment be rent by the subterranean forces slumbering below. From time to time a hollow murmur underground or a sudden spurt of flame into the air tells us of what is going on beneath our feet. Now and then the polite world is startled by a paragraph in a newspaper which tells how in Scotland an image has been found stuck full of pins for the purpose of killing an obnoxious laird or minister, how a woman has been slowly roasted to death as a witch in Ireland, or how a girl has been murdered and chopped up in Russia to make those candles of human tallow by whose light thieves hope to pursue their midnight trade unseen.[26]

In such a passage Frazer the editor of Cowper seems to join hands with Frazer the admirer of Gibbon. The nightmare vision of civilisation collapsing, with its significant reference to "superficial" accretions of religion and culture, is very much of a piece with his Enlightenment horror of the abyss. "He had", wrote Lionel Trilling, "the old lost belief in the virtue and power of rationality. He loved and counted on order, decorum, and good sense." This decorum had, however, a sinister dancing-partner: a fear of the darkness that may at any moment engulf us all. How Augustan it is, how close to the culminating nightmare of Pope's *Dunciad*:

> Religion blushing veils her sacred fires,
> And unawares morality expires.
> Nor public Flame, or private, dares to shine;
> Nor human spark is left, nor Glimpse divine!
> Lo! thy dread Empire, CHAOS! is restored;
> Light dies before thy uncreating word:
> Thy hand, great Anarch! lets the curtain fall;
> And Universal Darkness buries All.[27]

There is, of course, a problem which Frazer disguises. If anybody was dampening religion's sacred fires, it was he. If morality was dependent upon religion, and religion in turn was enshrined magic, what then? Trilling speaks of Frazer "counting on" order, decorum and good sense. But this is to put it at its lowest. There is surely an obscure sense, of which Frazer always seems dimly to have been aware,[28] in which this Enlightenment poise and stability relied on religious belief: not on explicit dogmas so much as on a compunction towards self-restraint which itself rested on religious foundations. Such compunctions were so much part of Frazer's emotional make-up that he seems not to have worried unduly about their origins. Yet nobody can read his letters to friends such as Jackson, Housman and Gosse without being struck by an overactive and not always comfortable conscience, a conscience never more alert than in small matters. In his life and correspondence he took a hair-splitting morality so much for granted that he seems at times to have been blissfully unaware what havoc his undermining of the religious foundations might unleash. Frazer regarded himself as a scientist; scientists, he seemed to argue, should ply their trade unhindered by sentiment or fear of the social consequences. This too now seems naïve, but it was a sentiment very much of the period. It is thus that in the Preface to the Second Edition he is moved to speak of himself as a battery of guns mounted against the ivy-mantled bastions of faith:

> It is indeed a melancholy and in some respects thankless task to strike at the foundations of beliefs in which, as in a strong tower, the hopes and aspirations of humanity throughout the ages have sought a refuge from the storm and stress of life. Yet sooner or later it is inevitable that the battery of the comparative method should breach those venerable walls, mantled over with the ivy and mosses and wild flowers of a thousand tender and sacred associations. At present we are only dragging the guns into position: they have hardly begun to speak. The task of building up into fairer and more enduring forms the old structures so rudely shattered is reserved for other hands, perhaps for other and happier ages. We cannot foresee, we can hardly guess, the new forms into which thought and society will run in the future. Yet this uncertainty ought not to induce us, from any consideration or regard to antiquity, to spare the ancient moulds, however beautiful, when these prove to be out-worn. Whatever comes of it, wherever it leads us, we must follow the truth alone. It is our only guiding star: *hoc signo vinces.*[29]

This is stirring stuff, but it is also slightly ingenuous. It is all very well to speak of stripping ivy from the stonework, but to talk of bombarding the walls is surely to invite them to collapse around your head, particularly if, like Frazer, you happened to be living in Whewell's Court at the time. When the towers fell in, when the courts of Trinity faded from view, when the clock stopped chiming the quarters and the college servants ceased making the beds, when Latin grace was no longer said in the Great Hall, what star would be left to steer by? One might call on the Cambridge police, but in 1900 the police still went to church; that, it might be said, is why one could call on them. If the faith of our fathers ceased to be taken with any seriousness, what then protected Cambridge dons in the dark? A Calvinist conscience was so deep-set in Frazer that he seems never seriously to have contemplated a world in which its claims might fall on deaf ears. And yet such a world there might be, and such a world had arguably existed in the not-so-distant past.

The question of the origin of morality is one which Frazer seems never systematically to have debated. Yet in the Second and Third Editions it is implicit in his discussion of religion and the subjugation of man's personal needs to the gods. The gods demanded respect; they also demanded obedience. When this was not forthcoming, reparation was due, and it is thus that Frazer is led to see propitiation as the cardinal characteristic of all religious, as opposed to magical, systems. It is to Frazer's treatment of religion as more narrowly defined that we must now apply our minds.

CHAPTER X

THE MAN OF SORROWS

NOT ALL of Frazer's family had been stay-at-homes. In the 1870s, during the university vacations, he and his sister Christine would ramble southwards to the estate of Lafine in Ayrshire, where, in Miss Havisham-like seclusion, lived an unmarried relative of their mother's. Lafine was a gaunt house in plain stone standing amid 6,000 acres at the head of its own lake. It had descended through their mother's family for generations. The current occupant, a Miss Martha Brown, was a woman of commanding but far from inflexible disposition who had recently lost a brother. From 1873 until her death in 1897 she and James corresponded regularly, and, from hints dropped in these letters together with much that his mother had already told him, the young man was able to piece together the worldwide exploits of his grandmother's people, the Bogles. Two pieces in this jigsaw puzzle were provided by family heirlooms. One was a box of eighteenth-century manuscripts which had reputedly been in the possession of James's great-great-uncle, George Bogle. The other was a necklace of unique and exotic design.[1]

First the necklace. It consisted of a single row of reddish-orange carnelian beads from which were suspended a set of pendants: a trio of green beads, terminating in a single carnelian set in gold, and others compounded of blue stones. From each end of the necklace hung sashes of silk braid: one terminating in an oval piece of blue glass set in gold, the other in a pear-shaped unset stone. The whole ornament was apparently the lower third of a larger necklace which had once hung around the neck of the Teshu Lama, one of the Grand Lamas of Tibet. What was it doing in Lafine?

Like so many Scots, the Bogles were wanderers. George Bogle of Daldowie, James's great-great-grandfather, had earned a brief notoriety in 1746 by provisioning Bonnie Prince Charlie's army. Of his nine children John had established an estate in Virginia and Robin a sugar plantation in Grenada, while George sailed to Bengal, where he rapidly attracted the attention of Warren Hastings, the Governor. When in 1774 an envoy to the as-yet unfrequented kingdom of Tibet was needed, it

was this young Scot whom Hastings chose. Bogle set out in the company
of a Scottish companion – another Alexander Hamilton, this one a
doctor – and in August wrote back from Bhutan to sister Elizabeth at
Daldowie:

> We are scattered all over the face of the earth, and are united only by
> hope and a tender remembrance. While you are passing your cheerful
> evenings with friends and relatives at Daldowie, while Robin, with his
> negroes (and happy they are under him), is planting the sugar cane,
> while I am climbing these rugged mountains, there is a secret virtue,
> like a magnet, which attracts us together, and cheers and solaces us.[2]

He was right about the dispersion, though less prescient about Robin's
blacks. A century later, in October 1865 – well after the Emancipation –
a rebellion broke out in Morant Bay, Jamaica. The leaders were a Free
Baptist deacon called Paul Bogle, his brother Moses, and a half-cast Scot
named George William Gordon. Paul Bogle made a pact with the
Maroons in the hills, and then walked the many miles to Spanish Town
to register his dissent at the chronic land shortage for freedmen.
Subsequently he created mayhem in Morant Bay itself. Betrayed by the
Maroons, he was arrested and strung up from the arch of the very court
house that he and his followers had gutted. Where, in the iconography
of Caribbean nationalism, he still remains: the hanged god of colonial
Jamaica.[3] Truly, whether of the blood or not, these Bogles were made of
sterling stuff.

But George Bogle carried on over the mountains to Teshu Lumbo.
On the eve of his departure the Great Lama made him a present from
off his own person of a necklace, the bottom strand of which was
dispatched back to Daldowie, whence it eventually descended to Cousin
Martha at Lafine. Meanwhile, back in Bengal, George wrote an account
of his travels which he sent to Dr Johnson, saying that his trip had
reminded him of Johnson's *Journey to the Western Islands of Scotland*,
published that same year. How Johnson reacted we do not know, but a
century later, when Frazer was in his second year at Trinity, the
manuscript was published in London by arrangement between Martha
Brown and the editor, Sir Clements Markham. In it occurs this description
of New Year's Day in Teshu Lumbo, Tibet, as Frazer's great-great-uncle
witnessed it in February 1775:

> On the first day of the Tibetan year everybody, except the Lama,
> assembled in the large court which is under the palace. All the galleries

which run round it were crowded with spectators. I was placed, as usual, next to the Chanzo Cusho in the highest balcony. The exhibitions began with dancing by Merry Andrews in masks. Then a number of banners were set up, and a crowd of gylongs dressed in various coloured habits, with their cymbals and tabours, and with trumpets, hautboys and drums, marched in procession round the court. Next about twenty gylongs, in visors resembling the heads of various, mostly wild animals, and in masquerade dresses, danced with antic motions, in the same manner (but better performed) than I had seen in Tassisudon. After this, the figure of a man, chalked upon paper, was laid upon the ground. Many strange ceremonies, which to me that did not understand them appeared whimsical, were performed about it, and a great fire being kindled in the corner of the court, it was at length held over it, and being formed of combustibles, vanished in much smoke and explosion. I was told it was a figure of the Devil, but am not sufficiently skilled in the Tibetan mythology to enter into particulars. One thing is certain, it was painted white with regular features, and whether or no it was intended to represent that being who "goes to and fro upon the face of the earth seeking whom he may devour", I could not help sometimes fancying that it much resembled a European.[4]

A gylong is a Buddhist priest, though as to the identity of the chalked devil we cannot be so sure. Bogle thought him a European; to Frazer, however, he was a vehicle for what he chose to term the expulsion of evils, the means whereby the people rid themselves of the contamination, moral and physical, which had accumulated during the course of the year. It is no coincidence that his most dramatic example of such expulsion – the contest in Lhasa between the Jalno and the King of the Years – was eventually to come from Tibet.[5] In the meantime, in the very first edition of *The Golden Bough*, we are offered this leaf from the family's past, this echo from the dead.

Frazer had touched fleetingly on expulsion rituals in 1890, but passed on to other matters, embarrassed perhaps by the implications. The expulsion of evils, after all, might seem to raise uncomfortable questions. What, to begin with, *were* evils? In a magical universe the term would, it seems, possess little meaning. What worked would be commendable, what did not work would not. The birth of morality was dependent upon the begetting of religion.

Somewhere along the march of the mind the moral idea had dawned, but it was no instant sunrise. Frazer had described the first glimmering of it in the First Edition. For, though his earlier tendency was to see all sacrifice as magical, this clearly could not apply in all contexts. Some sacrifices were clearly of another kind: a propitiatory kind. Frazer's most telling example of such propitiatory sacrifice had come from Japan.[6] The Ainu are a Mongolian people from the north Japanese island of Hokkaido, whither they probably migrated from north-east Russia, and their habits and customs certainly have far more in common with the Koryak of the Kamchatka Peninsula than they have with the southern Japanese. Until recently their entire economy was based on hunting the bear. The bear was their staple diet, their ecological partner, and they were quite used to killing it. But once a year they exceeded themselves. They took a bear cub and raised it in captivity, feeding it on the choicest meats. Then, at the time of the annual bear sacrifice, they took it out of its cage, made profound obeisance before it, and after begging its forgiveness, killed it. The festival in an innocuous form is still performed for tourists, and there exists to this day an exceedingly scratchy record of the original event on film.

Now, the bear-sacrifice could not conceivably be magical. If bears were habitually killed, what virtue or power could possibly accrue from one more symbolic death? And so we get a crucial distinction:

> The primitive worship of animals conforms to two types which are in some respects the opposite of one another. On the one hand, animals are worshipped, and are therefore neither killed nor eaten. On the other hand, animals are worshipped because they are habitually killed and eaten. . . .
>
> Corresponding to the two distinct types of animal worship, there are two distinct types of custom of killing the animal god. On the one hand, when the revered animal is habitually spared, it is nevertheless killed – and sometimes eaten – on rare and solemn occasions. Examples of this custom have already been given, and an explanation for them offered. On the other hand, when the revered animal is habitually killed, the slaughter of any one of the species involves the killing of the god, and is atoned for on the spot by apologies and sacrifices, especially when the animal is a powerful and dangerous one, and in addition to this ordinary and dangerous atonement, there is a special annual atonement, at which a select individual of the species is slain with extraordinary marks of respect and devotion.[7]

Put like this it is clear that the bear-sacrifice was an attempt to placate guilt. It was thus purely and simply a religious celebration. There were other instances of such placatory animal sacrament: the Kamtchatkans for example placated sealions.[8] Matters were not always, however, that clear-cut. The more usual state of affairs was for a religious significance to be foisted onto an existing magical rite. We have already observed the sacrifice in ancient Egypt of the Apis bull. Here the death of the god was clearly magical and intense sorrow was expressed at his demise. Lucian says that the celebrants used to shave their heads, and the general aspect of the proceedings was one of intense mourning. But Herodotos also says that the worshippers heaped the head with curses before flinging it into the Nile or else flogging it to the Greek traders. This hardly consorts with feelings of love or veneration, so why did the Egyptians behave so inconsistently?

As Frazer explains this aspect of the ritual it is expiatory, though in a different sense from the Ainu rite. The Egyptians were not placating Apis; rather were they taking advantage of his death as a means of ridding themselves of all manner of moral and physical unpleasantness (a distinction ancient man seems to have made but rarely). If Apis was to die in any case, why not use the opportunity to heap all kinds of noxious influences – moral culpability, disease – on his unfortunate head?

Now, if the Apis sacrifice was not propitiatory, another term was needed. The ritual therefore came to be seen as a double one. In so far as Apis died to release his strength into another and fitter bull, his slaughter was magical. In so far as he was laden with curses, however, it was religious. In this second capacity, and this capacity alone, Apis died as a scapegoat.

Scapegoat rituals abounded far and wide, and already in the First Edition Frazer had listed some of them. In an early chapter we noted the learned fragment in which Petronius evokes the tribulations of the individual selected in ancient Marseilles to be fed at public cost and then cast out of the city walls.[9] Why, after being so honoured, was he thrown out without succour or resource? The simple answer was that his expulsion conformed to a variety of public exorcism whereby people rid themselves both of disease and of their own transgressions. Once a year the people of Creek Town in Old Calabar performed a hue-and-cry in which the noxious influences of the old year were driven from every corner and then dumped unceremoniously in the river.[10] In Timor the people unloaded smallpox onto a small boat – a proa – and then towed it out to sea.[11]

There were a number of variables in the way such rituals were performed. They might be performed whenever the need arose or else at fixed intervals. The most usual interval was supplied by the agricultural year: seedtime or harvest. They might also be performed by direct assault upon the supposed evil or by the use of a surrogate, which in turn may be inanimate, bestial or human. Frazer's accounts cover all of these kinds, but he was especially interested in types of ritual expiation which were both seasonal and mediate – that is to say, kinds employing a substitute.

Of such substitution the best-known instance was biblical. Leviticus 16 sets down provisions for the annual Day of Atonement, upon which the High Priest was required to select two he-goats by lot.[12] One of the goats was to be consecrated to the Lord and sacrificed at the door of the temple. The second was to be dedicated to a desert demon called Azazel and led away to perish in the wilderness. Azazel reappears in the second century BC in the pseudepigraphical *book of Enoch*, where he is one of the two hundred fallen angels who descend from Heaven to Mount Hermon to seduce the daughters of men. His particular offence seems to have been to teach women how to paint their eyebrows. His punishment is to be well and truly trussed and bundled into the desert:

And again the Lord spake to Rafael: "Bind Azazel head and foot, and place him in the darkness. Make an opening in the desert, which is in Dudael, and place him therein. And place upon him rough and jagged rocks, and cover him with darkness, and let him abide there for ever."[13]

It is to consort with this desert demon that the scapegoat was led away. Its fate is most graphically described in the *Mishnah*, a guide to Temple practice written down one and a half centuries after the destruction of the Temple, but still the fullest guide to its codes. The High Priest identified Azazel's goat by placing around its horns a strand of wool crimson with the people's sins. After laying his hands on its head and wishing on it all the iniquities of Israel, the High Priest then entrusted it to the layman designated to lead it away:

And they made a causeway for it because of the Babylonians who used to pull its hair, crying to it "Bear our sins and be gone!" Certain of the eminent folk of Jerusalem used to go with him to the first booth. There were ten booths from Jerusalem to the ravine, which was a distance of ninety *ris* [about seven and a half miles]. At every booth they used to say to him "Here is food, here is water!" and they went from him from booth to booth; for none used to go with him to the ravine, but they stood at a distance and beheld what he did. What did he do? He divided the thread of the crimson wool and tied one half to the rock and the other half between its horns, and he pushed it from behind, and it went rolling down and before it reached half the way down the hill it was broken in pieces. He returned and sat down beneath the last booth until nightfall.[14]

Until the late nineteenth century, the passage in Leviticus was widely misunderstood. The saintly Jerome could make neither head nor tale of the name Azazel, so in the Vulgate rendered the unfortunate animal as "caper emissarius".[15] When William Tyndale translated the Pentateuch into English in about 1530, this then became "scapegoat", a coinage which was incorporated in the Authorised Version to yield the translation most commonly known.

The Committee for the Revision of the Authorised Version, on which Robertson Smith had sat, advised a return to "Azazel".[16] "Scapegoat", however, was too good to lose, and eventually became the title of the volume in the Third Edition of *The Golden Bough* in which Frazer describes the ubiquitous nature of expulsion rites, and implicitly their relevance to the treatment of Christ. "The Scapegoat" was not, however, his original title. From 1900, when he first set out these ideas at length in the edition we are currently considering, until the very eve of the publication of the relevant section of the Third Edition, he thought of this portion of the argument as "The Man of Sorrows".[17] "The Man of Sorrows" it very nearly became.

The Christian parallel was therefore of the essence. Eventually Frazer lost heart and banished his discussion of the scourging of Jesus to a discreet appendix at the back of the book,[18] but in 1900, when these passages were first written, the Passion of Christ, whom conventional theological wisdom had always viewed as the "Man of Sorrows" of Isaiah 53, was emphatically the climax of the whole. In the Second Edition, where it appears towards the end of the long chapter "Killing the God", it is very much the *coup de théâtre* up to which the whole foregoing discussion leads.[19] It is worth bearing this in mind as we read.

The Victorians were inclined to sentimentalise the scapegoat: in his canvas of 1854 William Holman Hunt twisted the crimson wool round the goat's horns so that the poor demented creature resembles nothing so much as a refugee from Crufts. The rationale behind such rituals had long been a source of bafflement. We have observed Ovid's puzzlement over the behaviour of the Salii during the month of March.[20] These odd clerics were to be seen prancing through the streets, clashing their spears against their shields and executing wild leaps in the air. The leaps Frazer thought were probably a form of imitative magic to encourage the corn to grow. Since the dance was performed twice yearly, in March and October, and since the Roman planting year had two seasons, this would seem to fit the facts. But in their dances the Salii also invoked a god called Mamurius Veturius, who was apparently a form of Mars. And on the day following the Ides of March a skin-clad man representing a god of that name was driven through the streets of Rome, beaten with rods and thrown out of the city.[21]

Nor were the Romans alone in this. The Athenians kept two criminals who were stoned to death at times of public calamity. The ritual was repeated every May at the Thargalia, when the victims were obliged to wear around their necks strings of figs.[22] Greek flautists of the sixth century were familiar with a melody known as "Kradiēs Nomos". It was to be performed during the beating of a sacrificial victim with the branches of, among other trees, the fig. He had previously been fed with a dole consisting of cheese, a barley loaf and, again, dried figs.[23]

From the outset Frazer recognised that, in many of these classical accounts, figs were a recurrent element. An explanation for this had already been offered by the German mythographer Wilhelm Mannhardt, who thought that the beating by figs, usually in the vicinity of the groin, had been intended to release the human scapegoat's reproductive powers.[24] In 1907 W. R. Paton amplified this suggestion by reference to the horticultural process of caprifaction, whereby dried figs were hung amid the branches to stimulate a tree's growth.[25] This, thought Frazer, might help explain why the Roman scapegoat was a form of Mars. Mars, like Saturn, had once been a god of vegetation, or, more especially, of the sown seed. By thrusting him from the gates of the city the Romans were ridding themselves both of public contamination and of the previous year's growth. The Roman year previously began in March; by throwing out the old Mars, that is the old seed, the Romans were both treading out the husk of the previous harvest and issuing in the spring.

In the First Edition Frazer left it at that: Mamurius Veturius was a scapegoat, but he was also a dying god of vegetation. But there was obviously more to it. Before ancient man rid himself of the consequences of his baser instincts, he often felt a need to indulge them. It was this impulse which gave rise to festivals such as the Roman Saturnalia and later the European Carnival, of which in the main text of 1890 there is no mention. The thought, however, had not passed Frazer by. Beneath his discussion of the Salii, and across two pages, he trails a footnote pregnant with afterthoughts:

> It is to be observed that in the "Lord of Misrule" who reigned from Christmas until Twelfth Night we have a clear trace of one of the periods of general licence and suspension of ordinary government which so commonly occur at the end of the old year or beginning of the new one in connection with a general expulsion of evils. . . . Analogy suggests that at Rome the Saturnalia, which fell in December when the Roman year began in January, may have been celebrated in February when the Roman year began in March. Thus at Rome, as in so many places, the public expulsion of evils at the New Year would be preceded by a period of general licence, such as the Saturnalia was.[26]

The Saturnalia and the Carnival between them represent one of the largest growth points in the Second Edition. The origins of this elaboration are easy to trace. Frazer's own interleaved copy of the First Edition survives,[27] and in its margins while preparing the Second Edition Frazer has entered suggestions for amplification. Here he is especially concerned by the seasons at which the dances of the Salii occurred: spring and autumn. Could other festivals be explained by reference to these fixed points of the year? Our own ritual expulsion arguably occurs at Hallowe'en:

> Are the Feasts of All Souls (ghosts of the dead come to visit their friends) always at the end of the year and always followed by a general expulsion of the souls, after they have been feasted? Was Twelfth Night the time of the expulsion of the ghosts who had been feasted during the preceding period of twelve days?[28]

The manuscript note in question goes on to discuss Miller's *Scenes and Legends of the North of Scotland*, yet as a Lowland Scot Frazer needed no authority to remind him of a period of licence occurring, if not at Twelfth Night, then at Hogmanay. 1 January was Frazer's birthday. The reference to Feasts of All Souls is another matter. The Catholic feast of that name falls on 2 November. Now 2 November was the second day of the ancient year of the Celts, their New Year being 1 November, now the Feast of All Saints. These Catholic festivals represent successive attempts by the Church to eclipse and hence obliterate the earlier pagan feast.[29] Hallowe'en, then, which All Souls replaced was also at root a New Year Festival. It also had the merit of suggesting a whole new explanation of the expulsion of evils. The objects of expulsion were traditionally sin and pestilence. Feasts of All Souls opened up a second possibility: that what were in effect being driven out on such occasions were the spirits of the dead.

We shall return to this anon, but in 1899, when he turned his attention fully to these facts, the placation of the unruly departed was only one of the thoughts that went rushing through Frazer's brain. So fertile did the field now appear that it threatened to hold up the Second Edition more drastically than his digression on magic. The new sections on the Saturnalia and related festivals expended four whole months, a woefully slow rate of progress for Frazer. But they turned out well enough. On 1 April, All Fools' Day (what would he have made of that?), we find him writing to Macmillan in a state of modest elation:

> I have nearly finished the Saturnalia business for the new G. B. It has turned out fairly well, I think, and ought to make some impression. It occurred to me that I might anticipate the publication of the book by publishing the part on the Saturnalia as a series of articles for the *Fortnightly*. Would this help or hinder the book?[30]

The sections in question were indeed printed in the *Fortnightly* in the months immediately preceding the publication of the book.[31] They were to serve as a taster, a strategy which was to tempt Frazer more than once. Why were they so appetising? The answer has partly to do with the passages concerning the Crucifixion, but there was more to it than that. The whole nature of the Roman Saturnalia had, he felt, been misunderstood. We have to go back to early November 1899, when Frazer first started working out these ideas. On the 4th we find him writing to Macmillan, thanking him for a gift:

> I am very much obliged to you for so considerately and kindly sending me a copy of Mr Warde Fowler's new book, to the publication of which I have been looking forward for years. I have only as yet been able to glance at it, but it seems, as I should have expected and did expect, a very careful, accurate and sensible piece of work. It also pleases me to note that he seems to have found my book useful.
> But between ourselves I am surprised and selfishly rather pleased that he appears to have overlooked a piece of new evidence as to the

Saturnalia which I regard as of the utmost importance not only for that festival but even for ancient religion in general, perhaps not even excluding the rise of Christianity. This will prove the most novel and striking feature, I think, in my new edition, as it confirms in a remarkable way my interpretation of the priest of Nemi. But please do not say anything about this. I am afraid of the cat jumping out of the bag and am rather grateful that Warde Fowler does not even suspect what a remarkable animal is in the sack.[32]

Warde Fowler's book was *The Roman Festivals of the Period of the Republic*, which Macmillan had just issued. The Saturnalia was clearly the sack, but what is this creature that writhes and purrs so invitingly within the sacking? Well, we have to turn back to the Roman rite as conventionally construed. Here, rather tamely, is Fowler's account:

To turn to the Festival. If the God was obscure and uninteresting, this was not the case with his feast. It seems steadily to have grown in popularity down to the time of the empire, and still maintained it when Macrobius wrote the dialogue supposed to have taken place on the three days of the Saturnalia, and called by his name. Seneca tells us that in his day all Rome seemed to go mad on this holiday (Ep. 18.1). Probably its vogue was largely due to the accident of fashion, partly to muddled ideas about the Golden Age and the reign of Saturn (Virg. *Georg*. ii, 538) but it seems to be almost a general human instinct to rest and enjoy oneself about the time of the winter solstice, and to show one's goodwill to all one's neighbours. In Latium, as elsewhere, this was the time when the Autumn sowing had come to an end, and when all farm-labourers could enjoy a rest. Macrobius alludes to the completion of all in-gathering by this date: "Itaque omni iam fetu agrorum coactu ab hominibus hos deos (Saturnus and Ops) coli quasi vitae cultioris auctores" (*Sat*. i, 10, 19 and 22). The close coincidence of the Consualia, Opalia and Saturnalia at this time seems to show that some final inspection of the honest work of the Autumn may in reality have been coincident with, or have immediately preceded, the rejoicings of the winter solstice.

There are several well-attested features of the Saturnalia as it was in historical times. On December 17 there was a public sacrifice at the temple (formerly the *ara*) of Saturn by the Forum, followed by a public feast in breaking up from which the feasters shouted "Io Saturnalia!" (Macrobius, 1.10.18). . . . On the 18th and 19th, which were general holidays, the day began with an early bath, then followed the family sacrifice of the sucking pig, to which Horace alludes (*Odes*, 3.17) ... Then came calls on friends, congratulations, games, and the presentation of gifts (Macrobius, 1.14). All manner of presents were made as they are still at Christmas; among them the wax candles (*cerei*) deserve notice, as they are thought to have some reference, like the yule log, to the returning power of the sun's light after the solstice.[33]

Now these *cerei* or wax tapers are very interesting. Looked at in a magical light they furnished an example of imitative magic; like the midwinter fires of which Frazer elsewhere speaks, they looked very like attempts to encourage the sun in its onward flight towards the spring. Regarded as religious emblems, however, they were even more interesting. Macrobius, the fourth-century author who is our principal source on these midwinter festivities, allows us to look at them in this way through his use of an obscure Greek pun.

The *Saturnalia* of Macrobius is a late Roman dialogue in which the main subject of discussion consists of the merits of the poet Virgil. One of the speakers, however – Praetextatus – has an explanation for the origins of the Feast of Saturn, on which their deliberations are depicted as taking place. On being forced to flee from Greece, he says, the Pelasgians sought counsel of Zeus at Dodona and were told to find a floating island in a stream. There they should settle and offer yearly thanksgiving to Saturn in the form of φωτα, a word they took to mean men. The island they found near Rome, where, assuming residence, they sacrificed men to Saturn annually, before Hercules arrived and told them that φωτα meant "lights":

For many years they thought to propitiate Dis with human heads and Saturn with the sacrifice of men since the oracle had bidden them offer heads to Hades and a man (φωτα) to the Father. But later the story goes, Hercules, returning through Italy with the herds of Geryon, persuaded their descendants to replace these unholy sacrifices with others of good omen, by offering to Dis little masks cleverly fashioned to represent the human face, instead of human heads, and by honouring altars of Saturn with lighted candles instead of with the blood of a man; for the word φωτα means "lights" as well as "a man". This is the origin of the custom of sending round wax tapers during the Saturnalia.[34]

These were the candles or *cerei* which the latter-day Romans handed round as gifts. The significance of Macrobius's wordplay here – φώς for φῶς – was that it alerted Frazer to one very interesting fact.[35] Along with the legends surrounding the origins of the feast, a dim memory apparently had been handed down of periodic human sacrifice. This unpleasant proceeding, it was safe to assume, had been commuted by the later Romans into a harmless exchange of gifts. In Macrobius, then, Frazer found what he had earlier discovered in Alexander Hamilton: evidence of the mitigation through a gentle custom of an earlier and far crueller one. The Saturnalia, like so many seemingly innocuous festivals, had its roots deep in blood. This may not have been a cat, but it was most certainly a kitten.

Now for the cat. The hint from Macrobius was strengthened by something Frazer considered a far more significant find. In 1897, three years before the Second Edition, Franz Cumont, a Belgian scholar, published *Les Actes de S. Dasius*, a recension of an eleventh-century manuscript concerning an obscure martyrdom in the Roman fort of Durostorum, situated on the Danube near the town of Silistra in what is now Bulgaria. The incident took place on 30 November 303, during a month-long period of licence prior to the Saturnalia. In introducing his find Cumont had written,

> From the very first words we happen upon some very quaint sidelights on the Saturnalia, which are almost certainly authentic. The soldiers in the garrison, so our anonymous author tells us, observed a custom during the Feast of Chronos [Saturn], a custom which they celebrated every year, of drawing a king by lots. Dressed in all the finery of his office, this personage issued forth at the head of an immense company and flung himself upon the town in all manner of debauchery. The licence according him on this occasion passed for a prerogative of the god, since this temporary king was considered his terrestial equivalent.[36]

Continental readers will confirm that even to this day the custom of *tirer le roi*, drawing a king by lot, is observed in France at New Year. The monarch so elected chooses his queen and rules for the day, much as in medieval times the Lord of Misrule lorded it until Twelfth Night, or much as on the Feast of Innocents (28 December) in the cathedrals of England a boy bishop occupied the *cathedra* for the duration of Childermas.[37] All this interests Frazer and enables him to make a vital connection between the Saturnalia and Christmas festivities, and later with the European Carnival. He is even more interested, however, in the sequel.

It is not clear what fate the soldiers of Durostorum had in mind for their temporary Saturn. The manuscripts are divided as to what was supposed to happen next, but at least two of them state that at the close of his fleeting reign the earthly Saturn was required to cut his own throat. But Dasius, a baptised Christian, considered the debauch an infamy and though elected would not serve. He was therefore tried by court martial and executed at four o'clock that Friday morning, on the twenty-fourth day of the moon.

Cumont had concluded that the information gleaned from these documents confirmed what the Roman authors Macrobius and Lucian have to tell us about the conduct of the Saturnalia. Since, however, he was editing the Paris manuscript, where the fate of the temporary king is ambiguous, he had drawn no consequences from the ritual suicide which according to other versions was supposed to ensue. For Frazer, however, this was the crux of the matter. The part which Dasius was so reluctant to play was that of the mock king whom Lucian and Tacitus describe lording it in somewhat squalid fashion over the yearly rites. Neither Macrobius, nor Lucian, nor Tacitus gives an inkling that this mock king had to die: by the time of the Republic he almost certainly did not. The garrison at Durostorum, Frazer thought, must have been harking back to an earlier, cruder version of the rite, such as Macrobius's fanciful wordplay projects.

Frazer drew three conclusions. The first was that the Priest of Saturn was considered by his votaries to be a temporary impersonation of the god. The second was that, as a god, he was doomed to die for the people. The third was that, as time progressed and the manners of the age grew more lenient, his fate was modified, finally losing all suggestion of severity, until by the time of the Caesars he had dwindled into a harmless, if beguiling, buffoon. If these speculations were right, then the Saturnalia was itself a feast of the dying god, and so were all festivals descended from it.

With the cat straining at the noose, Frazer now proceeds to the next stage of his argument. After briefly considering the Carnivals of Catholic Europe, he passes on to equivalent festivals in Western Asia: the Babylonian Zagmuk and Sacaea and the Jewish Purim. Disappointingly, none of this appears in the 1922 abridgement. Though denied to the common reader, however, these sections undeniably represent the pith of Frazer's case, since these festivities, so close in spirit to the Roman festivities, represented for Frazer a crucial ingredient in the religious heritage of the Near East, without an appreciation of which the mentality of the Mediterranean peoples in the years before Christ was incomprehensible. His further, albeit tactfully phrased, conclusion was that this evidence was essential to an understanding of Christ, for all his apparent uniqueness.

The trouble was that the available information about these rituals was quite extraordinarily scanty. The Zagmuk was a New Year festival at which the king renewed his strength by grasping hold of a vast statue of the god Marduk in the state temple. Our sources for this festival come in the form of inscriptions which in Frazer's time had only just been construed. For the Sacaea, which the Persians borrowed from the Babylonians, there were two sources, both fragmentary. The first was the *Babyloniaka*, a history of Babylonian society and religion dedicated to Antiochus I by its author Berosus, a priest of the god Bel; and second the *Persika* of Ctesias, a Greek doctor at the Persian court.

Now, in the first book of Berosus, and the second of Ctesias, a feast called the Sacaea, resembling in certain respects the Roman Saturnalia, was apparently described. Strabo tells us that the Sacaea was inaugurated to celebrate the victory of King Darius over a people called the Sacae. The relevant passages in Berosus and Ctesias are missing, so for information about the festival we are forced to rely on much later paraphrases in the Greek authors Athenaeus of Naucratis and Dio Chrysostom. Athenaeus cites Berosus to the effect that the Sacaea was a summer festival lasting five days in which slaves enjoyed privileges normally reserved for their masters. One of the slaves was given the title Zoganes and allowed to lord it over the house. So far the Sacaea seems rather like the Saturnalia. For Frazer, however, the clinching clue was supplied by Dio Chrysostom, whose fourth discourse takes the form of a dialogue between Diogenes, upright in his barrel and cynical as ever, and the young Alexander, who is about to invade Persia. In the passage in question Diogenes is goading him for his lack of humility. Would he not like, even for a while, to doff his kingly garments and adopt the guise of a servant? Even the Babylonians do this:

> They get hold of a condemned criminal, place him on the throne, dress him in the state regalia and allow him to issue edicts, to swill and guzzle to his heart's content, even, during the period allotted, to make use of the royal concubines. Nobody dare gainsay him. Afterwards though they strip him, scourge him, and string him up. [ἐκρέμασαν].[38]

The last verb could mean "crucify him", though it could equally mean "hang him". Frazer of course would like it to mean "crucify", though he concedes the ambiguity. Whatever form the execution took, however, it was close enough to the ritual described in *Les Actes de S. Dasius* to be suggestive. Might not the Zoganes too be the representative of a dying god, and might not the god in whose stead he died be the king? It was a slender thread, but it was enough to hold on to. On 1 April Frazer wrote to Macmillan, "The feature in the Saturnalia part which is likely to attract the most attention is a new theory of the mockery and crucifixion of Christ, into which I have been led by the new evidence as to the Saturnalia."[39]

But it was a long way from ancient Babylon to the bare hillside outside Jerusalem. How was he to traverse the distance 'twixt Susa and Golgotha? Only by identifying the Sacaea with a relevant Jewish feast. Now the Sacaea was without doubt a very early festival. Robertson Smith had identified it with the Feast of Tammuz, held at the height of summer, in the Babylonian month of Tammuz, our July. In that case it could not conceivably coincide with the Zagmuk, which took place earlier, probably in March. The uncertainty concerning the date was unhelpful, but it enabled Frazer to perform some of his most breathtaking bits of jiggery-pokery with the calendar. It enabled him to see both feasts as vegetation festivals and as celebrations of the life and death of Tammuz. More importantly, it enabled him to identify the Feast of the Sacaea – which itself, he thought, incorporated the Feast of Zagmuk – with the Feast of Purim celebrated by the Jewish people at least since the Babylonian exile, and possibly before it.

These equations seem outlandish in the extreme until one looks at Frazer's sources. Our principal source for the legend surrounding the origins of Purim is the biblical book of Esther. Now, Esther is a problematical work which has always been more popular with scholars than with priests. Luther, who was both, was tempted to throw it out of the canon. The reason is simple: it is the only book in Holy Scripture never to mention God. Instead it describes a power struggle in Susa, capital of ancient Persia at the time of Xerxes. The period is historical, but the story, it is agreed on all counts, pure fiction. Like the book of Exodus, it depicts a fray between the Jews and their captors, in this case the Persians. Overcome by modesty, Queen Vashti refuses to unveil herself before a raucous company at the behest of her husband Xerxes, here called Ahasuerus. She is hence supplanted by Esther, a Jewess chosen for her incomparable beauty. But Haman, the royal steward, is jealous of her influence at court and attempts to discredit her by spreading gossip of a plot involving Esther and her cousin Mordecai, who, denied access to the harem, squats at the palace gate. The Jews are just about to be slaughtered in reprisal for the rumoured uprising when Esther unmasks Haman for the villain that he is and has him executed in Mordecai's stead. Mordecai is made steward, his people are saved, and they are enjoined to keep Purim ever after as a memorial to their salvation.

Apart from Xerxes, the human characters in this story are apocryphal, as are their names. But in 1892 the German orientalist Peter Jensen was examining some Elamite tablets when he came across the name Humman. The Elamites were traditional enemies of the Babylonians, who had once had their capital in Susa, and Humman (compare "Haman") appears to have been their chief deity. Could the story of Esther describe the Babylonian conquest of Elam, relayed by the Persians to the Hebrews and reworked so as to make the heroes the Jews? "Esther" (Hebrew "Hadassah") is very close to "Ishtar", the name of the Semitic and hence Babylonian mother goddess, and "Mordecai" sounds like the god "Marduk". If it is correct to make these connections, the story of Esther may have originated in an attempt by the Babylonians to account for the origin of one of their own festivals, which Jensen refused to identify.

Frazer got all this not, initially, from Jensen himself, but from Theodor Nöldeke, who had concluded his summary of Jensen's evidence in the *Encyclopaedia Biblica* with an invitation hard to refuse:

> It is true that hitherto no Babylonian festival coinciding, like Purim, with the full moon of the twelfth month has been discovered, but our knowledge of the Babylonian feasts is derived from documents of an early period. Possibly the calendar may have undergone some change by the time the feast of Purim was established. Or it may be that the Jews intentionally shifted the date of the festival which they had borrowed from the heathen. We may hope that further discoveries will throw further light on this obscure subject.[40]

When Frazer read these words, something in him seems to have snapped. What if Purim were in fact the Sacaea, which the Persians had enshrined at the heart of their religious system after the conquest of Babylon in 538 BC? True, Purim was in April, the Sacaea in July, but the calendar was lunar and might have rotated. The Zagmuk festival, which (on very slight grounds) Frazer believed to underlie the Sacaea, had itself been a spring festival. If he could persuade himself that Purim were a Hebrew Sacaea, he could legitimately search for a victim who like the Zoganes was allowed to run amok before being killed. He found this victim in Haman.

Thus armed, Frazer pounced on the crucifixion of Christ. Like the Zoganes, Christ was crowned, scourged and then crucified. If Purim were the Sacaea, and Haman, who was regularly destroyed in effigy at Purim, a sort of Zoganes, and if – a very big if – the Passover that year happened to coincide with Purim, then the soldiers who subjected Jesus Christ to this singularly brutal treatment may simply have been honouring custom. They may have been Roman soldiers gone native, or they may, as St Luke implies, have been Jews. In either case, they may have seen Jesus, the Man of Sorrows, as the ideal Haman figure and scourged and crucified him in consequence. For Jesus read Haman; for Haman read the Zoganes; for the Zoganes read the King of Babylon, or someone who had died in his stead. Christ forfeited his life in the guise of a dying god of the Semites. *Quod erat demonstrandum.*

Some bag; some cat. It is certainly a very sleek creature, if a little wobbly on its pins. Frazer's mixture of elation and apprehensiveness is amply demonstrated by his suggestion to Macmillan in April 1900 that the relevant sections of the Second Edition be printed in the *Fortnightly Review* in advance of publication. It would help display the goods, and it might also help draw the enemy's fire. The sections were indeed so published with no apparent ill-effect. In November Frazer wrote to Macmillan in some relief: "From what you say I gather that my Saturnalia articles have not scandalised the orthodox, as I thought it just possible (though not very probable) that they might do."[41]

He spoke too soon. The book appeared, and then there was a deathly hush. But in April 1901, stung to the quick by the implied sacrilege and ever ready to find fault with an illustrious countryman, Andrew Lang rode to the attack in the columns of the *Fortnightly.*[42] The Feast of Zagmuk did not coincide with the Sacaea. The Sacaea did not coincide with Purim. Who was the Zoganes anyway? Was he the dying Tammuz, as Frazer asserted on p. 254 of volume II, or was he a substitute for the king, as he claimed on p. 152 of volume III? If he was Tammuz, and the Sacaea, as Smith held, his feast, how could the Jews have borrowed it from the Persians, since Ezekiel saw the women of Jerusalem mourning Tammuz well before the conquest?

With that Frazer's case did not exactly collapse, but it faltered. He later said that he was unaffected by Lang's review. Nevertheless, when

The Scapegoat appeared in 1913, the "Crucifixion" section was tucked into an appendix along with an apologetic little note. It does not belong there, since, as any reading of the Second Edition makes clear, it was intended as the apex of the argument. Was it for this reason that, in an acerbic passage in *The White Goddess*, Robert Graves took Frazer to task for his cowardice?

Lang and Graves are both right in one respect: the paragraphs on Christ's execution in the Second Edition are intended as the final skirmish in the underlying military campaign against unwarranted belief outlined in the Preface. The trouble is that, though the arguments concerning the Saturnalia are impressive and the setting of the ministry of Christ in a wider Semitic context profoundly valuable, Frazer's attempts to explain away the Crucifixion are an abject failure. The connections with the Zagmuk and the Sacaea are just too remote. Nor do his attempts to explain the coincidence of the Passover and Purim in the year in question by suggesting that at some earlier date the latter was moved command uncritical assent. In fact they look like special pleading. Areopagite Frazer might be, but on this occasion the accused has got away scot-free.

But Frazer had also provided Christian apologists with a convenient escape route. There are various ways of looking at precedents. Either they can be seen as robbing the sequel of its uniqueness, or else they can be viewed as trumpeting the way. History, for those so inclined, could still be viewed as a meaningful sequence of events orchestrated to a fine point. Christians were still free to claim the earlier parallels as anticipations – nay, portents – of a conclusive and definitive act of revelation. Frazer was aware of all this, leaving us, his readers, to judge for ourselves:

In the great army of martyrs who in many ages and many lands, not in Asia only, have died a cruel death in the character of gods, the devout Christian will doubtless discern types and forerunners of the coming Saviour – stars that heralded in the morning sky the advent of the Son of Righteousness – earthen vessels wherein it has pleased the divine wisdom to set before hungering souls the bread of heaven. The sceptic, on the other hand, with equal confidence, will reduce Jesus of Nazareth to the level of a multitude of other victims of a barbarous superstition, and will see in him no more than a moral teacher, whom the fortunate accident of his execution invested with the crown, not merely of a martyr, but of a god. The divergence between these views is wide and deep. Which of them is truer and will in the end prevail? Time will decide the question of prevalence, if not of truth. Yet we would fain believe that in this and all things the old maxim will hold good – *Magna est veritas et praevalebit*.[43]

And so, to the mingled strains of the *Te Deum* and Bacon's *Essays*, Frazer brings this most difficult and contentious of dissertations to a close. The tone is auspicious, wry and also oddly affectionate. If the doctrine of revelation is an error, it is a sublime one whose pathos Frazer records. There are also fresh buds, suggestions of subtleties to come. Frazer speaks of the noble army of martyrs who throughout history have died "in the character of gods". Man of Sorrows, divine Thespian, Christ was one – some would claim, the culmination and fulfilment – of these. The dramatic metaphor is astute, and would help set the tone for the Third Edition. It is to this edition, the last and arguably most magnificent, that we now turn.

CHAPTER XI

THE THEATRE OF MYTH

BEFORE LONG ominous noises were emanating from the Hôtel Printemps. A mere two months after the submission of the last manuscript, Frazer was at work again. The stimulus was Rome itself, the *locus classicus* in more than one sense. No sooner was he installed in the *pensione* than the eminent among the scholarly community began leaving their cards, among them Gordon Rushforth, who was determined to recruit Frazer's support for a British School in the city on a par with that in Athens,[1] and Giacomo Boni, the Director of Excavations at the Forum. Boni was keen to acquire the new edition, and so Mrs Frazer wrote to Macmillan requesting one more complimentary copy:

> The book will be in excellent hands with Signor Boni – he is an ardent admirer of my husband's work and has brought wonderful confirmation to light about one of Mr Frazer's theories – namely he has found in the Temple of Vesta pieces of charred oak and immense layers of ashes which, analysed, are found to be of oak, thus confirming Mr Frazer's suggestion that the sacred fire was always made of oak. Mr Frazer therefore has new evidence coming in for a third (+ enlarged???) edition of *The Golden Bough*.[2]

This was Frazer's kind of holiday. It was not simply *The Golden Bough* which was threatened with extension; with the insatiable thirst of a true workaholic he was also plundering the museums for material for a bigger and better Pausanias. With Signor Boni he at last visited the lakeside site at Nemi, and made notes for the fuller physical description of it which adorns the Third Edition. The Second Edition in any case was fast selling out – a phenomenon that was to occur with ever-increasing frequency to Frazer's books as his fame, or notoriety, spread. Macmillan would welcome a third edition, provided it could be kept within decent bounds. In the meantime there were some personal difficulties to attend to. Frazer was having problems with his eyes. His doctors advised

Germany, so Frazer obliged – was Germany after all not the *fons lucis*? – and went to Wiesbaden, where he sat in a steam bath composing a Preface for the yet-to-be-commenced definitive *Golden Bough*: "It is characteristic of my husband that while being treated (a kind of *torture* of vapour and steam bath etc.) he has just now composed a passage for the preface of the third edition of *The Golden Bough*."[3]

The steam clearing, promises were soon forthcoming to Macmillan, though by March 1903 "I have found so much to read for the new G. B. that I have not yet begun to write."[4] By July "my reading is almost complete",[5] but the auguries of impending size are sounding more and more alarming. Already Frazer is speaking of himself as an elephant about to bring forth – "like the elephant I produce at long intervals, and the result is apt to be proportionately large".[6] Macmillan is looking to his cages and receiving sympathetic bellows from the mother: "The reading that I have done is for my subsequent books as well as the new edition, so that once I have begun writing I expect to go on nearly continuously writing for some years – a dreadful prospect for you and the reading public."[7]

But then come the lectures on the kingship, separately issued, and by the time the elephant is about to deliver again – triplets this time: the Eastern gods Adonis, Attis and Osiris – publication of a third edition *en bloc* seems to be a receding prospect. Could *Adonis, Attis, Osiris: Studies in Eastern Religion* possibly also be issued as a monograph on the strict understanding that it is to be considered part of the forthcoming Third Edition? And could Messrs. R. & R. Clark possibly be prevailed upon to desist from inserting a conjunction in the title?

> My account of the Adonis, Attis and Osiris worships in the new edition of the G. B. has expanded to such an extent that it could form a volume by itself of the same size as the "Kingship". If you are not deterred by the experience of that book, will you consider the possibility of issuing "Adonis, Attis, Osiris" as a separate book on the same plan as the other? While the contents will not be so varied, and there will be nothing amusing in them, the interest might to many people be greater.[8]

And so it transpired. R. & R. Clark managed to omit the offending conjunction, but they also omitted any reference to *The Golden Bough* on the title page. Naturally Frazer was being modest: *Adonis, Attis, Osiris* is one of his most drily witty as well as most enduringly popular books. Within a year a second enlarged edition was called for and this time the printers got the title page right.[9] For Lady Frazer, however, it was all proving far too much. It was all very well bringing elephants into the world but somebody had to look after them. With the alarm bells ringing in her head, she wrote secretly to St Martin's Street requesting an urgent summit conference:

> I have the gravest anxiety! I fear a repetition of the Pausanias worry & extension & shall advise calling a meeting in regard to this matter as soon as the MS for the volume *Attis, Adonis & Osiris* [sic] has gone to the printer. I will advise you of it. My fear is that the G. Bough will extend so much that it would become a mere reference book etc. – It would be a pity.[10]

Fears of unreachable erudition were soon quelled by talk of an eventual abridgement, but as an interim measure Frazer and Macmillan hit on the plan of issuing each and every part of the work – some of them containing two volumes – as distinct monographs with each title page indicating that this was an instalment of a greater work in progress. Mrs Frazer need not have feared: sales were greatly increased thereby, many of the individual parts being reissued more than once before the work was complete. One interim plan was for the jumbo edition to be christened "Editio Major" and the planned abridgement – a dwarf elephant – "Editio Minor". By this stage it was 1907, and the master design already contained five parts. But then work was held up by *Totemism and Exogamy* and the Liverpool professorship. By the time they returned to the issue in December 1910 the five parts had grown to six:

Part   I   *The Magic Art and the Evolution of Kings*
Part   II   *Taboo and the Perils of the Soul*
Part   III   *The Dying God*
Part   IV   *Adonis, Attis, Osiris*
Part   V   *The Man of Sorrows*
Part   VI   *Balder the Beautiful*[11]

The aggregate of parts eventually grew to seven. In the meantime, something quite extraordinary occurred. The departure from Liverpool had left Frazer low in spirits and in funds. He and Mrs (not quite yet Lady) Frazer left for a brief continental holiday, sending SOS calls back from each stop – Baden-Baden, Switzerland, Paris – imploring some form of financial assistance. Finally a loan from Macmillan of £300 and a further £200 from the Civil List saved the day, and by September, with one massive act of the will, Frazer had pulled himself together and could write to his publisher, "I am about to fall tooth and nail on *The Golden Bough*." There then ensued the most remarkable period of sustained creativity in Frazer's working life. It was a sort of Indian summer – the break in the clouds of which every writer dreams and which he knows all too rarely. Not even an invitation to deliver two sets of Gifford Lectures in 1911–12 could arrest his progress. The lectures rotated round the Scottish universities and on this occasion were to be in St Andrews, his chosen subject being *The Belief in Immortality and the Worship of the Dead*. For once Frazer took the lectures in his stride, made arrangements to publish them, and, most significantly, made their thesis a mainstay of his thinking. Their influence on the Third Edition itself is, as we shall see, incalculable.

"It was a wonderful summer", he wrote in October 1911, and then in one long, fluent fanfare came the remaining volumes. Already *The Man of Sorrows* had divided into *The Scapegoat* and *Spirits of the Corn and of the Wild*. By June of the following year he felt sufficiently relaxed to take a break of six weeks in Switzerland. Then, the very next month, "I am nearing the end of Part VI",[12] and by March "The G. B. is now practically finished. If I died tomorrow (which I have no intention of doing) the book could still be published in its complete form."[13]

There remained one last task, more a pleasure than a duty. The 1907 edition of *Adonis, Attis, Osiris* had already exhausted itself, and enough fresh material had arrived to justify splitting it into two volumes. With their publication in 1914 the Third Edition as we now have it lay complete. Frazer dispersed his library, got knighted, and made for the continent. He had effectively begun the Third Edition with *Adonis, Attis, Osiris*, and with it he finished. Behind stretched all the variegated riches of his mind. *The Dying God, The Scapegoat, Balder the Beautiful* may constitute the Treasure House of Atreus of this his greatest achievement, but *Adonis, Attis, Osiris* is decidedly the Lions' Gate.

There were, however, staging-posts. At the head of the edition stands a quotation from Macrobius in which that fourth-century eclectic compares himself to a bee culling nectar from far and wide to store it in a thousand cells "and blending all their variegated juices into one flavour by adding some unique essence of his own".[14] In the Third Edition the juices are more variegated than before, and the essence contains something of

Frazer's perpetual scepticism combined with an enhanced dramatic sense, a heightening of physical evocation which seems to have been taken over from his Pausanias. There is also something else, which one can only define as a sublime sense of occasion. For, besides wishing us to understand his increasingly complicated interpretation of events, he also wishes us to visualise them with a keenness not always previously required of us. The new axis is especially evident in the enhanced description of Nemi, in his evocations of the scenery of the Near East – the Lebanon, Cyprus, Turkey – and in his descriptions of the ecstatic celebrations of various orgiastic cults. The purpose is partly reductive – excess turning to irony; it is also, as Frazer observes in the Preface to *Adonis, Attis, Osiris*, an attempt to see character – and through it character motivation – as a reflection of environment.[15] In a deeper sense, however, it is an aspect of the argument.

As before, that argument commences with the cult of Diana at Nemi. It is a misstatement of Frazer's intentions to view the mystery of the grove as less quintessential to the Third Edition than previously; the sections devoted to it, more especially in the second volume of *The Magic Art*, loom if anything more prominently than in the earlier versions. In 1905 the *Lectures on the Early History of the Kingship* had once more addressed the fundamental puzzle of the cult's meaning, which Frazer seems to have been unable to get out of his head. The visit to Rome, the conversations with Boni, the reviews of the Second Edition, many of which had concentrated on this facet of Frazer's discourse, had only intensified the fascination. During 1902–3 Frazer spent hour upon hour hammering out the mystery with Arthur Cook, a classical colleague from Queen's College, who in the *Classical Review* had submitted Frazer's reconstruction of the cult to perhaps its most searching scrutiny.[16] Frazer and Cook worried these points during endless afternoon teas in college, much to the dismay of the increasingly protective Mrs Frazer, who took Cook for an academic poacher.[17] There was nothing else for it: the problem of Rex Nemorensis would have to be re-examined from scratch.

The first attempt was entitled "Artemis and Hippolytus", published in the *Fortnightly* in 1904 and standing now towards the end of the opening chapter of *The Magic Art*.[18] In the Second Edition Frazer had stated that Rex Nemorensis impersonated the god of the grove, but which? Cook had looked hard at the paragraphs concerned, and for the life of him he could not work it out:

Dr Frazer believes that the Arician priest was the incarnation of a deity residing in the oak. But if we ask of what deity, we receive inconsistent replies. (a) Where Dr Frazer sums up his whole investigation he concludes that the King of the Wood lived and died as an incarnation of the Supreme Aryan God (GB iii, 346). On Italian soil that god was named Jupiter and "the image of Jupiter on the Capitol at Rome seems to have been originally nothing but an oak tree" (GB iii, 346). On Dr Frazer's showing, therefore, the Arician priest ought to be an incarnation of Jupiter. But we look in vain for any connection between Jupiter and the Arician grove. (b) Elsewhere it is Virbius, not Jupiter, who is described as "the spirit of the Oak on which grew the Golden Bough" (GB iii, 456). . . . (c) Earlier in his book Dr Frazer has implied that the immanent spirit was neither Jupiter nor Virbius, but Diana. . . .[19]

"Confusion", as Macduff would have put it, "now hath made his masterpiece." Assuredly Frazer had produced a masterpiece, but was he so confused? He got to work at once. No wonder Cook had harped on about Jupiter: his life's work was to be a five-tome *Zeus* (1914–40). But the confounding of Diana and Virbius was a more serious matter. Somehow these aberrant stars had to be enclosed within the same firmament. Cook had already made a start in his article "Zeus, Jupiter and the Oak", published in the *Classical Review* in 1903, but the knot needed to be pulled tighter. The problem was that Virbius was an elusive figure, local rather than cosmic, and Egeria was a country wench, fitfully associated with the Roman king Pompilius Numa. How, against all just impediments, were they to be joined?

It was here that the benevolent syncretism of the Roman cults came to Frazer's rescue. Virbius, both Cook and Frazer were agreed, was a soubriquet for Hippolytus, and Egeria for Diana. Now if Virbius, as according to Servius, was the consort of Diana, and if Diana, as all aver, was nothing but a Roman Artemis, then another shadowy couple could be perceived behind the Roman pair. For Virbius and Diana, read Hippolytus and Artemis. This was all well and good, but how yoke them? Hippolytus was worshipped at Troezen, where his name was linked with Aphrodite, at whose behest he was slain. Euripides, as we know, has him repulsing his step-mother Phaedra, who calls down Poseidon's vengeance on his head. But it need not have been any one mortal woman that he repulsed so much as the embraces of the amorous goddess. When Frazer visited Troezen in December 1895 he discovered a semi-circular declivity, the remains, it was said, of the stadium in which Hippolytus disported himself in manly pursuits, one of which was horse-riding.[20]

Within sight of this hippodrome had once stood a booth from which his infatuated foster-parent was supposed to have leered at him during his work-out. It was still there in the time of Pausanias, when it was called "The Temple of the Peeping Aphrodite".[21] By this token Phaedra and Aphrodite, the frustrated middle-aged matron and the eternal goddess of love, were one. Recognition of these facts had recently led to bizarre interpretations of the cult at Troezen which were much to Frazer's purpose. Of Hippolytus he states, "Every year a festival was held in his honour, and his untimely fate was yearly mourned with weeping and doleful chants." This has a familiar ring, and so he continues,

> It has been suggested, with great plausibility, that in the handsome Hippolytus, beloved of Artemis, cut off in his youthful prime, and yearly mourned by damsels, we have one of those mortal loves of a goddess who appear so often in ancient religion, and of whom Adonis is the most familiar type. The rivalry of Artemis and Phaedra for the affection of Hippolytus reproduces, it is said, under different names, the rivalry of Aphrodite and Proserpine for the love of Adonis, for Phaedra is merely a double of Aphrodite.[22]

So far, so good. But at Nemi Hippolytus was associated not with Venus but with Diana, which tones in well with the Greek legend according to which his devotion went to the woodland and the hunt. Besides, both Hippolytus and Artemis were notoriously virginal; so how could they have formed a pair? At Nemi Diana was invoked to aid childbirth, which might suggest a less ethereal role, but are not midwives often conceived of as sexless? None of this worried Frazer. It was Frazer's contention that the blameless reputations of these deities were the result of a modern misreading of the epithet Παρθένος habitually applied to both Artemis and Athene. *Parthenos* meant not so much chaste – a word with whose Victorian reverberations the Greeks might well have had difficulty – as "unmarried". Properly understood Artemis was the goddess of the wild things, of the greensward, the great outdoors, of teeming exultant life. Her statue at Ephesus depicted her ringed by breasts (so in their simplicity concluded the Victorians, though our more sophisticated eyes have taken them for eggs, even bulls' testicles). Artemis furthermore had a celebrated shrine on Delos, at whose entrance before their marriage maidens used to lay their tresses in honour of two girls who had died at this spot while bringing offerings to Delian Apollo.[23] This rite was duplicated at Troezen, where maidens gave up their tresses to Hippolytus. In his work on the Syrian goddess Lucian cites this custom in explanation

of an equivalent custom he had observed at the Phoenician shrine at
Byblos (now Jebail) where the shorn locks were dedicated to Astarte.[24]
In Hierapolis, five hundred miles to the east by the River Euphrates,
offerings of this kind were made to Atargatis, originally a Hittite goddess
whom Lucian appears to have confused with Cybele. Men too offered
the first bristles from off their chin. Lucian was a local lad from Samosata,
and his stubble still lay there in a casket:

> They have another curious custom, in which they agree with the
> Troezens alone of the Greeks. I will explain this too. The Troezenians
> have a law that their maidens and youths alike never marry till they
> have dedicated their locks to Hippolytus, and this they do. It is the
> same at Hierapolis. The young men dedicate the first growth off their
> chin, then they let down the locks of the maidens which have been
> sacred since birth; they then cut these off in the temple and inscribing
> the name on the vessel they depart. I performed this act myself when
> a youth, and my hair remains yet in the temple, with my name on the
> vessel.[25]

Now in Byblos the maidens offered their hair in preference to their
chastity, the alternative being submission to a form of sacred prostitution.
Was hair then a substitute for virginity? If so, the lasses who brought
their severed locks and lay them at the feet of Hippolytus were in effect
offering themselves. Sacred prostitution, Frazer thought, was a way of
reinvigorating the god or goddess by a variety of imitative magic. If this
was the case, Hippolytus was not quite as innocent as the legends made
him out to be. May he too not have been a god of fecundity, and in that
capacity united with Artemis? In that case the cults of Artemis and
Aphrodite were not rivals but complementary; both goddesses seem to
have been revered at Troezen. if Hippolytus and Artemis had mated at
Troezen, why not then at Nemi? In guarding the sacred oak, was the
King of the Wood defending, not merely his throne, but his possession
of Diana's favours?

That a literal union between the priest and a human embodiment of
the goddess regularly was consecrated at Nemi is an obvious corollary to
his argument to which Frazer nowhere explicitly commits himself.
However, in the chapter from the second volume of *The Magic Art*
entitled "The Sacred Marriage" there is an important concession:

> Now on the principle that the goddess of fertility must herself be
> fertile, it behoved Diana to have a partner. Her mate, if the testimony

of Servius is to be trusted, was that Virbius who had his representative, or perhaps rather embodiment, in the King of the Wood at Nemi. The aim of their union would be to promote the fruitfulness of the earth, of animals, and of mankind; and it might naturally be thought that the object would be more truly attained if the sacred nuptials were celebrated every year, the parts of the bride and bridegroom being played either by their images or by living persons. No ancient writer mentions that this was done in the grove at Nemi, but our knowledge of the Arician ritual is so scanty that the want of information on this count cannot be a fatal objection to the theory.[26]

There are two ramifications to this train of thought which have far-reaching implications for Frazer's theory as a whole. The first is that the union, like the contest for the kingly title, was real and that it was repeated. The charade of the duel was thus not the only dramatic performance mounted at Nemi: there was the Marriage Show, followed by the Death Show. There were recorded instances of trees getting married, for Pausanias describes such a wedding at Boethia.[27] But whether it was the tree that the priest married or a female embodiment of Diana mattered less than that the ritual was recurrent and actual. In either case, as long as the ritual lasted, the priest did not simply impersonate Hippolytus: he *was* Hippolytus. If a female counterpart was involved, she too *was* Diana.

This process of re-enactment, of a continual reinterpretation of ancient roles, is absolutely central to the vision of the Third Edition. Consider a late instance of it, taken over from earlier editions into *Spirits of the Corn and of the Wild*. There was a Greek legend according to which Dionysus was the illegitimate son of Jupiter, King of Crete. Such was his fondness for the child that in his absence he left him virtual regent in his place. But his stepmother Juno was tormented by jealousy and, luring the boy from the palace, had him torn limb from limb by the Titans, who then devoured him. His heart fell to his sister Minerva, who preserved it and presented it to the King on his return. So shameful was this episode that the Cretans annually re-enacted it to revive and salve their guilt. Our source for the Cretan story is Julius Firmicus Maternus, a fourth-century astrologer turned Christian, who describes the annual pageant thus:

To appease the anger of their monarch, the Cretans have elevated the anniversary of his death to the status of an annual festival which is conducted with especial pomp every other year. Blow by blow they re-enact everything the child did and all that he suffered on the fatal day. With their own hands they tear apart a live bull, reliving the baneful feast by this annual commemoration. Making the forests ring with cries of lamentation, they ape the writhings of demented souls, so as to give the impression that the misdemeanour was committed in an access of dementia rather than of treason. They carry aloft the container in which his sister sequestered his dismembered heart, and by the cooings of flutes and the tintinnabulations of cymbals imitate the musical blandishments by which the boy was enticed. All of this is performed by the servile populace for the sake of a despot, and in order to raise to godhead a baby who missed being decently buried.[28]

Of this bacchanal, so reminiscent apparently of that which Euripides describes in *The Bacchae* yet so different in purport, Frazer comments, "In this version a Euhemerist turn has been given to the myth by representing Jupiter and Juno (Zeus and Hera) as a king and queen of Crete."[29] What then, we may legitimately ask, did the bacchanal represent: (1) the fictitious death of a god called Dionysus, (2) an episode in the royal history of Crete, or (3) an annual ritual in which the participants staged a (presumably magical) ceremony? The truth is that at the time of writing the First Edition, Frazer's answer would have been that it was the third disguised as the first, a conjuring-trick decked out in bogus mythological colours. By the time he comes to write the Third Edition, however, his answer has become much more complicated. You have to distinguish, it seems, between the purpose for which the ritual was performed, the ritual itself, and the stories told about it. The god, in this case Dionysus, was killed annually. Because of this, an explanation for it evolved in the shape of a story-line, a scenario if you like, which enabled the events to be followed. This scenario identified characters in the plot. To begin with the *dramatis personae* consisted of the roles enacted, with the casting for that year as an incidental feature. But, as the rite persisted, and the story-line – call it a "myth" – entrenched itself, so the labels were increasingly seen to pertain to the actors themselves, who paradoxically grew in anonymity the more they fused with their roles. It was as if at the end of a very long run the critics started referring to Coriolanus when they meant Laurence Olivier (sometimes indeed they do). Thus myths which began life as accounts of the life and death of fictitious (in that sense mythical) gods and goddesses, came by association to designate the men and women who, year in and year out, took their parts.

An apt analogy might be to a cycle of medieval mystery plays. At the conclusion of *The Scapegoat*, as we have already seen, Frazer talks of "the great army of martyrs who in many ages and in many lands ... have died a cruel death in the character of gods". The give-away phrase here is the theatrical one: "in the *character* of gods". It is as if a member of the fifteenth-century Butchers' Guild had handed a modern person the script of the York Cycle of Mystery Plays with the telling addition of a stage direction at the end of *The Death of Christ* stipulating that Christ was to be killed. It is as if the modern had then asked, "What happened in this play?" and elicited the answer "Christ was killed." To the questioner this answer would manifestly be ambiguous: it would either mean "Jesus Christ was executed on Calvary" or "Every year we killed the man who impersonates our Saviour" or "Piers Bloggs died last time." It is as if the modern then asked which of these alternatives applied, only to receive the riposte that his question was meaningless. The actor died: *ergo* Christ died. To that extent at least, the play was about the actor.

It is in this sense that Frazer can talk about martyrs dying in the character of gods; it is in this sense too that he can reinvoke that discredited school of mythological interpretation known as Euhemerism. Euhemerus of Messina was a Sicilian in the service of Cassander of Macedonia (311–298 BC) and author of a novel of travel called Ἱερὰ ἀναγραφή, or "Sacred History", describing a visit to an apocryphal island in the Indian ocean called Panchaea. There a golden column informs him that Uranus, Cronus and Zeus were in their day great kings whom the people subsequently deified. The view that the gods had once been mortal became popular in the aftermath of Alexander the Great, once Diodorus Siculus had paraphrased Euhemerus's doctrine in his albeit-fragmentary sixth book. The doctrine then largely fell into abeyance until the eighteenth century, when it received occasional resuscitation in children's versions of myth such as for members of Frazer's generation were furnished in Lemprière's *Bibliotheca Classica*. Reprinted many times since its first appearance in 1788, this renowned "Classical Dictionary" had been one of the major sources of legendary knowledge employed by the Romantic poets: a work-shy Byron, a Greekless Keats. By the mid-Victorian period Lemprière was cheerfully perused by thousands of schoolboys, who thus absorbed their first passing acquintance with the gods of the antique world in the nursery. Among those who took their first Pierian drafts from Lemprière was Frazer's classical colleague A. E. Housman; they may have included Frazer himself. Now, in the Third Edition of *The Golden Bough*, Euhemerism had once more raised its hoary head. In order to understand how this state of affairs had come about we need to turn back to the very beginning of Frazer's career.

The theme of the dead was scarcely a novelty. The notion that the spirits of the departed were dreadful and needed to be placated comes from Tylor, who in *Primitive Culture*, Frazer's introduction to anthropology, had devoted an entire chapter to "Ancestor and Manes Worship". Two years after reading Tylor's book, Frazer's first excursion into the field of social anthropology was a lecture entitled "On Certain Burial Customs as Illustrative of the Primitive Theory of the Soul",[30] where thematically as well as stylistically he seems to draw on Sir Thomas Browne. When in 1911, like William James and James Ward before him, he was invited to deliver the Gifford Lectures on Natural Religion, he chose for his subject *The Belief in Immortality and the Worship of the Dead*; publication of the lectures got under way while he was falling into the swing of the Third Edition. Towards the close of his career he then returned to the subject for the three volumes of *The Fear of the Dead in Primitive Religion*.[31] The placation of the unruly departed was thus a lifelong preoccupation, one which moreover gradually pervaded other aspects of his thought.

In the meantime a fresh impetus had arrived in the form of changing ideas as to the origin of ritual and myth. In 1890 Frazer's thoughts seem to have run along these lines. Early man explained his environment by reference to magical principles, themselves misapplications of the Association of Ideas. He then attempted to influence the world around him by applying these principles in practice. Having evolved appropriate procedures, he then seems to have forgotten why he thought of them and tried to explain their persistence by the invention of myths. Myth, then, was a *post hoc* justification of ritual.

By the turn of the century Frazer had already grown sceptical of this programme. In the first place, too many myths referred to events which had in some sense emphatically occurred. The legends associated with Nemi were an example: nobody could doubt that the priest existed. In the second place, myths were known to survive long after magic had fallen into disrepute. The rituals associated with the cult of Adonis might serve as an instance. The Greeks of the time of Pericles still performed these rites, though their literal faith in magic had long since waned. There was clearly something missing: the magical account of ritual and myth had to be supplemented by a religious one. All this forced Frazer to adopt a diluted form of Euhemerism. In 1911, in the preamble to his Gifford Lectures, Frazer announced his conversion:

> The theory that most or all gods originated after this fashion, in other words that the worship of the gods is none other than the worship of dead men, is known as Euhemerism after Euhemerus, the ancient Greek writer who propounded it. Regarded as a universal explanation of the belief in gods it is certainly false; regarded as a partial explanation it is unquestionably true; and perhaps we may even go as far as to say, that the more we penetrate into the inner history of ancient religion, the larger seems to be the element of truth contained in Euhemerism. For the more closely we look at certain deities of natural religion, the more closely are we seen to perceive, under the quaint and splendid pall which the mythical fancy has wrapt round the stately figures, the familiar features of real men who once shared the common joys and the common sorrows of humanity, who trod life's common road to the common end.[32]

By the time he came to complete the last few volumes of the Third Edition, an implicitly Euhemerist interpretation of myth had also become central to the way in which scholars had come to view the origins of drama. In *The Origins of Attic Tragedy* (1910) Frazer's friend William Ridgeway had claimed that all theatre, not simply the Athenian, had arisen from festivals in honour of the dead. In support of his contention he had assembled evidence from New Guinea, from Africa, from India and from ancient Greece itself. A remarkable number of the greatest Attic tragedies took place, like the *Libation-Bearers* of Aeschylus, around the tomb of one of the great departed. Might not all drama be a re-enactment of the deeds of dead heroes, now rarefied as gods?

Much of this is implicit in Frazer's own writing, an early example being his treatment of the semi-mythical king Sardanapalus, who plays no small part in Frazer's discussion of the Asian Saturnalia, and who stages a prompt reappearance in *Adonis, Attis, Osiris*. Legends abound concerning Sardanapalus, who has always been a ripe case for Euhemerist treatment. Lemprière, for example, describes him as

> the fortieth and last king of Assyria, celebrated for his luxury and voluptuousness. The greatest part of his time was spent in the company of his eunuchs, and the monarch generally appeared in the midst of his concubines, disguised in the habit of a female, and spinning wool for his amusement. This effeminacy irritated his officers; Belesis and

Arsaces conspired against him and collected a numerous force to dethrone him. Sardanapalus quitted his voluptuousness for a while, and appeared at the head of his armies. The rebels were defeated in three successive battles, but at last Sardanapalus was beaten and besieged in the city of Ninus for two years. When he despaired of success, he burned himself in his palace with his eunuchs, concubines, and all his treasures, and the empire of Assyria was divided among the conspirators. Sardanapalus flourished about 770 years before the Christian era. He was made a god after his death.[33]

That at least is how the Greeks liked to remember him: an engaging and effeminate fop who spent his days in drunkenness and debauchery, and ended them on a funeral pyre rather than give himself and his womenfolk over to his assailants. This is the version of the story as it descended to Byron, who immortalised it in his poetic tragedy of 1821. Byron may have got his facts from Lemprière, who got his from Diodorus Siculus, but variations can be found scattered all over the Greek authors. Sardanapalus was supposed to have founded the twin cities of Tarsus and Anchiale, in what is now southern Turkey. Anchiale is no more, but outside its gates according to Strabo once stood a statue of Sardanapalus staring defiantly out to sea and proclaiming the virtues of hedonism. He was snapping his fingers at destiny while declaiming, "I, Sardanapalus, son of Anacyndaraxes, built Anchiale and Tarsus in one day. Eat, drink and be merry, for nothing else is worth this!"[34] The Assyrians, however, remembered him quite differently: not only did he found great cities, but as Ashurbanipal he was perhaps the greatest of their conquerors. The foppishness consorts ill with such renown and martial prowess, but much better with the attitude to be expected of the Zoganes, who at the annual Sacaea enjoyed the favours of the king's mistresses for a brief season before forfeiting his life. Does the myth of Sardanapalus, then, refer to the historical King Ashurbanipal or to the procession of actors who, year in and year out, impersonated him in the precincts of the palace, enjoying all the solace of luxury and riot till after a five-day reign their lives were for ever snuffed out in an act of summary execution, even of public burning?

Now, there is one facet of the Sacaea celebrations on which the German orientalist Franz Movers had placed great stress in the 1840s: the enjoyment of the king's concubines, such as in biblical times constituted a virtual claim to the throne.[35] It was Movers' belief that on these occasions the Zoganes impersonated none other than Sardanapalus, and that one of the concubines was chosen to reign by his side in the person of Queen Semiramis, who herself seems to have incorporated something of the Persian goddess Anaitis and the Semitic goddess Astarte. Now between the historic Semiramis and her legend there existed something of the same disparity as we earlier noted for Sardanapalus, for she is supposed to have reigned in Assyria and built the city of Babylon, after which she was transformed into a dove. Other reports of her are less flattering: she is supposed to have locked up her royal husband and then reigned in his stead, selecting her lovers from among the handsomest of her soldiers before peremptorily dispatching them to their deaths. This is the sort of behaviour attributed to the Empress Catherine of Russia, but it is even closer to what legend tells us of Ishtar, whose advances the mythical Gilgamesh rejected rather than be caught up in her fatal net. Might the myth then refer not to Queen Sammuramat, wife of King Shamshi-Adad V of Assyria, with whom the historians have been inclined to identify her, but to the sequence of consort–courtesans who took her part year by year at the annual feast day, mating with the putative Sardanapalus before he was engulfed by the flames? So thought Frazer, though not, apparently, Byron, who makes her Sardanapalus's grandmother.[36] If Frazer is right, the myths of Sardanapalus and Semiramis, which appear so complementary, might refer not to a set of historical circumstances at all, but to an annually recurring dramatic cycle. There were other facts which fitted this premise: Semiramis was associated with Astarte, whom Robertson Smith had identified with the Persian goddess Anaitis. Now, the chief shrine of Anaitis was at Zela, and was built, significantly enough, over one of Semiramis's burial mounds. Here, as at Nemi, an annual act of marriage, or at least concubinage, may have been performed:

> at the great sanctuary of the goddess at Zela it appears that her myth was regularly translated into action; the story of her love and the death of her divine lover was performed year by year as a sort of mystery-play by men and women who lived for a season and sometimes died in the character of the visionary beings whom they impersonated. The intention of these sacred dramas, we may be sure, was neither to amuse nor to instruct an idle audience, and as little were they designed to gratify the actors, to whose baser instincts they gave the reins for a time. They were solemn rites which mimicked the doings of divine beings, because man fancied that by such mimicry he was able to arrogate to himself the divine functions and to execute them for the good of his fellows.[37]

The original justification for these rituals must once have been magical, to instil fertility into the natural world by the influence of imitative magic, and something of that feeling still remained. But the rationale accorded to the rites in later times must have been for the most part – or observably entirely – religious. The mortal actors stepped into the sandals of the gods, thus transcending for a while their mortality and serving as a focus for supplicatory worship. This is the theory as Frazer whispers it in the closing pages of *The Scapegoat*, but in the opening paragraphs of *Adonis, Attis, Osiris* he sounds it out as his principal subject, his stirring and abiding theme:

Thus the old magical theory of the seasons was displaced, or rather supplemented by a religious theory. For although men now attributed the annual cycle of change primarily to corresponding changes in their deities, they still thought that by performing certain magical rites they could aid the god, who was the principle of life, in his struggle with the opposing principle of death. They imagined that they could recruit his failing energies and even raise him from the dead. The ceremonies which they observed for this purpose were in substance a dramatic representation of the natural processes which they wished to facilitate; for it is a familiar tenet of magic that you can produce any desired effect by simply imitating it. And as they now explained the fluctuations of growth and decay, of reproduction and dissolution, by the marriage, the death, and the rebirth or revival of the gods, these religious or rather magical dramas turned in great measure on these themes. They set forth the fruitful union of the powers of fertility, the sad death of at least one of the divine partners, and his joyful resurrection.[38]

The underlying object of all these dramas was to aid and abet the burgeoning of the natural world in the spring. Death therefore was not the climax to the whole. The Marriage Show was followed by the Death Show, which in turn, rather like an Aeschylean tragedy bringing in its train the satyr play, was followed by the Resurrection Show. These dramas, with their rotating cast, sometimes of effigies but more usually of human beings, and their weird, half-explicable plots were performed year in and year out round the eastern segment of the Mediterranean and further afield. One of Frazer's most trenchant examples, for instance, comes from the Kanagra district of India, where the god Siva and the goddess Pârvatî were married in effigy each spring at the festival of *Ralî Ka mela*. The images were then thrown into the river and mourned.[39] But by far the most impressive examples of these ceremonies originated in the Near East, from that complex interweaving mesh of cultic extravagance observable in classical times throughout western Syria, Turkey and the Aegean. The source of many of these mystery cults was Semitic, or more narrowly Babylonian, though there were Hittite and even Persian admixtures. It is these Eastern cults and their diffusion into the highly literate Graeco-Roman world which it is Frazer's reverent and meticulous purpose to examine in the volumes *Adonis, Attis, Osiris*.

CHAPTER XII

THE FLUTES OF TAMMUZ

PERHAPS the most vivid extant account of the Resurrection Show comes from Julius Firmicus Maternus. This fourth-century convert is addressing the emperors Constantius and Constans, whom he wishes to take a firmer hand in suppressing the perfidious practices of the heathen. Do their majesties appreciate just what these pagans get up to in their perverse, clandestine way? Up and extirpate them! In their unthinking perversity they even travesty the Opening of the Tomb:

On a certain night they lay an idol to rest on a funeral bier, weeping over it with a dying fall. Once they have given full vent to their sorrow, they carry the bier out into the light. Then the priest rubs holy oil into the necks of each of the worshippers, and after performing this unction murmurs the words:

Be of good cheer, brother. The Lord is saved.
For us too tribulation is the portal to bliss!

Why do you incite these miserable human specimens to rejoicing? Why do you drive men into a state of ecstasy by such subterfuges? Why bewilder them with vain promises? The death of your God is self-evident; he betrays no sign of life. No divine augury has foreshadowed his resurrection, nor has he shown himself to the people after his death that they should so believe in him. He has given them no advance warning of his intervention, nor has he produced proof or witness that these things shall come to pass.[1]

"Habet ergo diabolus christos suos", continues Firmicus Maternus: "the devil too has his ointments" or "the devil too has his Christs". The exact rite to which he is referring is uncertain, though it is probable that he is addressing himself to the cult of Attis, which by the fourth century had well and truly entrenched itself in the Western Empire, to the extent that uncomfortable parallels were for ever being drawn between it and the newer but fast-growing cult of Christianity. No wonder Firmicus Maternus is so concerned, so defensively dismissive. No wonder too that, when Frazer first sedulously applied himself to an extensive study of the Attis ceremonies in 1906, we find him excitedly writing thus of the new volume to George Macmillan:

> The subject is the death and resurrection of these Eastern gods, and I show grounds for thinking that their ritual has influenced that of the Christian Easter ceremonies, as these are observed by the Catholic and Greek churches.[2]

Over no festival of the Christian Church has controversy waxed more heatedly than over Easter. Originally it was celebrated on the fourteenth day of the Jewish month of Nisan, the date of the Passover as given in the Pentateuch. Accordingly the primitive Church observed it as a fixed feast which possessed no necessary connection with Sunday. It was kept in this position by the Church in Asia until the Council of Nicaea in the year 325 declared the practice of the "quartodecimans" (those who observed the fourteenth day) illegal, moving Easter to the Sunday following. This disparity between the Eastern and Western patterns of paschal observance became a recurrent feature of ecclesiastical history: even now they are out of step. When the quartodeciman method was abandoned, the date had to be fixed by the moon. The oldest system of such calculation in Rome ran on a cycle of eight years. There was another system of calculating it according to a twenty-eight-year cycle; this was maintained by the Church in Britain until the Synod of Whitby in 664 decided to fall in with Roman practice. By then Rome had moved on to a nineteen-year cycle, which fixed the date of the feast between 21 March and 25 April, around the time of the vernal equinox (25 March according to the Julian calendar). There is even evidence that in the earliest times Easter was invariably observed at the spring equinox in Gaul and even it seems in Rome.

The disparity between the Roman and Greek ways of calculating Easter is an integral part of Frazer's argument, for Easter remains one of the most engagingly local of Christian feasts. He might have drawn his illustrations from almost anywhere in Southern Europe, but chose to concentrate on those locations where a connection with the older, pagan cults is easiest to ascertain. On Good Friday in Sicily the figure of Christ is carried on solemn procession through the streets until, reaching the place of crucifixion, sometimes called Calvary, it is deposed and ceremonially buried. On the sepulchre are placed sprigs of fresh vegetation done up as miniature gardens which have previously been tended in the dark and regularly watered.[3] In Greek churches the pageant of crucifixion is followed by one of resurrection; at the exact stroke of midnight the bishop appears to the people and announces the glad tidings, whereupon the whole company burst into a spontaneous cacophony of release and of rejoicing.[4]

Now, in the Greek world the rites of Attis and of his consort Cybele, the Great Mother, had little purchase. Originating in Pessinus in Phrygia, they were taken up by the Romans when the oracle advised their adoption as a means of expelling the invader Hannibal. The ruse worked, and ever after the cult of Cybele entrenched itself in Roman life; she had her shrine towards the bottom of the Palatine Hill, and her castrated priests, or Galli, could be seen mincing around the backstreets of the capital, much to the dismay of more virile citizens. If in Rome Easter had indeed once coincided with the spring equinox, then it would have fallen on precisely the same day as the Feast of Attis. But in Sicily, a former Greek colony, and in the eastern Mediterranean, Easter seems for some time to have fallen later, and may even have incorporated certain aspects of the Feast of Adonis, which in Cyprus fell on 2 April.[5]

Adonis was a Syrian – that is as much as to say a Phoenician – god, the principal centre of whose worship in Asia was at Byblos, about five miles to the north of present-day Beirut and just to the north of the Nahr Ibrahim, which in ancient times was known as the River Adonis. He had another imposing shrine at Aphaca, several miles inland on the tableland overlooking the Nahr Ibrahim basin. Lucian, who grew up in Syria, saw the river flushing red as it gushed seawards in the early spring, as in 1861 did Ernest Renan, who was in Lebanon investigating the Phoenician sites.[6] The votaries explained this phenomenon by the god's annual demise, gouged in the thigh by a boar on Mount Lebanon, though one of Lucian's informants, a wise old buzzard by the sound of things, held a more mundane view:

Such is the legend vulgarly accepted; but a man from Byblos, who seemed to me to be telling the truth, told me another reason for this marvellous change. He spoke as follows: "This river, my friend and guest, passes through the Libanus; now the Libanus abounds in red earth. The violent winds which blow regularly on these days bring down into the river a quantity of earth resembling vermilion. It is this earth which turns the river red. And thus the change in the river's colour is due not to blood as they affirm, but to the nature of the soil."[7]

Be that as it may, the discoloration issued in the eight days of the annual Adonia, when women gave to their hair, or else or themselves, and when the recumbent god was mourned to the cooing melody of flutes called γίγγρας after one of the names of Adonis.[8] There was also a strong connection with the Egyptian cult of Osiris, whose coffin had supposedly once been wafted across the eastern Mediterranean to Byblos, where it was turned into a pillar in the royal palace before being recovered by the tearful Isis. The sea-passage was supposed to recur every year, when on the eighth day of the Adonia the women of Byblos went down to the shore to receive his head, which had apparently drifted across from Alexandria. No wonder Adonis and Osiris were often confused.

Something of the plangency of Isis's attitude seems to have worked itself into the ambiance of the Phoenician cult; Astarte too, the divine mistress of Adonis, was a *mater dolorosa*, and according to Macrobius her melancholy figure was cut into the rockface above Byblos.[9] Each year as her lover was wounded anew and the red anemone, his flower, blossomed out by the bay, she mourned him with all the women of the city. Little baskets of spring verdure, Gardens of Adonis, were cast into the water along with his effigy, which was later fished out and "revived". In the Alexandria of the Ptolemies, Adonis and Aphrodite were displayed side by side on adjacent palanquins, and after a form of marriage Adonis was taken to the seashore amid the keening of the people.[10] This lamentation according to Renan was "une sorte de soupir larmoyant, un sanglot étrange". Gradually it insinuated itself into the Greek mind and thence into the literary imagination of Europe, for which Adonis has always been the type of youthful promise blasted in its prime:

> Oh, weep for Adonais – he is dead!
> Wake, melancholy Mother, wake and weep!
> Yet wherefore? Quench within their burning bed
> Thy fiery tears, and let thy loud heart keep
> Like his, a mute and uncomplaining sleep;
> For he is gone, where all things wise and fair
> Descend; – oh, dream not that the amorous Deep
> Will yet restore him to the vital air;
> Death feeds on his mute voice, and laughs at our despair.[11]

Though the Phoenicians knew him as Adonis, to the Babylonians he was Tammuz, and it was under that name that the women of Jerusalem mourned him in Ezekiel's day.[12] "Adonis" is nothing but an honorific, since *adon* in the Semitic languages means "lord". Lord of Byblos and of Aphaca, he was, then, arguably Lord of Jerusalem too, for the Jews used *adon* or *adonäi* (my lord) as a soubriquet for Yahweh, and even in the Christian tradition the title has remained current:

> O come, O come, Adonaï,
> Who in thy glorious majesty
> From that high mountain clothed with awe
> Gavest thy folk the elder law.

The cult of Adonis spread rapidly in the Greek world until by the fifth century BC much of Athens was plunged into mourning on his annual feast day. Plutarch says that the Sicilian expedition heard the moans of women echoing through the streets as it made its way down to Piraeus;[13] the date of the sailing is given by Thucydides as June, whence we conclude that the festival fell later in Attica.[14] At Paphos on the southern shore of the island of Cyprus, his greatest shrine in the Greek world, it fell in April, when swine were sacrificed to the god – a fact which Robertson Smith had noticed, comparing it to equivalent practices elsewhere that he took to be totemic:

> My own belief is that the piacular sacrifice of swine at Cyprus on April 2nd, represents the death of the god himself, not an act of vengeance for his death, just as in Crete the sacrifice of a bull by tearing it in pieces with the teeth (Firmicus, cap. 6) represented the death of the Bull-god Dionysus. Adonis, in short, is the swine god and in this, as in many other cases, the sacred victim has been changed by false interpretation into the enemy of the god.[15]

Accordingly his myth had him gored by a jealous Ares in the guise of a boar, and dispatched to the world of the dead, whence he is intermittently rescued by the plaints of the infatuated Aphrodite. In Lebanon his assassination was supposedly re-enacted annually at Aphaca, whence his blood gushed down to the sea. For the Babylonians, as the *Epic of Gilgamesh* confirms, his consort was Ishtar; for the Phoenicians, Astarte; for the Romans (and hence for Shakespeare) she was Venus. But, whatever her name, her grief and her music seem instilled into the elegiac consciousness of Europe and inform Frazer's own style. Ernest

Renan too had mourned with her on Mount Lebanon, for there he had succumbed to malarial fever shortly after visiting the Holy Land to collect materials for *La Vie de Jésus*. When he recovered at Amschit on 20 September 1861 he learned that his beloved sister Henriette, the companion of his travels, had in the interval expired of the same complaint.[16] No wonder that the religion of Adonis became for Renan essentially a cult of the dead, a view with which Frazer sympathised but from which he finally demurred, finding it too abstract for his liking.

There were thus various ways of regarding Adonis. For Smith his legend had been a camouflage for a totemic sacrament, with the swine by a well-attested process of transposition converted into his enemy. For Frazer this was doubtful. The rite was a vernal one, possibly as the annual immersion suggested a rain charm. By the time the cult spread westwards it had changed dramatically into a fully fledged mystery religion sustained by a round of ceremonies or mystic dramas in which the love of the god and goddess, and the death of the former, were portrayed for the rapt assembly of the faithful, just as the descent of Persephone and a form of mystic marriage were once performed at Eleusis. The myth described the ritual, not the ritual the myth. The characters in the story were *personae* in this tragic cycle, their roles being taken each year by a different set of participants who took on the afflatus of divine beings and perhaps suffered the consequences.

Frazer supports this interpretation by a whole phalanx of parallel instances, not all of which appear immediately relevant to his case. We have already mentioned Sardanapalus. He was, Frazer believed, annually wedded to Semiramis, but he was also known as Hercules, and a Hercules figure, known locally as Melcarth or Melkart, was annually incinerated at Tyre.[17] The prophet Ezekiel railed against the kings of Tyre for walking on live coals; but, if the story holds, they received a lot more than blisters.[18] The Greek legend had Sardanapalus immolating himself on a funeral pyre, so once again it looked as if the fable was a plot for the sacred drama: each year Sardanapalus married and then died in the flames.[19] Sardan, a figure in some ways closely associated with Sardanapalus, was annually burned in Tarsus, a city Sardanapulus was supposed to have founded.[20] At Gades (Cádiz), a Phoenician settlement in Iberia, Melkart was regularly burned, while from Carthage ambassadors were dispatched annually to observe the rite in Tyre.[21] Dido, their queen, expired on a funeral pyre on the departure of Aeneas, though Sylvius, glossing Virgil, thought it her sister Anna.

It therefore looked very much as if the death of the god, as Smith had remarked, was a common feature of Semitic and more broadly of Eastern religion, as was a form of marriage or at least concubinage between representatives of the god and the goddess. Sacred prostitution was practised in the temple at Byblos, where maidens probably gave of themselves before the expedient arose of offering their hair. Herodotos records the same custom in Babylon and in Cyprus. The shrine of Anaitis at Zela was almost entirely populated by sacred prostitutes presided over by a supreme pontiff who, possibly donning the vesture of Sardanapalus, annually coupled with one of them.[22] At Boghaz-Keui in the hinterland of Turkey stand two processions of figures, one of each sex, let into the rockface. They meet in the centre of the frieze, where a semi-divine figure stands at the head of each: can this represent a form of sacred marriage, such as may possibly have been celebrated at one time between the kings and queens of Tarsus?[23] Were the recorded instances of sacred prostitution always a tribute to the god, and were the more elaborate marriage celebrations simply an extension of the same principle, whereby in an act of human coupling the actors fertilised the earth?

All of this Frazer surveys at lightning speed, but with a reverence of attention which is barely held in check by his irony. For the dying Adonis, one senses, Frazer had an ungrudging respect. Had his yearly demise not instilled itself into the elegiac literature of the West? Had it not worked itself into the grain of the Christian religion, the poetry of the *Stabat Mater*, the pathos of the Michelangelo *Pietà*? When he comes to Attis, however, his tone changes. Attis was an obscure god of a mountain-pent people, unnaturally bumped up into prominence when the Sibylline books, that sublime farrago of nonsense, advised the Roman Senate to accept the image of the Idaean goddess Cybele, the Great Mother, into the city as an antidote to Hannibal. The decision seems to have been a response to some form of mass hysteria: superstition was rife, portents tore across the skies; panic gripped the city. Livy describes the moment when the sacred image arrived on Roman soil to be greeted by the delegates of the people:

> The women . . . passed the Goddess from hand to hand, one to another in succession, while all the population came thronging to meet her; censers were placed before the doorways on her route with burning incense, and many prayers were offered that she might enter the city of Rome with kindly purpose and benignant thoughts. So the procession moved on, till they brought her to the temple of Victory on the

Palatine. It was the day before the Ides of April, and that day was held sacred. People crowded to the Palatine with gifts to the Goddess, and there was a Strewing of Couches, and Games called the Megalesia.[24]

So the Romans took the nostrum and Hannibal to his heels, but ever afterwards they were stuck with the goddess and her epicene consort. Until the reign of Claudius, Attis himself held a subsidiary place in the cult, but grew in prominence as the Empire declined, eventually holding equal place with the Great Mother. For Frazer this was the beginning of the end, the inception of the empire's slow decline, and he waxes eloquent on the consequences: the orgiastic concentration on the self, the neglect of material interests, the apathy towards worldly responsibilities and the exigencies of child-rearing. The tide was on the turn: the Sea of Faith, to reverse Arnold's metaphor, was swelling upwards, bringing down in its mad career all the carefully constructed dams of civilisation. They were not to be properly repaired until the Renaissance, and the tide would not ebb until the nineteenth century in its wisdom commenced that onslaught upon religion whose lieutenant-general Frazer had enthusiastically proclaimed himself in the Preface to the Second Edition. Attis is the enemy, and on him Frazer opens the full battery of his irony and his scorn.

The rites were truly ridiculous, food for a Roman satirist or perhaps comedian. We have already witnessed the god's resurrection, but it was the manner of his death that was the trouble. On 22 March he was strapped in effigy to a pine-tree (like Marsyas, a possible double), and on the 24th he was doused with blood from the arm of the officiating priest. The effigy was kept for a year and then burned along with the tree. The laceration of the priest's arm seems to have been notional: far worse ensued. Lucian, who had observed a form of the rite, describes the awful moment when the incision was made and the whole assembly of worshippers was suddenly seized by a self-denying bloodlust, and young lads whose enthusiasm had got the better of their reason dashed forward and, seizing one of the ceremonial swords thoughtfully provided for the purpose, unmanned themselves on the spot. They then ran screaming through the streets of the city and flung the severed genitalia into any house at random, obliging the occupants so favoured to provide them with a set of women's garments which they wore thereafter.[25] Catullus describes the dreadful moment when the postulant came to:

So, roused from gentle slumber and of feverish frenzy freed,
As soon as Attis pondered in heart on his passionate deed,
And with mind undimmed bethought him where he stood and how
    unmanned,
Seething in soul he hurried back to the seaward strand;
And he gazed on the waste of waters, and the tears brimmed full in
    his eye;
And he thus bespoke his fatherland with a plaintive womanish cry . . .
Shall I be our Lady's bondmaid? a slave at Cybele's hand?
Shall I be a sexless maenad, a minion, a thing unmanned?
Shall I dwell on the icy ridges under Ida's chilly blast?
Shall I pass my days in the shadows that the Phrygian summits cast,
With the stag that haunts the forest, with the boar that roams the
    glade?
Even now my soul repents me: even now is my fury stayed.[26]

In 1906, when Frazer first describes these momentous events, his
account is barely factual; in 1907 it is amplified; in 1914, perhaps
conscious of the relative humourlessness of the earlier versions, he opens
up the full diapason of his irony. *Adonis, Attis, Osiris* contains some of
his most gripping descriptive writing; it also sees him at his most
Gibbonian. It is, after all, the long twilight of classical clarity and grace
that he is expounding, that grandly Gibbonian theme: the crumbling of
the elegant Corinthian columns into a mess of broken marble and
shattered architraves. Here he is in 1914 on the concurrence of the
Roman Easter with the Feast of Attis and the resulting dispute between
the adherents of the two sects, a matter which had in the meantime
been discussed by Franz Cumont in *Les Religions orientales dans le
paganisme romain* (1909):

In point of fact it appears from the testimony of an anonymous
Christian, who wrote in the first century of our era, that Christians
and pagans alike were struck by the remarkable coincidence between
the death and resurrection of their respective deities, and that the
coincidence forced a theme of bitter controversy between the adherents
of the rival religions, the pagans contending that the resurrection of
Christ was a spurious imitation of the resurrection of Attis, and the
Christians asserting with equal warmth that the resurrection of Attis
was a diabolical counterfeit of the resurrection of Christ. In these
unseemly bickerings the heathen took what to a superficial observer
might seem strong ground by arguing that their god was the older and

therefore presumably the original, since as a general rule an original is older than its copy. This feeble argument the Christians easily rebuffed. They admitted, indeed, that in point of time Christ was the junior deity, but they triumphantly demonstrated his real seniority by falling back on the subtlety of Satan, who on so important an occasion had surpassed himself by inverting the usual order of nature.[27]

This is Frazer's satire as its keenest; the veritable absurdity of the heathen rubbing off on the Christians – both the primitive sort and by implication their nineteenth-century successors – who, puffing themselves up with the overweening superiority of the saved, are seen nevertheless to succumb to an intellectual preposterousness which would put the most uncouth unbeliever to shame. David Hume would have been very proud of that sentence.

Little, however, would have shamed the adherents of Osiris. With Syrian Adonis and Phrygian Attis, the significance might have been subject to doubt, but the sources at least were unambiguous. When Frazer broached the dim domains of Egyptian Attis, he entered a quagmire. We have already recounted the Osiris myth as relayed to us by Plutarch, but this story was only one strand in his worship, much overlaid by the successive encrustations of time. The Pharoah Akhenaten, whom Frazer refers to by his original title of Amenophis IV, was so determined to subjugate all polytheistic cults, including those of Isis and Osiris, to the supreme sun god Ra (or, more strictly, to his disk or *aton*) that he incorporated their worship into a national solar religion, thus laying many a false trail. Later Osiris joined hands with the Apis cult at Memphis to produce the syncretic deity Serapis, under those generous parasol Osiris was worshipped by the Romans. Plutarch connects Osiris emphatically with Isis, who had, however, her own rituals and her own sphere of influence. In the second century AD Apuleius has Lucius, his human-turned-ass, beseeching Isis to return him to human form at her annual festival, yet hardly spares a thought for Osiris. Yet Osiris reigned supreme in the Egyptian pantheon, and from the earliest times was revered as a god of the dead. In early times deceased kings were referred to as Osiris, and from the Eighteenth Dynasty this privilege was extended to all the departed, whose bodies were wrapped round with papyri containing the 189 chapters of *The Book of the Dead*, an early passage in which is a hymn to Osiris:

Hail to you, King of Kings, Lord of Lords, Ruler of Rulers, who took possession of the Two Lands even in the womb of Nut; he rules the plains of the Silent Land, even he the golden of body, blue of head, on whose arms is turquoise. O Pillar of Myriads, broad of breast, kindly of countenance, who is in the Sacred Land: May you grant power in the sky, might on earth and vindication in the realm of the dead, a journeying downstream to Busiris as a living soul and a journeying upstream to Abydos as a heron; to go in and out without hindrance at all the gates of the Netherworld. May there be given to me bread from the House of Cool Water and a table of offerings from Heliopolis, my toes being firm-planted in the Field of Rushes. May the barley and emmer which are in it belong to the ka [soul] of the Osiris N [that is, the deceased].[28]

But, magisterial as this presidency over the world of the dead may seem, it did not exhaust Osiris's possibilities. At times he seems to have run the whole gamut of significance and to have rubbed shoulders with many other gods, both indigenous and alien. Plutarch makes confusion doubly confused by associating him with the moon. His temporary peregrination to Byblos has already been recalled: there is something indeed to be said for the view that the entire resurrection motif in the Adonis cult was nothing but a transmogrification of the Osiris myth. One element in this was the raising of Osiris's coffin into a pillar in the palace at Byblos apparently carved out of the *erica* tree, and the tree-raising motif recurs in inscriptions depicting the annual raising of the *Dad* tree, reputedly another effigy of the god, who in that case was arboreal. The permutations seemed endless.

Of one thing Frazer was certain: Osiris was a seasonal deity whose behaviour had much to do with the rise and fall of the Nile. The river began to swell in early June and continued until September, when it slowly subsided. In August the waters were dammed and released onto the expectant fields. The sowing itself took place in November just before the river shrank to its habitual course; the harvest ensued in April before the annual inundation began again. It was in November too that the festival of Osiris fell, once the Egyptian year, which due to the disparity between the lunar and the solar calendars had traditionally rotated, stabilised itself at the insistence of the Ptolemies. It thus made a lot of sense to regard Osiris as a god of the sown seed, like Saturn or Mars, with the qualification that his fluctuations followed the very different agricultural regime of the Nile delta, and that his crops were sorghum, maize and millet.

Now Plutarch had noted one unusual feature of the November sowing season: the farmers wept as they placed the seed in the earth and said that they were mourning for Osiris. The Platonist in Plutarch was indignant at this: you did not commit idolatry by attributing a soul to mere grain.[29] It was the god who brought the grain, and the god if anyone whom the farmers should be mourning. Plutarch thought the people must have recognised this at first and then, forgetting it, transferred the divinity to the seed. For Frazer this view of Plutarch's represented sacrilege of a different sort, since it was to misconstrue history by placing the religious cart before the magical horse. It was, moreover, to indulge in a fallacy similar to the so-called "disease of language", propagated in Frazer's own day by men such as Max Müller, according to which men originally invented religious metaphors which they then persuaded themselves into taking literally, thus giving rise to myth.

Frazer had always been absolutely insistent that no such transfer of association had ever taken place. Men in the animist stage did indeed anthropomorphise the crops. Only later, when a religious consciousness took hold, did they learn to ascribe the abundance of the harvest to the intervention of the gods. It is at this later stage that they must have devised the myth and set up shrines to Osiris and his divine consort. Mythology, then, did indeed represent a sort of disease of language (though Frazer would have given up the ghost rather than use this term), but a disease which ran the opposite course from that diagnosed by Plutarch or later by Max Müller. Men began by emphasising the life and death of all natural creatures, whether vegetable or animal, but later detached the soul from the substance, kicking it upstairs into some ineffable and unreachable sphere of the divine. Osiris religion, then, was a superimposition upon Osiris magic.[30]

Some support for this avenue of approach had come from recent advances in Egyptology, a field in which Frazer had been interested since the 1880s. Egypt was an area of concern he had in common with Smith, and some of their earliest communications involve it. As early as 1889, while working on the first *Golden Bough*, Frazer had been alerted by the manner in which modern Egyptians greeted the annual appearance of the flood. They apparently raised a pile of earth called "the bride", upon which a sample of grain was placed as an offering to the river. The name bestowed upon the pile suggested an origin in human sacrifice. Frazer fired off one of his rapid communications to Smith: was this suspicion justified, and had Smith ever witnessed anything of the kind? Smith sent a postcard in reply, directing him to A. W. Lane's *Modern Egyptians*:

Lane describes the large boat which is vulgarly believed to represent a magnificent vessel in which the Egyptians used, before the conquest of the country by the Arabs, to convey the virgin whom it is said they threw into the Nile. The sacrifice was made when the river began to rise to a plentiful inundation. A pillar or truncated cone of earth called the bride is set up near the dam. On its flat top a little maize or millet is set. The tide washes it away as the river rises, a week or more before the dam is cut.[31]

All of this took place while the waters were rising in August, but this was not the only occasion on which the Egyptians made oblations of the seed. During the 1890s the tombs of the great Valley of the Kings at Thebes were excavated, and certain remarkable finds came to light. Among them was the tomb of a royal fan-bearer whose sepulchre contained a mattress painted with a man-sized Osiris figure; inside it was a vegetable mould which by the time the tomb was opened had sprouted to a length of two or three inches. Similar discoveries were made at Cynopolis, where the finds were of Osiris-shaped mummies filled with grain and swathed in cloth. These finds were supported by pictorial evidence gathered from elsewhere. At Denderah, for example, a bas-relief showed Osiris ascending into Heaven to be received into the loving arms of Isis, while at Philae his recumbent body was shown sprouting tendrils while a priest dutifully watered him from a pot. At Denderah too was an inscription describing his obsequies performed during the month of Choiak, the Egyptian month which after the revisions of the calendar came to coincide with November. They began with a ceremonial sowing, after which water was sprinkled on a miniature garden which seems to have fulfilled much the same function as the Gardens of Adonis. Then on the twenty-second day of the month gold images of the god filled with vegetable mould were loaded onto a flotilla of papyrus boats and, attended by a waterborne illumination, carried downstream, until on the last day of the month a statuette of the god in a mulberry-wood coffin was laid to rest in a tomb shaded by *Persea* trees. Diodorus Siculus tells us that red-haired men were once sacrificed on the Feast of Osiris, and their ashes scattered on his grave.[32]

These discoveries confirmed what earlier writers had asserted, that Osiris was primarily conceived of as a god of the dead. Herodotos describes his feast day as celebrated in Bubastis, Busiris and Sais between 13 and 16 November.[33] The mystery of his disappearance was enacted by the carrying-out of a golden calf, its gilded horns shaped like a burnished sun. The cow probably represented Isis searching for her sire, just as Demeter had searched for Persephone, and the goddess's bereavement was imitated by the worshippers, who beat their breasts in a frantic mimicry of loss "in whose honour, however, I do not feel it proper to say". The object of bereavement was certainly Osiris, Herodotos's bashfulness being caused by the marked similarity to the Greek rites. As Sais the climax of the festivities took the form of a grand nocturnal illumination which reminded Frazer of All Souls' Days worldwide, wherein the spirits of the deceased were hosted at the homes of their relatives by night. Was it not simply Osiris who was being mourned at Sais, but along with him the whole community of the dead?

This view of the Osiris cult as essentially a form of commemoration of the dead had recently received dramatic support from Egyptologists. In the winters of 1901–2 and 1902–3, the great temple of Osiris at Abydos was at last excavated. A door and passage led into one long chamber covered in inscriptions and showing clearly the cartouche of the Pharaoh Merenptah. On one wall, between an image of the vivification of Osiris and another of Merenptah offering up incense, was inscribed chapter 142 of *The Book of the Dead*, the passage known as "Chapter of Knowing the Names of Osiris";

> The hair of Osiris Ba-en-Ra mer-Neteru, [true] of voice, is as Nu;
> The face of Osiris Hotep-her-Maat Merenptah [true] of voice, is as Ra.
> The two eyes of Osiris Ba-en-Ra, mer-Neteru, [true] of voice, are as Hathar;
> The two ears of Osiris Hotep-her-Maat Merenptah, [true] of voice, are as Upuaut . . .[34]

Upuaut was a jackal-headed god, brother and near double of Anubis, the god of embalming. It was the opinion of Margaret Murray, who had taken down the inscriptions at Abydos, that Upuaut, who invariably appears in scenes of judgement and transfiguration, was the original deity presiding at Abydos, his functions gradually being subsumed by Osiris.[35] The two gods invariably appear together on inscriptions depicting the great gathering or feast day called the *sed*, which had recently been reinterpreted in a fashion very flattering to Frazer's theories. The Rosetta Stone apostrophises Ptolemy V, to commemorate the anniversary of whose accession it was set up, as "lord of the Thirty-Year Festivals", an apparent reference to the *sed*. In that case the interval between festivals coincided with a shift of one week in the old Egyptian year, calculated before 30 BC by the rising of the dog-star Sirius, which the Egyptians associated with Isis. So on one in four occasions the shift would have corresponded to a lunar month. Accordingly once every 120 years the sed was denominated sed tep sed heb, "chief celebration of the tail festival".

For the actual content of the celebrations we are dependent upon depictions of it on the seals of the Egyptian kings. The mace of Narmer, the first monarch to rule over the whole of Egypt, shows the king of Osiris enshrined in a dais at the top of a flight of nine steps. Before him is a palanquin bearing a figure called "the royal child". Beneath stand oxen for some sacrificial slaughter, and at the head of an opposing procession stands Upuaut. On the seal of the Pharaoh Zer the king is confronted with Upuaut's standard, while before him floats on ostrich feather on which traditionally the souls of the Pharaohs were supposed to be transported to Heaven. In the tomb of the Pharaoh Den (1875 BC), a second royal is seen dancing with his back to the first, who as in other instances is depicted as Osiris. The sed was also held in the reign of Amenophis III, Akhenaten's father, in the year 1401 BC. Portrayals of this occasion show the ostrich feather being borne aloft on a separate standard which immediately precedes that of Upuaut.

Most of these facts may be gleaned from Margaret Murray's indispensable monograph of 1904 The Osireion at Abydos. But Frazer's inferences are drawn not from Murray but from Professor Flinders Petrie, who directed the excavations and who in 1906 paraphrased the evidence, adding to it one crucial ingredient: Strabo's observation that in the kingdom of Meroë the priests sometimes dispatched messengers to the king requesting him to terminate his life.[36] Was this the "tail" or "end" of which the title of the sed festival spoke? With this slender branch to lean on, Petrie is off:

> The conclusion may be drawn thus. In the savage age of prehistoric times the Egyptians, like other African and Indian peoples, killed the priest-king at stated intervals in order that the ruler should, with unimpaired life and health, be enabled to maintain the kingdom in its highest condition. The jackal-god went before him to open the way to the unseen world; and the ostrich feather received and bore away the king's soul in the breeze that blew it out of sight.[37]

And what has driven Petrie to a conclusion at first sight so bizarre? It is with no small surprise that we discover his source cited as the writings of a certain J. G. Frazer, whose book The Golden Bough he thoughtfully summarises for us at some length. Out it all comes: Meroë, Sofala, Calicut

. . . Virgil's bough has by now spread its protective shade over a neat colony of saplings – the writings of Petrie, on which Frazer primarily leans for his interpretation of the Osiris death cult, being one of the more promising growths.

This sort of incestuous doubling-back of evidence – depending like a Shelleyan image precariously upon itself – was a growing feature of Frazer's writing from the time of the publication of the Second Edition in 1900 to the completion of the Third in 1915, the originator feeding self-generated instances into his text when and as they were brought to his appreciative attention. To a remarkable extent by 1906 he is feeding us with his own theories parroted back by a whole generation of orientalists, ethnologists and classicists whose notions owed much to his thinking. In much the same sort of way, by 1913, when *The Scapegoat* was published as a separate volume, the dramatic theory of ritual had come to lean on Ridgeway, who in turn had got it from the Second Edition. By the time Frazer came to wind up the Third Edition *The Golden Bough* had turned the corner from innovation to convention. It had established an orthodoxy which would guide scholars of early society until the Second World War, after which there would break across its bows a great tide of distrust, from which it has not yet fully recovered.

Despite its passages of sheer conjecture, its use of informed and sometimes not so informed intuition, its occasional fits of grumpiness, *The Golden Bough* had by the outbreak of the Great War become the anthropological bible of its age. Before we turn to consider the aftermath, there is, however, one last matter we must briefly consider. Osiris had not, it seems, always been a grain god. By all accounts he is among the oldest of Nilotic deities, and the Egyptians cannot always have been farmers. There is a passage in Firmicus Maternus which sheds some light on this matter. Once more he is railing against the practices of the heathen. Not only do these worthless people deify the elements – earth, water, fire and air; they even deify the trees. Could anything be more absurd?

In the Phrygian rites supposedly dedicated to the Great Mother they cut down a pine every year, and the image of a young man is attached in the middle. In the ceremonies as performed in Asia, they split the pine down the centre, then they fill it up with an effigy of Osiris made from grain. In the cult of Proserpine they cut down a tree, then give it the aspect and shape of a young girl, then lead it into the town where they weep over it for forty nights. On the fortieth, they burn it. But the other trees of which I have spoken also end in the flames, because after a year they are made up into a ceremonial pyre and burnt.[38]

And a good thing too, Firmicus Maternus seems to be telling us, as he warms his hand at this bonfire of the gods. Persephone is no stranger in this company: she was goddess not simply of the seed as at Eleusis, but more generally of vegetation, including trees. Attis too has been recruited by Frazer into the ranks of tree spirits. If the Egyptians like other peoples had passed though a stage in which they worshipped the occupants of trees with which at one time their land must have been much more thickly crowded, to view Osiris as a quondam arboreal spirit was only just.

Frazer had been preoccupied with tree spirits since his inclusion in the First Edition of the theories of Wilhelm Mannhardt, on whose studies of European folk traditions he had largely then relied, but nothing annoyed him more than the suggestion by some critics that trees and trees alone were his obsession, still more that they were the theme of his greatest work.[39] The suggestion in its most insidious form had dropped from the poisoned pen of Andrew Lang, who in his book *Magic and Religion* of 1901 had elected Frazer to the life presidency of "the Covent Garden School",[40] though he might more aptly have spoken of Kew Gardens. Had he done nothing but reduce all human achievement to oaks and pines? True, in the First Edition, in which the focus is more assuredly Aryan, the tree-trunks cluster thickly within the ancient forests. But emotionally and intellectually Frazer was a pluralist: he had not dismantled other monisms – solar theory, the disease of language – simply in order to replace them with one of his own. In order to understand his arboreal theories aright, it is important to see them in proportion to the rest of his thinking. The chapters concerning Balder are of particular relevance here.

CHAPTER XIII

"SEXTA LUNA"

LET US look once more at Turner's picture *The Golden Bough* of 1834. To the left of the canvas and bathed in sunshine a robed woman holds aloft a sprig of mistletoe, while from her right hand hangs a sickle. Behind her rises an escarpment, halfway up which a pedimented Corinthian façade overlooks a lake shrouded in mist in a deep declivity to her left. On the slopes rising from the lake, recreations are in progress: a circle of figures gambol to the woman's left while immediately in front of her, and beneath a tall Italian pine to the far side, two women feast on victuals spread before them on the grass. Beyond them and into the far distance stretch turreted buildings dissolving out of sight. The whole scene is irradiated with that mellow light which Turner seems to have discovered in Italy.

"Who does not know Turner's picture of the Golden Bough?" runs Frazer's opening sentence, yet he continues with a mistake. Turner's source was the passage in the sixth book of the *Aeneid* in which the Sybil at Cumae tells Aeneas that, in order to visit his father Anchises in the Underworld, he must cull a sprig of vegetation glowing brightly like the mistletoe in the depths of the forest.[1] In the picture Aeneas has just arrived clutching the branch, and the Sybil, who will act as his guide, beckons him on towards the depths of Lake Avernus, seen in the dell below. On the greensward to the right loll the Shades, while amidst the dark pigment in the foreground lurks a snake, signifying the difficulties he will encounter on his path. Much of this can be found in Virgil, but the only translator to mention a "golden bough" is Christopher Pitt, from whom the title of the canvas, and thence Frazer's book, is derived. It is the Sybil who speaks:

> But since you long to pass the realms beneath,
> The dreadful realms of darkness and of death,
> Twice the dire Stygian stream to measure o'er,
> And twice the black tartarean gulph explore:
> First, take my counsel, then securely go;

A mighty tree, that bears a golden bough,
Grows in a vale surrounded with a grove,
And sacred to the queen of Stygian Jove.
Her nether world no mortals can behold,
Till from the bole they strip the blooming gold.[2]

There is no reference, either here or elsewhere in the *Aeneid*, to Nemi.
The one and only source for this connection is a brief gloss in Servius's
fourth-century commentary on the *Aeneid* in which the sprig of foliage
that Aeneas wields as a passport to the infernal regions is identified with
the branch which the aspirant to the office of Rex Nemorensis had
perforce to break before issuing his challenge:

> Those who write about the mysteries of Proserpine hold this branch
> to be mystical, but rumour states otherwise: that after killing King
> Thoas in Taurica Orestes . . . fled with his sister Iphigenia, and near
> Aricia re-established the effigy of Diana, in whose temple the rite was
> transformed. There was a certain tree whose branch none might
> disturb, except that a prerogative was granted to runaway slaves that
> whosoever broke this branch might challenge the fugitive priest to
> single combat, and so become priest himself in commemoration of the
> original flight.[3]

Frazer assumed that Turner knew of this passage and hence intended
the setting in his painting to be the grove at Nemi, but, despite a
superficial physical resemblance, there is no evidence that Turner had
Nemi in mind. Frazer then goes on to assume that Aeneas's branch was
the mistletoe, to which Virgil merely compares it. The identification
comes from Jacob Grimm, who had, however, felt bound to point out
that Virgil describes the bough as "aureus", whereas he describes
the mistletoe as the colour of saffron ("croceus").[4] Frazer needs the
identification because he is determined to connect the story of the grove
with the story of Balder.

Balder was a Norse divinity who kept to his native fjords until the
mid-Victorians discovered him and made him their own, Matthew Arnold
writing a famous mini-epic on his death in 1855. The youngest and most
beautiful of the gods, Balder was troubled with dream-born intimations
of mortality, but was protected by the goddess Frigg from vulnerability
to all earthly things. Owing to her forgetfulness and the malice of Loki,
he succumbed at last to a sprig of mistletoe flung at him in all innocence
by the blind dupe Hother (Old Norse Höðr), upon which in a manner

characteristic of the sagas, but possibly of Aryan provenance, his body was consigned to the deep in a flaming ship.[5] It is a tale in which the principal elements of Frazer's work – wood, fire, and water – peculiarly combine: wood in that both the ship that formed the bier and the mistletoe which was Balder's undoing were arguably oak-bred; fire because the flames that consumed both body and ship were, Frazer argued, one with the other seasonal fires with which the European peasantry to his day sought to encourage the sun on its onward flight; and water because water spells benediction, lustration and cleansing.

1890 had been the year of the oak. On Wednesday 30 April Frazer, who after finishing the First Edition was retracing the steps of Pausanias for his resumed commentary, left Vourkano in the company of a monk and climbed Mount Ithome, on the highest peak of which they found a monastery inhabited by a solitary hermit. They lunched in the courtyard, "I on the food I had brought with me, the monk on black olives and black bread. The latter supplied me with some villainous resinato, of which I took a few mouthfuls. I gave him a drachma, with which I think he was dissatisfied." The following morning he struck out across the Messenian plain:

> On the ridge we passed through the remains of a fine oak forest. They were the first oaks I had noticed in Greece, and ... their sturdy gnarled trunks and fresh green leaves (for the leaves appeared just to be out) were like old friends in a foreign land.[6]

Oaks had not always been foreign to Southern Europe. It was Frazer's persuasion that much of the continent had at one time been covered by oak forest. If much of Europe, why not Italy, and, if Italy, why not the glade at Nemi? Even now the slopes beneath the village of Nemi are covered by holm-oaks, but in classical antiquity oaks must have stretched as far as the eye could see, almost as far as the coast. Only later were they supplanted by the olive, the tamarisk, and the Italian pine which Turner seems to have found everywhere he looked. The dispersal of the oak in ancient times was as ubiquitous as the dispersion of the Aryan people themselves.

Later Frazer was to grow annoyed when anybody wrote him off as a sort of vicarious tree-fetishist,[7] but there is little doubt that in 1890 the arboreal aspect of his argument was of architectural importance. He had just been reading Grimm, according to whom the original religion of the European peoples was a variety of tree-worship:

> At a time when rude beginnings were all that there was of the builder's art, the human mind must have been roused to a higher devotion by the sight of lofty trees under an open sky than it could feel inside the stunted structures reared by unskilful hands. When long afterwards the architecture peculiar to the Teutons reached its perfection, did it not in its boldest creations still aim at reproducing the soaring trees of the forest? Would not the abortion of miserably carved or chiselled images lag far behind the form of a god which the youthful imagination of antiquity pictured to itself throned on the bowery summit of a sacred tree? In the sweep and under the shade of primeval forests the soul of man found itself filled with the nearness of sylvan deities.[8]

These suggestions had been amplified by Wilhelm Mannhardt whose researches among the Central European peasantry had demonstrated just how resilient were the pieties of their forefathers, and just how deeply the festivities of farming folk in the third quarter of the nineteenth century were rooted in seasonal fluctuations, and more especially in the veneration of trees.[9] Of all trees in the greenwood the oak was esteemed the most venerable. Tacitus had described the oak cults of the primitive Teutons, and such forms of devotion were not unknown to Greek or to Roman. When Odysseus wished to discover by what means he should travel back to his island home, was it not the rustling branches of the oak at Dodona, through which Zeus was presumed to speak, which he consulted:

> The man himself had gone up to Dodona
> to ask the spelling leaves of the old oak
> the will of God: how to return, that is,
> to the rich realms of Ithaka after so long.[10]

Was not the residence of Jupiter upon the Capitol in Rome the spreading limbs of an ancient oak-tree, as Livy had declared?[11]

By Ovid's time the grove at Nemi was esteemed an offshoot of the national religion of Rome, with which in any case it probably had a common ancestor in the primordial worship of the Latins, and even of the Etruscans. Frazer is thus justified in seeking for connections between it and the oak-worship of the Romans. But from this it is a large inferential step to the assertion, found nowhere in classical literature, that the tree before which the priest prowled was an oak, a still larger one to the proposition that the priest personified the tree and Jupiter who was immanent within it. Both of these steps are balletic feats of the comparative method. For whether as in earlier versions he is depending upon diffusion as a means of dispersing customs, or as in later versions on spontaneous and simultaneous invention, the final proposals concerning the Arician priesthood depend very much on a set of parallels from places far distant from Nemi. Indeed, by the closing chapters of the First Edition it is clear that his whole theory is dependent on a sort of continental shelf of the mind running from the tip of Italy to the Baltic. However construed and modified, the meeting of Balder with the King of the Wood rests foursquare on the parity of the Aryans.

The notion of an Aryan diaspora was common enough in the late nineteenth century for Frazer to have caught a whiff of it, and, however suspicious he later grew of such thinking, in 1890 he was still markedly influenced by the theories of William Jones and his successors concerning the parity of Indo-European cultures. The mythological argument and the ethnographic come together in their common cousin, philology. According to Grimm *Nemi*, from the Latin for a pastured woodland glade (*nemus*), was cognate with the German *nimidas*, the word used by his Latin source *Indiculus Paganiorum* for the sacred woods known to the Teutons whose tree cults had been described by Tacitus.[12] Frazer's familiarity with Scottish place-names was sufficient to inform him that the common Celtic root for oak, *daur*, sprang from the same root as the Greek δϱυς; the Welsh for door is *drws*, presumably originally signifying a door made of oak.[13] A *dryad* is an oak spirit, and Pliny has it that the *Druids* of ancient Britain took their name from the oak-trees which they revered. Once a month, he says, they staged a ceremony in which they culled mistletoe from the trunk of an oak in the recesses of the forest. And now we come to a further spectacular blunder by Frazer. In 1890 he had translated the passage from Pliny thus:

> The mistletoe is very rarely to be met with; but when it is found, they gather it in a solemn ceremony. This they do especially in the sixth month (the beginnings of their months and years are determined by the moon) and after the tree has passed the thirtieth year of its age, because by that time it has plenty of vigour, though it has not attained half its full size. After due preparations have been made for a sacrifice and a feast under the tree, they hail it as the universal healer and bring to the spot two white bulls, whose horns have never been bound before. A priest clad in a white robe climbs the tree and with a golden

sickle cuts the mistletoe, which is caught in a white cloth. Then they sacrifice the victims, praying that God may make his own gift prosper with those upon whom he has bestowed it.[14]

The beauty of this passage for Frazer lay in the date: the culling of the mistletoe was apparently a midsummer festival. Now, Mannhardt had recorded a number of seasonal fires that occurred at midsummer, and all of them seem to have been kindled by the friction of the oak.[15] If both Mannhardt and Pliny were right, the twin facets of the Balder myth – the mistletoe and the burning – described consecutive events. The story of Balder Frazer believed belonged "to that class of myths which have been dramatised in ritual".[16] Just as the myth had two stages – the death of the god and his burning – so the ritual had two phases. In the first the god was slain by a parasite of the very oak which his sacred person epitomised. In the second he was burned to death like an oak-tree itself in the midsummer fire.

This ritual must, Frazer thought, have been a midsummer feast common to all Aryans. There were remnants of it still. Grimm had noted that the mistletoe was still plucked at midsummer in Sweden;[17] and Mannhardt had recorded many instances, both in Germany and France, in which an effigy, often a wicker man, was burned to death either at midsummer or at some other strategically significant point in the agricultural year. The collation of these instances enabled Frazer to piece together what had occurred at Nemi. The mistletoe on the sacred oak-tree represented the priest's life; when it was plucked, the priest knew himself doomed. Originally he would then have been burned to death in much the same manner as Balder, until the humane practices of a later age commuted this verdict to a hand-to-hand fight in which he had a chance of survival or, if not, of a relatively speedy demise. The peasants whose festivals Mannhardt described were also implicitly burning the god. By that token Balder was the oak; and the priest of Nemi exemplified the same equation.

Imagine then Frazer's dismay when on 4 November 1891 he received a courteous letter from the Oxford Latinist Warde Fowler informing him that Pliny's phrase "omnia sexta luna" meant not "in the sixth month", but "on the sixth day of the moon".[18] The Celtic feast was not, then, a midsummer celebration but a monthly feast, and the culling and the burning did not coincide at all. With that Frazer experienced one of those moments of self-lacerating panic to which he was always prone when led to question his own veracity. He first wrote an open letter in *The Athenaeum* – the very organ in which Savile's discoveries had been announced – abjectly apologising for his own ineptitude.[19] He then went to H. Montagu Butler, the Master of Trinity, and offered his resignation and with it his only regular means of financial support. The Master handed back his note with Luther's phrase "pecca fortiter": "sin more strongly".[20] Frazer recovered his composure and *The Golden Bough* lived to fight another day, but the mistletoe theory, and with it the connection with midsummer fires, were never quite the same again.

The oak-tree, however, was more resilient. In the Second Edition the oak theory is substantially the same, though Pliny has been retranslated and the conjunction of fire and mistletoe leans rather precariously on the fragmentary modern evidence. But the oak had struck deep roots in the classical mind, and more especially in the minds of two scholars who were to do much to enable Frazer to recast his theory for the Third Edition: A. B. Cook, who had reviewed the Second Edition for the *Classical Review*, and Warde Fowler, who had broken the news about Pliny. With the help of these two gentlemen Balder was to appear in the Third Edition in shining new colours.

Cook's review had been so astringent that he feared he had alienated Frazer for ever. He little knew the man. The Frazers had recently returned from Rome bearing photographs of Nemi, and, when Frazer received a contrite note from Cook stating his earnest hope that the great man had not been offended by his comments, the result was an invitation to inspect these trophies over tea.[21] It was the beginning of a fruitful collaboration that was to last several years.

To begin with Cook was unrepentant. All this business about the priest personifying an oak which at the same time lodged Jupiter was surely folly. Jupiter was the supreme sky god; how came he to get entangled in something as mundane as a tree? Frazer deluged him with facts.[22] The Romans got much of their religion from the Etruscans, whose kings wore crowns of oak-leaves interwoven with acorns and precious stones. The common cult of the Latins had been that of Jupiter Latiaris, whose habitation was a grove of oaks on the Alban Mount. Moreover, Latinus, the eponymous king of the Latins, actually went so far as to identify himself with Jupiter Latiaris. Virgil describes the victorious warriors of Alba Longa as crowned "civili . . . quercu", "with wreaths of civic oak".[23] The trophies raised by Roman victors on the field of battle were nothing but stylised oaks. The perpetual fire on the Vestal hearth, as Boni had affirmed, was fed by oak-wood, which would seem to have been nothing

because by that time it has plenty of vigour, though it
has not attained half its full size. After due prepara-
tions have been made for a sacrifice and a feast under
the tree, they hail it as the universal healer and bring
to the spot two white bulls, whose horns have never
been bound before. A priest clad in a white robe
climbs the tree and with a golden[1] sickle cuts the
mistletoe, which is caught in a white cloth. Then
they sacrifice the victims, praying that God may make
his own gift to prosper with those upon whom he has
bestowed it. They believe that a potion prepared
from mistletoe will make barren animals to bring forth,
and that the plant is a remedy against all poison.

In saying that the Druids cut the mistletoe in the
sixth month, Pliny[2] must have had in his mind the
Roman calendar, in which the sixth month was June.
Now, if the cutting of the mistletoe took place in June,
we may be almost certain that the day which witnessed
the ceremony was Midsummer Eve. For in many
places Midsummer Eve, a day redolent of a thousand
decaying fancies of yore, is still the time for culling
certain magic plants, whose evanescent virtue can be
secured at this mystic season alone.* For example, on
Midsummer Eve the fern is believed to burst into a
wondrous bloom, like fire or burnished gold. Who-

---

[1] It is still a folk-lore rule not to cut
the mistletoe with iron; some say it
should be cut with gold. Grimm,
Deutsche Mythologie,[4] ii. 1001. On the
objection to the use of iron in such cases,
see Liebrecht, *Gervasius von Tilbury*,
p. 103; and above, vol. i. p. 177 *sqq.*

[2] Pliny, *Nat. Hist.* xvi. § 249 *sqq.*
On the Celtic worship of the oak, see also
Maximus Tyrius, *Dissert.* viii. 8, Κελτοὶ
σέβουσι μὲν Δία ἄγαλμα δὲ Διὸς Κελτικὸν
ἰψηλὴ δρῦς. With this mode of gathering the mistletoe compare the following.
Branches of the sacred olive-tree at
Olympia which were to furnish the
victors' crowns were cut with a golden sickle
by a boy both of whose parents
were alive (Schol. on Pindar, *Olymp.* iii. 60).

In Cambodia when a man perceives a
certain parasitic plant growing on a
tamarind-tree, he dresses in white and
taking a new earthen pot climbs the
tree at mid-day. He puts the plant in
the pot and lets the whole fall to the
ground. Then in the pot he makes a
decoction which renders invulnerable.
Aymonier, "Notes sur les coutumes et
croyances superstitieuses des Cambod-
giens," in *Cochinchine Française, Ex-
cursions et Reconnaissances*, No. 16, p.
136.

but a way of focusing the fire of heaven itself, the heat of the sun, just as the ancient Teutons and their modern European successors lit the need-fire by friction of oak upon oak.

By 1904 Cook was sufficiently convinced to publish a virtual recantation of his early criticisms in a series of articles in which Jupiter appeared as a triple god one of whose attributes was the oak.[24] So mesmerising had Frazer's influence been that Cook even went so far as to intepret the rule of succession to the priesthood of Zeus at Dodona along much the same lines as Frazer had proposed for Nemi. It was a temporary mood, and by 1914, when he published the first volume of *Zeus*, Cook seems to have forgotten much of it, but it had renewed Frazer's confidence in the basic strength of some of his most cherished theories, and it led, moreover, to a momentous extension of the oak-wood within the enclosure of the Third Edition.

During those endless sessions over the tea, a new version of the oak theory emerged, one much less dependent than it had been previously on some greater Aryan dispersion, much more firmly grounded in the ancient soil of Latium. The new theory took its bow in *Lectures on the Early History of the Kingship*, where Cook's influence is especially marked. Here the contest for the kingship at Nemi is seen as just one realisation of tendencies throughout Latium. For the King of the Wood was not the only Roman monarch to suffer an untimely death. Very few of the kings of ancient Latium, whom Virgil called the Silvii, met natural deaths, and few were succeeded by their sons. The dynasty veered violently with each succession, and the circumstances of the transfer of power sometimes bore an uncanny resemblance to the grim combat by the lakeside. This is true of the ancient kings of Latium and Etruria, for many of whom we have nothing but the names. It is even truer of the kings of Rome themselves:

> Servius Tullius came to his end in circumstances which, as Mr. A. B. Cook has pointed out, recall the combat for the priesthood at Nemi. He was attacked by his successor and killed by his orders, though not by his hand. Moreover, he lived by the oak groves of the Esquirine Hill at the head of the slope of Virbius, and it was here, next to the sanctuary of Diana, that he was slain.[25]

The resemblance did not stop there. Like the Kings of the Wood, the kings of Rome impersonated a god, and that god was Jupiter. And, just as the victor in the woods would seem to have enjoyed the favours of the goddess or else her human representative, and to have celebrated his union with her in an act of consecrated marriage, so had the kings of Rome.

How were all these facts to be connected? Some help was forthcoming from the ancient marriage system. Republican Rome, as Maine had observed, was solidly patriarchal, but early societies, among them the Rome of the ancient kingdom, had, as M'Lennan asserted, been matrilinear. If descent was through the mother, then the hand of the King's daughter would be avidly sought. Might her favours have been contested for in some form of combat? There was one Roman custom, a survival from past ages, which might provide a clue here. Once a year, on 24 February, the *rex sacrorum*, a successor of the ancient kings, fled through the Roman streets away from the Forum after offering a sacrifice in the Comitium.[26] Conventionally this was interpreted as a pageant representing the flight of Tarquin Superbus (an explanation offered by Ovid, and one to which, despite Frazer, more conventional Latinists like Fowler still clung[27]). Might this act of flight now be seen as a ritualistic re-enactment of a race between aspirants to the throne, the prize being the hand of the king's daughter and with it the kingship? If that were the case, the patterns of succession at Rome in ancient times might have been very much closer to those at nearby Nemi than Frazer himself had dreamed in 1890.

There were indeed remnants of a sacred marriage in the Rome of classical times. Another remnant of monarchical institutions at Rome was the Flamen Dialis, the taboos surrounding whom had been of such interest to Frazer in 1887–90. But the taboos covered both the Flamen, a priest of Jupiter, and his wife, the Flamenica. The very intensity of these rules, so reminiscent of those surrounding royalty, suggested that in this priestly pair we have a pale reflection of the ancient kings and queens of Rome, and that their marriage might in fact be a form of the marriage of ancient kings, which itself embodied the union of Jupiter and Juno:

If at any time of the year the Romans celebrated the sacred marriage of Jupiter and Juno, as the Greeks commonly celebrated the corre-sponding marriage of Zeus and Hera, we may suppose that under the Republic the ceremony was either performed over images of the divine pair or acted by the Flamen and the Flamenica. For the Flamen Dialis was the Priest of Jove, indeed, ancient and modern writers have regarded him, with much probability, as the living image of Jupiter, a human embodiment of the sky-god. In early times the Roman king, as representative of Jupiter, would naturally play the part of the heavenly bridegroom at the sacred marriage, while his queen would figure as the heavenly bride, just as in Egypt the king and queen masqueraded in the character of deities, and as at Athens the queen annually wedded the sky-god Dionysus. That the Roman king and queen should act the parts of Jupiter and Juno would seem all the more natural because these deities themselves bore the title of King and Queen.[28]

Frazer then cast his mind back to the very beginning of his career, and remembered his speculations concerning the prytaneum in 1885. The prytaneum held a perpetual fire, but so did the temple of the Vestal virgins in the Forum, and it was Frazer's contention in 1885 that those who tended the sacred flame in its precincts, namely the Vestals themselves, had once been the daughters of the king, whose palace the temple represented. He then recalled the circular stylobate which Savile had discovered in Nemi. In 1890 he had preferred to interpret this as the base of a sacrifical altar, but might it not also be the cradle of a perpetual fire? One of Diana's titles, at Nemi as elsewhere, was Hestia, and that in itself reinforced the connection. Were the priestesses of Diana in the sacred grove, then, the equivalents of the virgins who tended the sacred flame in Rome? And was the flame itself the sacred fire in which the god, that is the priest, was once ceremonially burned? As Boni had so usefully confirmed in 1900, the fire in the Vestal temple had been fed by oak wood. Was the fire at Nemi also so fed? If so, the much-needed connection between fire, the oak and the priest, which had been so crippled in 1891 by Frazer's recognition of his mistranslation of Pliny, was re-established and confirmed from sources not hundreds of miles away in the gloomy Northern forests, but across the Alban Hills in the heart of Roman civilisation.

That substantially was the theory of the divine kingship as it appeared in Frazer's lecture series of 1905 and as it flowed into the third *Golden Bough*. With its help Frazer was able to reinterpret his earlier ideas without leaning quite so heavily on the Balder myth and the mistletoe, neither of which do the lectures mention. But there is no sign that Frazer had lost interest in The Plot. The King of the Wood is still there, his plight as poignant as ever. If he bears a more Roman appearance now, is less a sort of Aryan mascot, all to the good. And this is not all: he has discovered a second self. In February 1911, in the nick of time for volume III (*The Dying God*), Frazer's continuing inquiries amongst ethnographic field-workers provoked an answer from an unexpected quarter.

Charles Seligmann was to make a reputation as one of the constellation of younger anthropologists who gathered around Malinowski at the London School of Economics. In 1911 he was engaged in research among the peoples of the White Nile: the Dinka and Shilluk. Seligmann was one of a whole generation of younger anthropologists profoundly influenced by Frazer's writings. Metaphorically or physically he kept *The Golden Bough* in his pocket, and in 1911 sent Frazer the typescript of a work of his own called *Divine Kings of the Shilluk*, the principal conclusions of which Frazer promptly incorporated in his text.[29] Such collaboration speaks well for the temper of the times: one wonders how many field-workers today would be prepared to do as much in advance of publication.

Seligmann's view of the Nilotic kings vindicated Frazer's conjectures in a dramatic manner. The Dinka rainmaker was buried alive as soon as he sickened, and, when one of the King of Shilluk's wives reported the slightest slackening of her husband's sexual powers, "which was regarded as an undoubted sign of senescence", the unfortunate monarch or *rēt* was walled up, his head couched for comfort in the lap of his favourite wench.

Thus far was the sacrifical theory of sacrifice vindicated, but this was not all. When Seligmann eventually obtained an audience with the king, he found that the wretched fellow could scarcely keep his eyes open for sheer fatigue. On inquiring why this was the case, he elicited the answer that the poor man had been up all night keeping watch. For, not only had the King of the Shilluk to consent to being immured when his virility deserted him, but like Rex Nemorensis he could, it seemed, be challenged to single combat at any time, the only difference being that in the Sudan the assailant had to be one of his sons:

But the attack on him could only take place with any propsect of success at night; for during the day the king surrounded himself with his friends and bodyguards, and an aspirant to the throne could hardly hope to cut his way through them and strike home. It was otherwise at night. For then the guards were dismissed and the king was alone in his enclosure with his favourite wives, and there was no man near to defend him except a few herdsmen, whose huts stood a little way off. The hours of darkness were therefore the season of peril for the king. It is said that he used to pass them in constant watchfulness, prowling round his huts fully armed, peering into the blackest shadows, or himself standing silent and alert, like a sentinel on duty, in some dark corner. When at last his rival appeared, the fight would take place in grim silence, broken only by the clash of spears and shields, for it was a point of honour with the king not to call the herdsmen to his assistance.[30]

The remarkable thing about this passage is that it comes almost verbatim from Seligmann's typescript. If it sounds like Frazer, it is because Seligmann had swallowed not only the theory but also the prose that went along with it. "It is clear", he wrote "that the *rēt* must be numbered among those rulers whom Dr J. G. Frazer called 'divine kings'." As in Petrie's observations in the Upper Nile, Frazer's theories had generated their own fiat.

The confidence thus induced is evident on every page of the Third Edition. The book has a scope, a grandeur and a subtlety of realisation apparent in neither previous version. The keenest difference is a lessening dependence on the Aryan connection, and a reliance instead on two foundations: an inner Roman core, and an outer ring of non-European parallels. The most obvious victim of this process is Balder. The weakness of *Balder the Beautiful* when compared to the earlier volumes of the Third Edition is manifold. In the first place, Frazer's old theory of fire festivals as magical interventions in the course of nature aimed at encouraging the sun on its onward flight has been supplanted by a new theory of fire as a means of purgation, or more narrowly of the dispersal of witches, which Frazer had gleaned from Westermark's researches in Morocco. Yet the solar theory of fire, with its sources in Mannhardt, is retained shorn of its strength. Secondly, the Depository Theory of totemism, in which by 1914 Frazer had long since lost faith, is also retained as a prop to the notion of the external soul, which itself is weakened in consequence.

Thirdly, the old idea of Jupiter as the god of the oak is retained, but along with it the idea of Jupiter as a sky god. The connecting link is through lightning, since Frazer had learned from his old friend Warde Fowler that oaks are more likely to be struck by lightning than any other tree in the forest, and that early man must therefore have regarded oaks as the special resting-place of the sky god. Fourthly, the reinforced oak theory, now well and truly wedded to Jupiter as the royal god of the Romans, arrives to occlude suggestions earlier in the book that the priest of Nemi is the representative of Hippolytus or of his Roman embodiment Virbius. Despite Cook's best efforts, it is no clearer in the Third Edition than it was in the Second which among the pantheon of Graeco-Roman gods the King of the Wood was truly meant to embody or impersonate.

It was almost Frazer's last word on the subject. He was to strip the book down to its essentials for the popular abridgement of 1922, and fourteen years later to add a volume of supplementary instances called *Aftermath*. The examples thus collected stretch from Uganda to ancient Russia, yet Rex Nemorensis is as Roman as ever. The paradox of the Third Edition is this: that within its pages the King of the Wood has wandered further afield than ever, only to stay more resolutely at home.

CHAPTER XIV

RETROSPECT: THE DYING SUN

WITH the publication of a bibliography and general index in 1915 the Third Edition came to rest. The First Edition had helped set the mood of the 1890s; the Second had seen the nineteenth century to its close. The Third swept to its conclusion as the storm clouds gathered over Europe, engulfing for ever the secure Victorian world in which Frazer had been raised.

He retreated to a flat in the Inner Temple and, closing his ears to the dinning enthusiasms around him, concentrated his mind on the folkloric legacy of the patriarchs. He looked out over the open spaces of the quadrangle beneath his window, and, hearing the men of the bar drilling for the front, thought with fond regret of the London of Addison. Meanwhile, back in Trinity, his friend A. E. Housman endeavoured to concentrate on Manilius while billeted soldiers thumped quadrilles on the floor above. "*Hoc signo vinces.*" Where had the light led?

But Frazer had said what he meant; there was no need to alter the design. The Third Edition is in a sense his definitive statement; his readers had no need to fear a fourth. For twenty years Frazer's reputation held steady. *Folklore in the Old Testament* held a certain appeal for a generation still bewildered by religious disquiet. In a world of collapsing certainties, ritual was something to hold on to. The classics too owned Frazer's sway as the Cambridge ritualists and Gilbert Murray interpreted Attic tragedy anew in a Frazerian light.

But more and more *The Golden Bough* appealed to imaginative writers rather than scholars. In 1890 Hardy read it and noted the similar habits of Dorset farmers and Asiatic peasants. In 1919 Mrs Yeats records page references to the Third Edition in the automatic writing she takes down from the spirits. Eliot cites Frazer in the notes to *The Waste Land*, and elsewhere calls him "unquestionably the greatest master".[1] Lawrence reads him during the war and uses him to boost his endless homilies to Russell about "blood-consciousness". One cannot think Frazer would have approved.

It was in the emerging social sciences that Frazer's credit declined

most steeply. To begin with, new evidence tended to confirm rather than
modify his theories. The monarchs of the Khazars in south-east Russia
were, it appeared, allowed to live for no more than a certain number of
years, the sum of which was variously reported by Arab travellers of the
medieval period. Mashona chiefs were obliged to forfeit their existence
after a set time. The same appeared to be true of the Banyankole of
Uganda. Between the White and Blue Niles lived a people called the
Fung among whom Evans-Pritchard found a similar rule by which the
king was executed when he sickened. Further evidence for Feasts of All
Souls came from Tibet, and for the external soul from San Cristóbal.
Frazer continued to tabulate it all with unwearying accuracy – enough
by 1936 to furnish a whole supplementary volume to the Third Edition.[2]
Aftermath was less an extension of the argument than a scrapbook into
which Frazer pasted further illustrations as they occurred to him. The
result was rather like a set of marginalia to a non-existent text. "I wear
my theories more lightly now", wrote Frazer in the Preface, and he was
more and more inclined to the view that the vitality of his writing resided
less in his theories than in his examples. *Aftermath* gives the lie to this
view: it is a storehouse of such examples, and it is lifeless.

With the growth of social anthropology as an academic discipline after
the First World War, a generation grew up with the idea that Frazer
had asked interesting questions, even if his way of answering them
seemed quaint. Bronisław Malinowski reviewed the abridged *Golden
Bough* flatteringly on its appearance in 1922, and promptly led the
subject off in a completely different direction.[3] With the growth of
opportunities for field-workers after the Second World War, and the
development of a tighter though more exclusive professional vocabulary,
vistas from the college window came to seem of less and less relevance.
It was the age of the sparrows, and Frazer had been an eagle.
Functionalism – the insistence on observing each society *in situ* and
principally in terms of its internal relations – appeared to sound Frazer's
knell. With the rise of more modish schools of thought, even students of
myth turned their attention elsewhere. By 1970, twenty-nine years after
his death, Geoffrey Kirk could describe Frazer as "this fallen colossus".[4]

If Frazer had ceased to bestride the world, his decline had more to do
with his methodology than his meaning. At the outset he had nailed his
colours to the comparative method, and with it he rose and fell. His
commitment to this method predated its application to any given field of

inquiry. In 1882, while preparing for the bar, we find him reading Maine's *Ancient Law*, on which he makes copious notes, citing M'Lennan against him. His enthusiasm for legal study temporarily deserting him, he doodles in the back of his notebook what looks like the inception of an elementary semiology: "Language, spoken or written, is a species of signs. Signs are modes of conveying thought between intelligent beings by means of sensible impressions. Signs are of two kinds: representative and symbolical. . . ."[5]

After a further page, the trail of speculation peters out. If its abandonment strikes us as an opportunity lost, it is because we have since come to the conclusion that language precedes culture, logically if not in time, and that sharper insights can be derived from an investigation of the two taken together than from an investigation of the second alone. Yet these two schools of thought – the Frazerian and the semiotic – share a common assumption. The parity of human behaviour – cultural or linguistic – is grounded in the common nature of the mind.

That the mind of man, under whatever circumstances and at whatever period, works in pretty much the same way was a conviction Frazer derived in the first instance from his empiricist forebears and in the second from Victorian evolutionary theory. His naïveté is that he applies the first to the second, as if a commonality of logical processes somehow guaranteed a common course of cultural development. The application of this equation to widely divergent societies in very different parts of the world constitutes his Achilles' heel. Deprived of the axiom of parallel evolution, the comparative method becomes a sort of sublime leap-frogging, the rules of whose operation are left up to the frog.

The arbitrariness of Frazer's reasoning is apparent from his structures. Deprived of evidence in one context he will always move sideways to supply it from another. Converted into a working hypothesis the transplanted fact then becomes a platform on which further conjectures are raised. *The Golden Bough* is a towering edifice of such conjectures. The putative horse-sacrifice at Nemi is just one example, but there are countless others.

Wittgenstein read Frazer in abridgement in 1930 and commented on the quirkiness of his logical procedures. The interchangeability of facts led in the end to a variety of phantasmagoria:

Just how misleading Frazer's accounts are we see I think from the fact that one could well imagine primitive practices oneself, and it would only be by chance if they were not actually found somewhere. . . . We can readily imagine that, say, in a given tribe no-one is allowed to see the king, or again that every man in the tribe is obliged to see him. . . . Perhaps no-one will be allowed to touch him, or perhaps they will be *compelled* to do so. Think how after Schubert's death his brother cut certain of Schubert's scores into small pieces and gave to his favourite pupils these pieces of a few bars each. As a sign of piety this action is *just* as comprehensible to us as the other one of keeping the scores undisturbed and accessible to no-one.[6]

This is very germane to Frazer's ideas on taboo. If anything despised is by the same token holy, and anything holy by the same token despised, it is clear that a given piece of ritual, a fragment of myth, can signify just about anything. Ultimately hypothesis and fact perform a kind of barn dance together, endlessly swapping partners.

Thus the essence of Frazer's arbitrariness inheres in his logic. His favourite word for a logical step is an inference, which earlier in the century Hamilton had defined as "the carrying out into the last proposition what was virtually contained in the antecedent judgements".[7] But Reid also used it in the sense of an implication felt to be persuasive, and it is in this looser sense that Frazer habitually employs it.

Armed with a logic so insecure, it seemed to Wittgenstein presumptuous of Frazer to characterise the ideas of early man as mistakes ("Was Augustine mistaken, then," he asks, "when he called on God on every page of the *Confession*?"). For, if Frazer is pinning his hopes on inductive logic, he is as mistaken as those whom he describes. In the *Tractatus Logo-philosophicus* Wittgenstein's word for all inductive inferences had been *Aberglaube* (superstition): "We *cannot* infer the events of the future from those of the present. Belief in the causal nexus is superstition."[8]

Commenting on this statement, Bertrand Russell observed that in that case there can be nothing binding about any natural law, or indeed expectation: "There cannot in Wittgenstein's logic be any such thing as a causal nexus . . . That the sun will rise tomorrow is a hypothesis. We do not know whether it will rise, since there is no compulsion according to which one thing must happen because another happens."[9]

Frazer thought that early man viewed the world magically, and modern man scientifically. But, if in a scientifically construed universe the sun may not rise tomorrow, where does that leave Frazer? With his Brahmin, casting spells to induce the dawn.

But Wittgenstein has his own error, which is to assume that Frazer did not recognise this. In reality Frazer was well aware of the insecurity of the inductive method. "After all," he wrote in 1890, "what we call truth is only the hypothesis which is found to work best."[10] The superiority of modern man, if such there was, rested simply in the length of time over which his ideas had been tested. Yet even the sharpest of scientific ideas had their magical foundations, and when contemplating the blundering steps of our forefathers it behoved us to be grateful. It did not always appear to Frazer as if our ancestors had been fumbling in the dark. *"Cum excusatione itaque veteres audiendi sunt"*: "with such a plea let the elders be heard."[11] Had nineteenth-century man fared so much better? A scepticism as to the ultimate worth of science is an integral part of the Humean inheritance that Frazer inbibed with his mother's milk, and in *The Belief in Immortality and the Worship of the Dead* he speaks of it most movingly. The weakness of scientific method lay just where Wittgenstein had put it – in the fallibility of the causal idea:

> Now when we analyse the conception of a cause to the bottom we find as the last residue of our crucible nothing but what Hume found long ago, and that is simply the idea of an invariable sequence. Whenever we say that something is the cause of something else, all that we really mean is that the latter is invariably preceded by the former, so that wherever we find the second, what we call the effect, we may infer that the first, which we call the cause, has gone before it. All such inferences from effects to causes are based on experience. . . . Once the ideas are by dint of repetition firmly welded together the one by sheer force of habit calls up the other, and we say that the two things which are represented by those ideas stand to each other in the relation of cause and effect. The notion of causality is in short one particular case of the Association of Ideas. . . . All this is as true of the savage as it is of the civilised man. . . . But the range of his experience is comparatively . . . narrow, and accordingly his inferences from it often appear to civilised man with the wider knowledge, to be palpably false and absurd.[12]

It follows that the superiority of science to magic is a matter of pure subjectivity. For the connections which scientific man perceives have no more necessity than those perceived by his forebears.

With this underlying epistemology, there is little wonder that Frazer often appeared to be unpersuaded of the binding force of the scientific view. At moments it seems as if the whole evolutionary scenario was a shadow-play which time would dissolve. In 1900, in the culminating moments of the Second Edition, he envisages history as a web woven of variously coloured strands: black for magic, red for religion, white for science. The future was a blur, a white and crimson stain:

Will the great movement which for centuries has been slowly altering the complexion of thought be continued in the near future? Or will a reaction set in which will arrest progress and even undo much that has been done? To keep up the parable, what will be the colour of the web which the Fates are now weaving on the humming loom of time? Will it be white or red? We cannot tell. A faint glimmering light illumines the backward portion of the web. Clouds and darkness hide the other end.[13]

Whatever eventual composition of the web, it was of limited extent. While a student at Glasgow in the early 1870s, Frazer sat at the feet of William Thomson, later Lord Kelvin, whose opinion it was that the sun, fired by no more than ordinary heat, would cool to extinction within a few thousand years. The poignancy of this view, foreshortening the vista of science at the very moment when it had seemed to open so dramatically, colours the culminating paragraphs of *The Golden Bough*. The Second and Third Editions close on a vision of the sun going out:

however vast the increase of knowledge and of power which the future may have in store for man, he can scarcely hope to stay the sweep of those great forces which seem to be making silently but relentlessly for the destruction of this starry universe in which the earth swims as a speck or mote. In the ages to come man may be able to predict, perhaps even control, the wayward courses of the winds and clouds, but hardly will his puny hands have strength to speed afresh the slackening planet in its orbit or rekindle the dying fire of the sun. Yet the philosopher who trembles at the ideas of such distant catastrophes may console himself by the reflection that these gloomy apprehensions, like the earth and the sun themselves, are only part of that insubstantial world which thought has conjured up out of the void, and that the phantoms which the subtle enchantress has evoked to-day she may undo tomorrow. They too, like so much that to common eyes seems solid, may melt into air, into thin air.[14]

This is the sombre side of Frazer's idealism. Hope is an illusion, thought an illusion, fear itself an illusion. Finally we know nothing. As one by one the cloud-capped palaces dissolve, Frazer stands there wand in hand, not yet quite prepared to drown his book. Is this the colossus who has fallen?

One strand in the baseless fabric of this vision is Frazer's rationalism, which at times he profoundly distrusted. For, if in Robertson Smith a ruthless evangelical honesty contrives to undermine the sanctity of the biblical text, in Frazer the idealistic premises of Humean empiricism turn in on themselves to make doubt itself an impossibility. To the end Frazer remained sceptical, even of his own scepticism.

This is nowhere truer than in his attitudes to religion. It is easy to make out a case for his apostasy, in support of which Robert Ackerman quotes his letter to Henry Jackson on 18 April 1904 explaining his rejection of a Visiting Lectureship at Didsbury College, Manchester. He would have been speaking to aspirants to the Christian ministry, and would have been obliged to disguise his views:

I am not a Christian, on the contrary I reject the Christian religion as utterly false. Yet if I accepted the post I should be expected . . . to say nothing that would offend the religious feelings of the students. That is, I should be implicitly bound to conceal my own firm belief in the falseness of Christianity and, I suppose, not to put before the students facts which might tend to undermine their faith. Do you think that would be honest? . . . the facts of Comparative Religion appear to me to be subversive of Christian theology; and in putting them before my students without any express reference to Christianity, I should still feel as if I was undermining their faith, contrary to my implied promise not to do so.[15]

But it is important to recognise of what Frazer is here speaking. He is talking about assenting to a body of doctrine, and in that sense he was manifestly not religious, church-goer though he was. But it is a large step from this to the claim that he had no sense of religion, or that he regarded religion as a whole as untrue. He certainly thought it had been superseded, but, as we have already seen, his feelings about the future were ambiguous. Certainly he liked to portray himself as a sniper at the religious establishment, but his delight in this activity was often pure fun. In the Preface to the Second Edition he compares himself to a field battery storming the bastions of faith, but each man kills the thing he loves, and many a man has stormed his own citadel. Plain rationalist he was not. Against the letter to Jackson one needs to put a slightly later letter to George Macmillan, commenting on a proposal by Edward Clodd, the arch-rationalist of the Folklore Society, to reprint *The Golden Bough* under the imprimatur of the Rationalist Press. Frazer's verdict was peremptory – have nothing whatsoever to do with it:

I do not suppose that you would entertain the proposal, and even if you were willing to do so, I do not think I would consent. I wish to keep aloof from all bodies, ecclesiastical and anti-ecclesiastical, who are committed to the propagation of certain definite opinions. I wish to maintain a position of complete independence, and think that any influence I may have might to some extent be compromised by committing myself to a set of any sort.[16]

Thus, though like Gibbon he loved to *épater les chrétiens*, Frazer was no mere partisan. Notice the terms of his refusal. The opinions to which he has been invited to subscribe are suspect because they are definite. Definition implies an end, or at least a circumscribed view, and of this Frazer wanted no part.

At times the impossibility of knowing anything for certain seems to have inspired in Frazer a sort of twinkling delivery, a sardonic self-scrutiny, a cat-and-mouse game with truth. He was not above playing to the gallery in this respect. It is an aspect of his deliciously self-deprecating humour. How much was tact, how much a genuine admission of ignorance? It is impossible even to guess. Was there a God, and if so was knowledge of him available to man? In the opening lecture of his Gifford series *The Belief in Immortality and the Worship of the Dead* he seems to throw up his hands in despair at the sheer obduracy of the question:

Now I desire to confess at once that an adequate discussion of these and kindred questions exceeds my capacity and knowledge; for he who would do justice to so arduous an enquiry should not only be endowed with a comprehensive and penetrating genius, but should possess a wide and accurate acquaintance with the best accredited results of philosophical speculation and scientific research. To such qualifications I can lay no claim, and accordingly I must regard myself as unfitted for the purely philosophical treatment of natural theology. To speak plainly, the question of the existence of God is too deep for me. I dare neither affirm it or deny it. I can only confess my ignorance.[17]

The Golden Bough was continually reworked and rewritten in the search for truth. That truth it never reached; nor, I think, would Frazer have embraced it if it had. Characteristically he always liked to see himself as at the beginning of a search: he was in a very real and a very humble sense a student all his life. He thought that posterity would consign his work to oblivion, but we know better. In many ways *The Golden Bough* is a great book because it is so flawed. Were it a cogent work of science it would long ago have been supplanted. But in the last resort Frazer is a poor scientist: he lacks the training and even the will. He would be a scientist if he could control his facts, but this he manifestly cannot do. The fissure in his logic lets religion in. It is clear that he thinks Nemi a holy place, and, since Nemi remains pre-eminently a region of the mind, it is clear that he finds the mind holy too.

Which brings us back to the bells. "The sound of sabbath bells," wrote Frazer in 1935, "even in a foreign land, still touches a deep chord in my heart." Now Exodus 28 stipulates that the High Priest should wear a fringe of golden bells around the hem of his scarlet robe, and in a remarkable chapter in *Folklore in the Old Testament* Frazer glosses the reference for us. He starts by citing the literary parallels. In the *Purgatorio* Dante compares the passing-bell to the Vesper bell heard by voyagers at sea. Byron heard the Angelus drifting over the tops of the pine forest near Ravenna, and in a memorable stanza in *Don Juan* evokes it, echoing Dante and Sappho as he does so.[18] Frazer continues,

A like sense of the power of bells to touch the heart and attune the mind to solemn thought is conveyed in a characteristic passage of Renan, in whom the austere convictions of the religious sceptic were happily tempered by the delicate perceptions of the literary artist. Protesting against the arid rationalism of the German theologian Feuerbach, he exclaims: "Would to God that M. Feuerbach had steeped himself in sources of life richer than those of his exclusive and haughty Germanism! Ah! if seated on the ruins of the Palatine or the Coelian Mount, he had heard the sound of the eternal bells lingering and dying over the deserted hills where Rome once was; or if, from the solitary shore of the Lido, he had heard the chimes of Saint Mark's expiring across the lagoons; if he had seen Assisi and its mystic marvels, its double basilica and the great legend of the second Christ of the Middle Ages traced by the brush of Cimabue and Giotto; if he had gazed his fill on the sweet far-away look of the Virgins of Perugino, or if, in San Domenico at Sienna, he had seen Saint Catherine in ecstasy, no, M. Feuerbach would not thus have cast reproach on one half of human poetry, nor cried aloud as if he would repel from the him the phantom of Iscariot!"

Or if, Frazer seems to add, he had once lingered by the shores of Lake Nemi. Late in his life Frazer acknowledged this passage as the source of his own Roman bells. The sense of it is this. Feuerbach had used his mind to plumb the mystery of other minds, or, more precisely, of their religious consciousness. In this he had failed because his own mind was incomplete. He was lacking in the Italy of his mind. Religion is part of the mind: the world cannot be understood without it.

We are now in a position to appreciate why Frazer adamantly refused to strike out the reference to the bells of Rome from the concluding paragraphs of *The Golden Bough*, even when their reverberation was shown to be impossible. He was in many ways very close to Renan, nor were there many intellectuals in the world of his time for whom he felt a stronger affinity. This one-time seminarian, renegade intellectual, eccentric visionary and idiosyncratic prophet seems to have appealed to him in a way that Edward Clodd and the monstrous regiment of the unfaithful could not. Renan had heard the bells of Rome echoing across the slopes of the Palatine and known his vision complete. To the extent that Nemi was a visionary terrain they needed to sound there too. To stop them resounding would have been to reduce oneself to the "arid rationalism" of Feuerbach.

Frazer had defined religion as what occurs when the mind is confronted by that which it knows it is powerless to control. In Frazer's case that which it cannot control is the facts. In that sense alone Frazer is seized by reverence towards his own subject matter. The world, *in fine*, is larger and more complicated than the mind.

It is part of Frazer's outstanding intellectual humility, and an aspect of his charm. It is time we took this man's measure again. We are further along the web than he, and the way ahead is no clearer. The past remains a quandary to which we have too easily consigned him. This intellectual mountaineer, this Moses of the Mind, bringer of broken tablets, finally claims to know very little. He is stranded on Pisgah still, peering through the mist. We have not found our Joshua.

NOTES AND REFERENCES

References to *The Golden Bough* are normally to the edition of first appearance, and are phrased thus: *GB 2*, II.216, i.e. p. 216 of Volume II of *The Golden Bough*, Second Edition. References to the manuscript collections in the Wren Library, Trinity College, Cambridge and the British Library are respectively phrased TCC and BL, followed by the accession number. Unless otherwise stated, translations are by the author.

CHAPTER I PROSPECT: "DIANA'S MIRROR"

1. Strabo, *Geographia*, v.3.12; tr. Horace Leonard Jones in *The Geography of Strabo*, Loeb Classical Library (London: Heinemann; New York: G. P. Putnam, 1923), II, 420–3.
2. Cicero, *De officiis*, I.44.
3. For recent interpretations of the site cf. T. F. C. Blagg, "The Cult and Sanctuary of Diana Nemorensis", in *Pagan Gods and Shrines of the Roman Empire*, ed. Martin Henig and Anthony King (Oxford: Oxford University Committee for Archaeology, 1986), pp. 211–19. It is now thought to date back to the fifth century BC, though the buildings Savile excavated, probably not Diana's temple, are believed to date from the first century BC.
4. For an account and transcription of some of these, see Savile's description of the excavations in the *Journal of the British and American Archaeological Society in Rome*, I, no. 2 (1885–6).
5. Jones's painting of 1785 is of the town of Nemi from the temple ruins, which Jones sketched in 1777.
6. For the history of the excavations cf. *Mysteries of Diana: The Antiquities from Nemi at Nottingham Museums* (Nottingham: Castle Museum, 1983), from which the map is also taken. See esp. A. G. MacCormick, "The Temple of Diana", and T. F. C. Blagg, "The Architecture of the Sanctuary". The biographical details concerning Savile are from the sketch by E. Horriben in the same publication.
7. *GB 3*, I, 12. *GB 1*, I, 4, has the simpler wording "it appears that she was especially worshipped by women desirous of children or of an easy delivery".
8. Nottingham Castle Museum, N 636.
9. Cf. Blagg, *Pagan Gods and Shrines*, p. 218.
10. In addition to Savile's account in the Society's journal, a full account also appeared in *Bulletino dell' Instituto di Corrispondenza Archeologica*, 1885, pp. 149ff (Otto Rasbach) and pp. 225ff (N. Hibbig). It is on the second of these which Frazer's observations are primarily based.

11. *The Athenaeum*, no. 3024 (10 October 1885) 477–8.
12. For the date of Frazer's discovery, see *GB 1*, I, ix; for the reference to southern Indian affinities, see *GB 3* I, vii. For a more precise identification of the Indian material, see Chapter IV.
13. Ovid, *Fasti*, III.260–76.
14. Statius, *Silvae*, III.55–60.
15. See Servius on VI.136. For a translation of this passage, and a discussion of its relevance to the myth of the Golden Bough, see Chapter XIII.
16. Juvenal, *Satires*, IV.113ff.
17. Persius, *Satires*, VI.55ff.
18. Suetonius, *Caligula*, 35.
19. *Pausanias's Description of Greece*, tr. with a commentary by J. G. Frazer (London: Macmillan, 1898), I, 112–13.
20. Ibid., III, 251.
21. Pausanias, *Guide to Greece*, tr. with an introduction by Peter Levi (Harmondsworth: Penguin, 1971), I, 195n.
22. Servius on the *Aeneid*, II.116 and VI.136.
23. Herodotos, II.65.
24.

> The barbarous Scythian
> Or he that makes his generation messes
> To gorge his appetite, shall to my bosom
> Be as well neighbour'd, pitied, and reliev'd
> As thou my sometime daughter.
>   (*King Lear*, I.i)

25. For Savile's account of Nibby's discoveries, see "Discovery of the Temple at Nemi" in *Illustrated Catalogue of Classical Antiquities from the Site of the Temple at Nemi with an Account by Lord Savile of the Discovery of the Temple and the Objects Found There*, ed. G. H. Wallis (Nottingham: Castle Museum, 1893).
26. Ibid., p. 10.
27. Ovid, *Fasti*, III.397.
28. Ovid, *Fasti*, III.260–1. Frazer's prose translation runs: "Who will now tell me why the Salii bear the heavenly weapons of Mars and sing of Mamurius?" *Publii Ovidii Nasonis Fastorum Libri Sex. The Fasti of Ovid*, ed. with a translation and commentary by J. G. Frazer (London: Macmillan, 1929), I, 130–1.
29. Ovid, *Fasti*, v.521ff, with Frazer's commentary (*The Fasti of Ovid*, III, 61–9).
30. Cf. Monboddo's *Antient Metaphysics* (1779–99).
31. Thomas Malthus, *Essay on the Principle of Population* (1798).
32. Thomas Love Peacock, *Headlong Hall and Gryll Grange*, ed. Michael Baron and Michael Slater (Oxford: Oxford University Press, 1987), pp. 57–8. Cf. also *Melincourt* (1817), where Sir Oran Hautton is distinguished by his civility.
33. Richard Whately, *On the Origin of Civilization* (1855).
34. See esp. Friedrich Max Müller, *Lectures on the Science of Language*, 2nd ser. (London, 1864).

35. E. B. Tylor, *Primitive Culture* (London, 1871).
36. Cf. J. G. Frazer, "Speech on Receiving the Freedom of the City of Glasgow", in *Creation and Evolution in Primitive Cosmogonies* (London: Macmillan, 1935), p. 126.
37. *GB 3*, XI, 308–9.
38. See Chapter XIV.

CHAPTER II THE EBBING TIDE

1. J. G. Frazer, "Memories of My Parents", in *Creation and Evolution*, p. 133.
2. Daniel Frazer, *The Story of the Making of Buchanan Street with Some Reminiscences of the Last Half Century* (Glasgow, 1885).
3. In 1900 the main body of the Free Church joined the United Presbyterians to form the United Free Church, which returned to the Auld Kirk in 1929. The present Free Presbyterian Church – the "wee frees" – stems from the remnant who refused to be reconciled. After its recent removal of the Lord Chancellor as an Elder, it is even more of a remnant.
4. Andrew Lang, *John Knox and the Reformation* (London: Longman, 1905), pp. 36, 64, 239.
5. Ibid., p. 116.
6. Ibid., p. 11.
7. See J. G. Frazer, *The Belief in Immortality and the Worship of the Dead*, I (London: Macmillan, 1913), 18–19.
8. *Boswell in Extremes, 1776–1778*, ed. Charles McWeiss and Frederick A. Pottle (London: Heinemann, 1971). Hume died on 25 August 1776. He was buried on Calton Hill.
9. The remote originator of the Association of Ideas was in fact one Revd. Mr Gray, Fellow of Sidney Sussex College, Cambridge, whose remarks were published in a preface to Archbishop King's *Origin of Evil*. Hartley's version of the theory made its first appearance in his *Observations on Man* (2 vols, 1749).
10. *GB 3*, II, 53. The relevance of associationism to the understanding of magic had already been pointed out by Tylor (*Primitive Culture*, I, 116), though he had refrained from specifying its branches.
11. The table reproduced here is that in *GB 3*, I, 54, though Frazer's nomenclature changed between editions. For a full account of this shift, see Chapter IX.
12. *GB 3*, I, 55.
13. *GB 3*, II, 176.
14. Thomas Reid, *An Inquiry into the Human Mind, on the Principles of Common Sense* (Edinburgh, 1764).
15. Frazer, *Creation and Evolution*, p. 123.
16. Frazer was admitted as a student of the Middle Temple at the age of twenty-four on 24 October 1878. He was called to the bar on 26 January 1882. He never practised, though his membership entitled him to reside in Brick Court, within the precincts of the Temple, from 1914. He was made an Honorary Bencher on 18 June 1931. *Register of Admission to the Honourable Society of the Middle Temple*, ed. A. A. C. Sturgess, II (London: Butterworth, 1949).

17. In 1816 Hamilton presented a case to a jury before the Sheriff of Edinburgh and was adjudged "heir male general" to Sir Robert Hamilton of Preston (1650–1701), their common ancestor being John Hamilton, who died before 1522. Thenceforth he styled himself "Sir William, baronet of Preston and Fingalton". Cf. *Dictionary of National Biography*, XXIV, 228.

18. Sir Henry Maine, *Ancient Law, its Connection with the History of Society, and its Relation to Modern Ideas* (London, 1861). Whilst a law student Frazer made copious notes on Maine's text, citing M'Lennan against him (TCC 0.11.39). Frazer's manuscript note on M'Lennan runs: "In other races a very different system has been found to exist, traces of which are not wanting even amongst Indo-European races. See M'Lennan's *Primitive Marriage*."

19. J. F. M'Lennan, *Primitive Marriage: An Inquiry into the Origin and Form of Capture in Marriage Ceremonies* (Edinburgh, 1865).

20. Maine's book has recently been reissued in New York by Dutton (1977) and in Tucson by the Arizona University Press (1986). It was a set book for jurisprudential courses in the University of London as late as the early 1960s.

21. J. J. Bachofen, *Das Mutterrecht* (Stuttgart, 1861).

22. Judges 20–1; Deuteronomy 20:10–14.

23. Deuteronomy 25:5.

24. Sir William Hamilton, *Be Not Schismatics, Be Not Martyrs by Mistake. A demonstration that "the principle of non-intrusion" so far from being "fundamental in the Church of Scotland" is subversive to that and even other Presbyterian church establishments* (Edinburgh, 1843).

25. Frazer, *Creation and Evolution*, p. 139.

26. J. D. Mackie, *History of Scotland* (Harmondsworth: Penguin, 1964), p. 328.

27. Reproduced as a frontispiece in J. S. Black and George Chrystal, *The Life of William Robertson Smith* (London: A. & C. Black, 1912), from which the following biographical details are taken.

28. J. S. Mill, *An Examination of Sir William Hamilton's Philosophy* (London, 1865).

29. Black and Chrystal, *Life of Robertson Smith*, p. 116.

30. J. F. M'Lennan, "The Worship of Animals and Plants" (3 parts), *Fortnightly Review*, October and November 1869, February 1870.

31. Black and Chrystal, *Life of Robertson Smith*, pp. 144–5.

32. The offending article appeared in the *Encyclopaedia Britannica*, 9th edn, III (Edinburgh: A. & C. Black, 1875), 634–48.

33. *Draft Form of Libel. The Free Presbytery Aberdeen against Mr William Robertson Smith* (Aberdeen: Free Church, February–March 1898).

34. The Appointment to a Lord Almoner's Readership in Arabic was partially obtained due to the intervention of a fellow Scot, William Aldis Wright, whom Smith had met on the committee for the revision of the Authorised Version of the Old Testament.

CHAPTER III A MEETING OF MINDS

1. The set of rooms Frazer occupied in his early years as a Fellow were on the first floor of the staircase immediately to the north of the Great Gate,

between it and the Chapel. Newton had once occupied the rooms opposite. See R. Angus Downie, *James George Frazer: The Portrait of a Scholar* (London: Watts, 1940) pp. 8–9.

2. Thomas Babington Macaulay, *The Lays of Ancient Rome* (London, 1842), pp. 102–3.

3. R. St John Parry, *Henry Jackson O.M. Vice-Master of Trinity College and Regius Professor of Greek in the University of Cambridge* (Cambridge: Cambridge University Press, 1926), p. 246.

4. Ibid., p. 165.

5. Frazer matriculated at Trinity in the Michaelmas Term of 1874. He was already a graduate of Glasgow. He completed the Cambridge Classics Tripos in March 1878.

6. Eventually published by Macmillan in 1930 as *The Growth of Plato's Ideal Theory*.

7. *The Dialogues of Plato*, tr. and ed. B. Jowett, 3rd edn (Oxford: Clarendon Press, 1892), p. xxxv.

8. Henry Jackson, "Plato's Later Theory of Ideas", *Journal of Philology*, 1881–6: X, 132–50, 253–93; XI, 287–331; XIII, 1–40; XIV, 173–230.

9. Aristotle, *Metaphysics*, I.6.

10. Frazer, *Plato's Ideal Theory*, p. vii.

11. Ibid., p. 68.

12. Ibid., p. 65.

13. A list of Frazer's undergraduate reading during his first year is preserved in the Wren Library at Trinity College, Cambridge (TCC Add. b.17.102).

14. An interesting sidelight on this is provided by a letter from Frazer to the Kennedy Professor of Latin, A. E. Housman, on 17 August 1930, in the wake of his edition of Ovid's *Fasti*. Frazer had noted certain minor errors, and writes beseeching Housman to deal justly with him: "If you prefer to publish your corrections in a review or otherwise, I would equally receive them gratefully and attend to them carefully, nor would I in the least object to any severity of language you might apply in laying on the rod, believing as I do that your severity is just and deserved" (TCC Frazer 1.42.1). This is rather like the standard Victorian schoolboy's speech to the headmaster before receiving a sound thrashing. No such thrashing occurred, but Housman possessed a ferocious reputation as a Latinist from his appointment to the Chair at University College, London, in 1892 until his death in 1936. Frazer's errors were indeed slight, but they evidently caused him much pain.

15. See Chapter I, note 19. The first volume contained the translation. The whole was reissued in a second, subscription edition in 1913.

16. Cf. his letter to George Macmillan of 8 November 1889 (BL Add. 55134).

17. Frazer's advance copy is marked on the fly-leaf "James G. Frazer, Athens, 21st May, 1890" (TCC Adv. 21.68). The book was published on 1 June.

18. *Pausanias's Description of Greece*, ed. Frazer, V, 158.

19. TCC R 844 (1) and RG 44 (2).

20. Levi, Introduction to Pausanias, *Guide to Greece*, pp. 2–3.

21. Cf. especially his letter of 18 April 1904 to Henry Jackson on refusing a Visiting Lectureship at Didsbury College, Manchester (TCC Add. c.30.47). For a full discussion of this letter and the whole vexed issue, see Chapter XIV.

22. "Sir James Frazer was able to keep his beautiful rooms in Trinity College, Cambridge, until his death by carefully sailing around his dangerous subject, as if charting the coastline of a forbidden island without actually committing himself to the declaration that it existed" – Robert Graves, *The White Goddess*, 2nd edn (London: Faber, 1961), p. 248. Graves, however, is even wrong about the rooms.

23. TCC o.11.43.

24. 1895 journal, entry for Wednesday, 2 October.

25. *Pausanias's Description of Greece*, IV, 250ff. Part of this is reproduced in *Pausanias and Other Greek Sketches* (London: Macmillan, 1900). The passage clearly meant a great deal to Frazer. The vacillation between the first persons singular and plural is evidence of his uneasy negotiation between the confessional and the objective.

26. Pausanias, VIII.21.1.

27. *Pausanias's Description of Greece*, IV, 265–6. "His knowledge of music was such that he had to be restrained from standing up when *Rule Britannia* was played" – R. Angus Downie, *Frazer and the Golden Bough* (London: Victor Gollancz, 1970), pp. 96–7.

28. Robert Ackerman, *J. G. Frazer: His Life and Work* (Cambridge: Cambridge University Press, 1987), p. 29.

29. Quoted in W. R. Sorley, *James Ward, 1843–1925* (London: British Academy, 1927), p. 3.

30. "Psychology", *Encyclopaedia Britannica*, 9th edn, XX, 37–85.

31. James Ward, *Naturalism and Agnosticism: The Gifford Lectures, 1896–8* (London: A. & C. Black, 1898). The "crux of faith" issue brought Ward close enough to the concerns of Henry Sidgwick for him to edit Sidgwick's *Philosophy: Its Scope and Relations* (1902) and his *Lectures on the Philosophy of Kant* (1905).

32. Ackerman, *Frazer*, p. 22.

33. *GB 1*, I, 3.

34. Cf. Frazer's obituary for his friend in the *Fortnightly Review* of June 1892, repr. in *The Gorgon's Head and Other Literary Pieces* (London: Macmillan, 1927); cf. esp. pp. 281–4.

35. Journal of a Tour in Spain, 1883, entry for 28 March, TCC RG 43.

36. Frazer to John F. White, 15 December 1897, TCC Frazer 1.40, quoted in Ackerman, *Frazer*, p. 60.

37. Like a number of his shorter articles for the *Encyclopaedia*, this one is unsigned. But the similarity to the wording both of his article on the Prytanis in the *Journal of Philology* and to his remarks on the Prytaneum in Athens in his Pausanias makes it virtually certain that it comes from Frazer's hand.

38. Pausanias, I.18.3.

39. J. G. Frazer, "The Prytaneum, the Temple of Vesta, the Vestals, Perpetual Fires", *Journal of Philology*, XIV (1885), 145ff, repr. in *Garnered Sheaves* (London: Macmillan, 1931), pp. 51–76.

40. Cf, letter from Lady Frazer, quoted in Ackerman, *Frazer*, p. 144. The pressure on the floors was, according to Downie (*Frazer: Portrait of a Scholar*, p. 9), the reason for Frazer's removal to Whewell's Court. Downie places the threatened floor in the Great Court, Lady Frazer in Nevile's.

41. A marvellous photograph of Smith in his Arab get-up is reproduced in Black and Chrystal, *Life of Robertson Smith*, opposite p. 336.

42. Smith was required to give one public lecture each Easter Term in his capacity as Lord Almoner's Reader. In each year of his tenure he in fact delivered "at least three". In the Easter Term of 1883 his subject was "Early Relations of Arabia with Syria and Palestine", and in 1884 "The History of Palmyra".

43. A case of special pleading, I fear, since Jackson published disgracefully little. The special pleading can be found in Jackson's letter to an unnamed correspondent, Black and Chrystal, *Life of Robertson Smith*, pp. 72–3.

44. *The Athenaeum*, no. 3024 (10 October 1885), pp. 477ff.

45. See Chapter I, notes 4 and 10.

46. J. G. Frazer, *Totemism* (Edinburgh: A. & C. Black, 1877), repr. in *Totemism and Exogamy* (London: Macmillan, 1910).

47. Published in the *Journal of the Anthropological Institute*, XV (1885–6), 64–101, and repr. in *Garnered Sheaves*, pp. 3–50.

48. Joseph Ernest Renan, *Le Prêtre de Nemi* (Paris, 1886). Ackerman makes great play with this as the *fons et origo* of *The Golden Bough*, but, though Frazer almost certainly read it, it was at most a small contributory factor in the making of Frazer's book. For other, more important factors, see Chapters I and IV.

49. *GB 1*, I, 3.

CHAPTER IV   THE KING IS DEAD

1. Sir William Rowan Hamilton (1805–65), Astronomer Royal of Ireland.

2. Alexander Hamilton, *A New Account of the East Indies* (Edinburgh, 1727), I, 306–8. Frazer seems not to have had access to the original edition, which is rare. Instead he read Hamilton's account in John Pinkerton's *General Collection of the Best and Most Interesting Voyages and Travels* (London, 1808–14), VIII, 374ff. Cf. *GB 1*, I, 224–5. He was subsequently to discover that Hamilton's evidence had been corroborated and extended in 1887 by William Logan, District Commissioner of Malabar Province. Cf. William Logan, *Malabar* (Madras, 1887), esp. I, 162–9. It is on Logan's account that the discussion of Calicut in subsequent editions is based.

3. On 15 November 1712, in Hyde Park. The anomaly is easily explained, since Hamilton "slew his opponent" Charles, Lord Mohun, before himself falling, it is suspected, to Mohun's second. See *Burke's Peerage and Baronetage*, 105th edn (London, 1970), p. 1217.

4. For the date of Frazer's discovery, see *GB 1*, I, ix; for the reference to southern Indian affinities, see *GB 3*, I, vii: "The explanation was suggested to me by some similar rules formerly imposed on the kings of Southern India." Calicut is the only example in *GB 1* in which such a rule was "*formerly imposed*".

5. Frazer to Macmillan, 8 November 1889, BL Add. 55134.

6. Frazer to Macmillan, 11 December 1889. BL Add. 55134.

7. For the firm's history at this period, see Charles Morgan, *The House of Macmillan* (London: Macmillan, 1943).

8. Frazer to Macmillan, 25 December 1889, BL Add. 55134.

9. Letter of 8 November. Middleton had been appointed Slade Professor of Fine Art in 1886. He later became Director of the South Kensington Museum (now the Victoria and Albert), was an expert on Roman antiquities, and had in his student years gone walking in Iceland with Morris, with whom he shared an enthusiasm for the sagas.

10. See note 8 above. At this period Frazer often worked a fourteen- or fifteen-hour day. The whole research for, and writing of, the First Edition took a little under a year, the Preface being dated 8 March 1890.

11. Frazer to Macmillan, 15 March 1890, BL Add. 55134.

12. Duarte Barbosa, *A Description of the Coasts of East Africa and Malabar in the Beginning of the Sixteenth Century* (London: Hakluyt Society, 1866). Cf. esp. pp. 172ff. Originally written in Portuguese, this account had previously been translated into Spanish and thence into Italian. The Hakluyt translation is Baron Stanley's.

13. *GB 1*, I, 241.

14. Strabo, *Geographia*, XVII.2.3. Tr. Horace Leonard Jones in *The Geography of Strabo* (London: Heinemann; New York: Putnam, 1932), pp. 143–9. See also Diodorus Siculus, III.6.

15. João dos Santos, "History of Eastern Ethiopa", in Pinkerton, *Voyages and Travels*, XVI, 684. Cf. *GB 1*, I, 45ff and 219–21.

16. *GB 1*, I, 12.

17. Cf. *GB 1*, I, 7.

18. Mannhardt was by this time dead, but his books had an intense effect on Frazer, and remained his principal source for the European peasantry. See esp. *Roggenwolf und Roggenhund* (1865), *Der Baumkultus der Germanen und ihrer Nachbarstämme* (1875), *Antike Wald–und Feldkulte* (1877) and *Mythologische Forschungen* (1884).

19. See *GB 1*, I, 50–2.

20. Esp. A. B. Cook in the *Classical Review* (1902). For this, and a discussion of the critical reaction to the Second Edition – the harshest Frazer received – see Chapter XI.

CHAPTER V   THE SACRED AND THE TABOO

1. Virgil, *Aeneid*, III.44–6.

2. Servius on the *Aeneid*, III.57.

3. *GB 1*, II, 212.

4. Macrobius, *Saturnalia*, III.7.6.

5. Isaiah 53:3.

6. James Cook, *Voyage to the Pacific* (1785), II.ix.

7. *Encyclopaedia Britannica*, 9th edn, XXIII, 15–18, repr. in *Garnered Sheaves*, pp. 80–92.

8. *Encyclopaedia Britannica*, 9th edn, XXIII, 16–17, repr. in *Garnered Sheaves*, pp. 91-2.

9. J. G. Frazer, *The Fear of the Dead in Primitive Religion*, III (London: Macmillan, 1936), 199–235.

10. *Encyclopaedia Britannica*, 9th edn; XXIII, 18; and *GB 1*, I, 117.

11. Diodorus Siculus, I, 70; *GB 1*, I, 116.

12. *GB* 1, I, 162.
13. *GB* 1, I, 161.
14. *GB* 1, I, 165.
15. *GB* 1, I, 181.
16. *GB* 1, I, 193.
17. *GB* 1, I, 110–12.
18. *GB* 1, I, 119.
19. *GB* 1, I, 109–10.
20. *GB* 1, I, 172.
21. *GB* 1, I, 168–9.
22. Tylor, *Primitive Culture*, I, 409ff.
23. *GB* 1, I, 127.
24. *GB* 1, I, 147.
25. *GB* 1, I, 146.
26. *GB* 1, I, 160–1.
27. *GB* 1, I, 190.
28. *GB* 1, I, 183–4.
29. Ovid, *Fasti*, III.265ff; Virgil, *Aeneid*, VII.761ff; Pausanias, II.27; *GB* 1, I, 6.
30. Pausanias, II.27.
31. *GB* 3, I, 24. For an entirely fanciful reconstruction of a horse-sacrifice at Troezen, see Mary Renault's hyper-Frazerian *The King Must Die* (London: New English Library, 1961), pp. 10–12.
32. *GB* 1, II, 64–7.
33. Wilhelm Mannhardt, *Mythologische Forschungen* (Strassburg, 1884), pp. 156–201.
34. *GB* 1, II, 62.
35. William Robertson Smith, "Ctesias and the Semiramis Legend", *English Historical Review*, II (1887), 308.

CHAPTER VI   TOTEMS AND TOTEM FEASTS

1. "The Worship of Animals and Plants", *Fortnightly Review*, October and November 1869, February 1870.
2. *C. Sallusti Crispi Catalina et Iugurtha*, ed. with notes by the late George Long, 2nd edn, rev. (London: George Bell and Sons, 1884).
3. Smith to J. S. Black, in Black and Chrystal, *Life of Robertson Smith*, pp. 494–5. But "Torture" stayed. What went was "Tory".
4. J. Long, *Voyages of an Indian Interpreter* (1791), p. 86. Cited in *Encyclopaedia Britannica*, 9th edn, XXIII, 467.
5. Frazer, *Creation and Evolution*, p. 126.
6. TCC Add. c.59.2(A).
7. The article to which Lang especially objected was Frazer's "The Beginning of Religion and Totemism among the Australian Aborigines", *Fortnightly Review*, July and September 1905. For Lang's riposte see his *The Secret of the Totem* of the same year.
8. Andrew Lang, *The Secret of the Totem* (London: Longman, 1905).
9. After the appearance of Frazer's paper "Burial Customs" in 1885, Wilken wrote to him and they had been in correspondence ever since. Among other

things Wilken had sent him his paper "De Simonsage", *De Gids*, 1888, no. 5, pp. 6ff, which Frazer had promptly acknowledged (*GB 1*, I, 326), only to be accused by Tylor of plagiarism. The correspondence can be followed by TCC Add. b.37.312.

10. *Folk-lore Journal*, II (1884), 288–303. See also Clodd's *Myths and Dreams* (London, 1885), pp. 188–98.
11. *GB 1*, II, 342–55.
12. Herodotos, I, 199. For Lydian evidence see Herodotos, I, 93.
13. Cf. Frazer, *Adonis, Attis, Osiris*, (1914), III, 59n.
14. For two accounts of this, see S. Krascheninnikow, *Beschreibung des Landes Kamschatka* (Lemgo, 1766), p. 259; and G. W. Steller, *Beschreibung von dem Lande Kamschatka* (Frankfurt and Leipzig, 1774), p. 346.
15. Cf. *GB 1*, II, 225–53.
16. TCC c.30.40–6.
17. *GB 1*, II, 358–9.
18. Ackerman, *Frazer*, p. 153.
19. Spencer to Frazer, 12 July 1897, in *Spencer's Scientific Correspondence with J. G. Frazer and Others*, ed. R. R. Marett and T. K. Penniman (Oxford: Clarendon Press, 1932), p. 4.
20. J. G. Frazer, "The Origin of Totemism", *Fortnightly Review*, April–May 1899, repr. in *Totemism and Exogamy*, I, 101.
21. Cf. Frazer to George Macmillan, 14 January, 22 April and 24 November 1898, BL Add 55135.
22. See note 20.
23. Baldwin Spencer to Frazer, 27 September 1897, in *Spencer's Scientific Correspondence*, pp. 12–13.
24. BL Add. 55134.
25. Cf. Tylor, *Primitive Culture*, II, 371 and 407–9.
26. Mary Kingsley to Frazer, 9 November 1899, TCC Add. c.58.80.
27. William Robertson Smith, *The Religion of the Semites* (Edinburgh: A. & C. Black, 1889). A second, expanded edition was published after Smith's death in 1894.
28. *GB 1*, I, xii–xiii.

CHAPTER VII   SACRIFICE AS EUCHARIST

1. *GB 1*, I, 52–3.
2. Oscar Wilde, *The Picture of Dorian Gray* (London: Ward, Lock, 1891), pp. 197–8. The story had previously appeared in *Lippincott's Monthly Magazine* in June 1890.
3. Genesis 15:7–17.
4. Genesis 20:1–14.
5. For a discussion of these see Frazer's *Folklore in the Old Testament* (London: Macmillan, 1918), III, 62n., 64, 70.
6. Black and Chrystal, *Life of Robertson Smith*, opposite p. 336.
7. Frazer, *Folklore in the Old Testament*, II, 481.
8. Black and Chrystal, *Life of Robertson Smith*, p. 333.

9. W. Robertson Smith, *Kinship and Marriage in Ancient Arabia* (Cambridge: Cambridge University Press, 1895), p. viii.
10. Smith, *Kinship and Marriage*, p. 186.
11. *Iliad*, v.738.
12. Pausanias, II.9.7 and II.19.3. See also Frazer's commentary in *Pausanias's Description of Greece*, III, 189–91.
13. Pausanias, I.24.4. For Smith's explication, see *Encyclopaedia Britannica*, 9th edn, XXI, 137.
14. Herodotos, II.39, 40, tr. Aubrey de Selincourt in Herodotus, *The Histories* (Harmondsworth: Penguin, 1954), pp. 144–5. The goddess is Isis–Hathor. See also *Encyclopaedia Britannica*, 9th edn, XXI, 137; and Smith, *Religion of the Semites*, p. 283.
15. Smith, *Religion of the Semites*, esp. pp. 407ff.
16. Ezekiel 8:10.
17. Smith, *Religion of the Semites*, p. 276.
18. Ibid., p. 338.
19. Isaiah 17:10. Cf. also Smith, "Ctesias", *English Historical Review*, II, 307, and *Religion of the Semites*, p. 180n; and see *Peake's Commentary*, 2nd edn (Edinburgh: Nelson, 1937), p. 448.
20. Judges 2:13.
21. Smith, *Religion of the Semites*, pp. 391–2.
22. Ibid., p. 392.
23. Cf. Frazer to Macmillan, 18 December 1889, BL Add. 55134.

CHAPTER VIII   SACRIFICE AS MAGIC

1. *GB 2*, I, xviii.
2. *GB 2*, I, xix.
3. Again, see Frazer's obituary notice for Smith, repr. in *The Gorgon's Head*, esp. p. 285.
4. *GB 1*, II, 58–9; *Encyclopaedia Britannica*, 9th edn, III, 137.
5. For an account of this dispute, see Ackerman, *Frazer*, pp. 224–35.
6. Though the word is rare in Smith, and he seems to have thought Christian sacrament as such non-sacrificial. For the *Britannica* he commissioned a completely separate article on sacrament, in which the sacrament of Holy Communion is interpreted in a wholly non-sacrificial light: *Encyclopaedia Britannica*, 9th edn, XXI, 131–2.
7. *GB 1*, II, 82–3.
8. Smith, *Religion of the Semites*, p. 393.
9. Plutarch, *Isis and Osiris*, 13–19.
10. Plutarch, *Isis and Osiris*, 8, tr. J. Gwynn Griffiths in Plutarch, *De Iside et Osiride* (Cardiff: University of Wales Press, 1970), p. 129.
11. *GB 1*, II, 59.
12. *GB 1*, II, 44–8.
13. *GB 1*, II, 38–41. For Smith's discussion of the Bouphonia see *Religion of the Semites*, pp. 304ff.
14. Porphyry, II.30.
15. Pausanias, I.24.4 and I.28.10.

16. Porphyry, II.29–30.
17. *GB 1*, II, 60–2.
18. Plutarch, *Isis and Osiris*, 57.
19. Frazer to Macmillan, 8 November 1889, BL Add. 55134.
20. *GB 1*, II, 90–2.
21. *GB 1*, II, 92–3; Herodotos, II.42.
22. *GB 1*, II, 47.
23. *GB 1*, II, 41.
24. *GB 1*, II, 51.
25. *GB 1*, II, 101–5.
26. *GB 3*, VIII, 58. For a fictional re-creation of this custom, see Chinua Achebe, *Arrow of God* (London: Heinemann, 1964).
27. *GB 3*, VIII, 89.
28. Macrobius, *Saturnalia*, 1.7.34.
29. *GB 1*, II, 83.
30. *GB 2*, I, 7–128.

CHAPTER IX   THE PROGRESS OF THE MIND

1. Frazer to Macmillan, 8 July 1899, BL Add. 55135.
2. Frazer to Macmillan, 6 August 1900, BL Add. 55135.
3. Frazer to Macmillan, 18 November 1900, BL Add. 55135.
4. Ibid.
5. Clodd's address took place on Friday, 30 November 1894, Lang's "Protest of a Psycho-Folklorist" on 19 June 1895. For all of which, see *Folklore*, VI (1895).
6. *The Letters of William James*, ed. Henry James (London: Longman, 1920), II, 139–40, quoted in Ackerman, *Frazer*, p. 175. But Frazer seems not to have noticed the asperity. See letter to Macmillan, 23 December 1900, BL Add. 55135.
7. Frazer to Macmillan, 19 August 1899, BL Add. 55135.
8. F. B. Jevons, *An Introduction to the History of Religion* (London: Methuen, 1896). The crucial distinction is discussed on pp. 24ff.
9. E. S. Hartland, *The Myth of Perseus* (London: Grimm Library, 1894), II, 63ff.
10. *Folkore*, VIII (1897), 65. The identification of the anonymous reviewer is Frazer's, *GB 2*, I, 10, n.2.
11. *GB 1*, I, 9–12.
12. A. B. Ellis, *The Tshi-Speaking Peoples of the Gold Coast of West Africa* (London: Chapman and Hall, 1887), p. 226, cited by Frazer in *GB 2*, I, 33.
13. Theocritus, II.11.53ff, cited in *GB 2*, II, 60.
14. Sir Alfred Lyall, *Asiatick Studies*, 1st Ser. (London: John Murray, 1899). The discussion of magical practices occurs in II, 99ff.
15. *GB 2*, I, 63–4.
16. Jevons, *Introduction to the History of Religion*, pp. 39–40.
17. *GB 2*, I, 16–17.
18. Frazer to Macmillan, 24 February 1905, BL Add. 55135.

19. TCC Frazer 33.3, manuscript of "The Evolution of the Kingship in Ancient Society", pp. 45–6.
20. Frazer to Clodd, 14 December 1918, TCC Add. b.35.
21. J. G. Frazer, *Condorcet on the Progress of the Human Mind*, the Zaharoff lecture for 1933 (Oxford: Clarendon Press, 1933).
22. "Kingship" manuscript, pp. 20–1.
23. Ackerman, *Frazer*, pp. 213–15.
24. J. G. Frazer, *Psyche's Task: A Discourse Concerning the Influence of Superstition on the Growth of Institutions* (London: Macmillan, 1909), pp. 83–4.
25. Frazer to Macmillan, 9 February 1909, BL Add. 55136.
26. *GB* 2, I, 74–5.
27. Alexander Pope, *The Dunciad*, IV, 648–56.
28. See esp. his remarks on this score in *The Belief in Immortality and the Worship of the Dead*, I (London: Macmillan, 1913), 4–5.
29. *GB* 2, I, xxi–xii.

CHAPTER X   THE MAN OF SORROWS

1. Frazer recorded his impressions of the Bogles in "Memories of My Parents" *Creation and Evolution*; see esp. pp. 143–6. The history of George Bogle's expedition is from *Narratives of the Mission of George Bogle to Tibet and of the Journey of Thomas Manning to Lhasa*, ed. Clements R. Markham (London, 1876), on p. cxl of which a drawing of the necklace appears.
2. *Narratives*, p. cxxxix.
3. For a fuller account see Clinton Black, *A History of Jamaica*, 2nd edn (London: Collins, 1965), pp. 173–83.
4. *Narratives*, pp. 106–7. An original manuscript is in the British Library (BL Add. 19283).
5. *GB* 2, III, 113–17.
6. *GB* 1, II, 101–5.
7. *GB* 1, II, 133–4.
8. *GB* 1, II, 110–11.
9. *GB* 1, II, 212, citing Servius on the *Aeneid*, III.57, following Petronius.
10. *GB* 1, II, 193, amplified in *GB* 3, VIII, 108, and IX, 203, where the source is Mary Kingsley. See her *Travels in West Africa* (London: Macmillan, 1897), pp. 494–5.
11. The whole subject of disease boats is treated at length in *GB* 1, II, 185–9.
12. Leviticus 16: 7–22.
13. *The Book of Enoch*, R. H. Charles (Oxford: Clarendon Press, 1893), pp. 71–2.
14. "Yama" (The Day of Atonement) 6:4–6, cited from Herbert Danby's translation of the *Mishnah*, (Oxford: Clarendon Press, 1933).
15. Leviticus 16:8.
16. See Leviticus 16.10 26 in the Revised Version.
17. Frazer to Macmillan, 23 December 1910, BL Add. 55137. In 1911 part V is advertised as "The Man of Sorrows" opposite p. 426 of the *The Magic Art*, I, (*GB* 3, I).

18. *GB 3*, IX, 412–23.
19. *GB 2*, III, 186–9.
20. *GB 1*, II, 208–10.
21. *GB 2*, III, 122.
22. *GB 1*, II, 212.
23. *GB 1*, II, 213.
24. *GB 1*, II, 214. Cf. also Mannhardt, *Mythologische Forschungen*, pp. 113ff.
25. *GB 3*, IX, pp. 257–8.
26. *GB 1*, II, p. 211.
27. TCC Adv. C.21.68.
28. Frazer's marginal comment runs along the top of II, 203.
29. For a later discussion of these facts, see *Adonis, Attis, Osiris* (1906), pp. 243–7.
30. Frazer to Macmillan, April 1900, BL Add. 55135.
31. In two instalments: *Fortnightly Review*, new ser., LXVIII (July–December 1900) pp. 653–76 and 825–49.
32. Frazer to Macmillan, 4 November 1899, BL Add. 55135.
33. Warde Fowler, *The Roman Festivals of the Period of the Republic* (London: Macmillan, 1899), pp. 270–1.
34. Macrobius, *Saturnalia*, I.7.31–2. I have used the translation by Percival Vaughan Davies (New York: Columbia University Press, 1969), pp. 60–1.
35. *GB 3*, II, 307 and n.2.
36. Franz Cumont, *Les Actes de S. Dasius, Analecta Bollandiana*, XVI (1897), 5.
37. For this cf. *GB 3*, IX, 336.
38. Dio Chrysostom, *Orationes*, ed. Ludwig Dindorf (Leipzig, 1857), I, 76.
39. Frazer to Macmillan, 1 April 1900, BL Add. 55135.
40. Theodore Nöldeke, "Esther", *Encyclopaedia Biblica*, T. K. Cheyne and J. Sutherland Black, II (Edinburgh: A. & C. Black, 1901), 1405. An intimate of the firm, which had been Smith's publishers, Frazer had access to Nöldeke's article prior to publication. Cf. *GB 2*, III, 159n. By the following year his own theory concerning the origins of Purim had achieved such currency that he was invited to paraphrase it as part of the article on Purim in volume III (1902). See pp. 3980–2, "Further developments in Golden Bough", initialled J. G. F.
41. Frazer to Macmillan, 18 November 1900, BL Add. 55135.
42. Andrew Lang, "Mr Frazer's Theory of the Crucifixion", *Fortnightly Review*, LXIX (1901), 650–62.
43. *GB 2*, III, 197–8.

CHAPTER XI   THE THEATRE OF MYTH

1. Frazer to Macmillan, 18 November 1900, BL Add. 55135.
2. Lady Frazer to Macmillan, 7 December 1900, BL Add. 55135.
3. Lady Frazer to Macmillan, 9 August 1901, BL Add. 55135.
4. Frazer to Macmillan, 8 March 1903, BL Add. 55136.
5. Frazer to Macmillan, 18 July 1903, BL Add. 55136.
6. Frazer to Macmillan, 19 May 1905, BL Add. 55136.
7. Frazer to Macmillan, 18 July 1903, BL Add. 55136.

8. Frazer to Macmillan, 8 March 1906, BL Add. 55136.
9. Frazer to Macmillan, 3 February 1907, BL Add. 55136.
10. Lady Frazer to Macmillan, 4 May 1906, BL Add. 55136.
11. Frazer to Macmillan, 23 December 1910, BL Add. 55137.
12. Frazer to Macmillan, 29 July 1912, BL Add. 55138.
13. Frazer to Macmillan, 8 March 1913, BL Add. 55138.
14. Macrobius, *Saturnalia, Praefatio*, 5 quoted in *GB* 3, I, iv.
15. *Adonis, Attis, Osiris* (1906), pp. v–vi.
16. A. B. Cook, "The Golden Bough and the Rex Nemorensis", *Classical Review*, XVI (1902), 365–80.
17. Downie, *Frazer and the Golden Bough*, p. 25. At least Cook did not suffer the indignity of Solomon Schechter, whose walks with Frazer to Grantchester and back came to an end when Lady Frazer bought her husband and herself bicycles.
18. *Fortnightly Review*, LXXVI (July–December 1904), 982–95.
19. Cook, in *Classical Review*, XVI, 372–3.
20. For Frazer's description of Troezen, see *Pausanias's Description of Greece*, III, 273 ff.
21. Pausanias, II.32.3.
22. *GB* 3, I, 25.
23. Herodotos, IV.33.
24. Lucian, *De Dea Syria*, 6. See also Smith, *Religion of the Semites*, p. 311.
25. Lucian, *De Dea Syria*, 60, tr. Herbert Strong in *The Syrian Goddess*, (London: Constable, 1913), 89.
26. *GB* 3, VII, 13.
27. Pausanias, IX.3.2, with Frazer's commentary (*Pausanias's Description of Greece*, V.19–20).
28. Firmicus Maternus, *De Errore Profanarum Religionum*, 5.
29. *GB 3*, VII, 13.
30. *Journal of the Anthropological Institute*, XV (1886), 64–101, repr. in *Garnered Sheaves*, pp. 3–50.
31. J. G. Frazer, *The Fear of the Dead in Primitive Religion*, I (London: Macmillan, 1933). Volume II followed in 1934 and volume III in 1936.
32. Frazer, *Belief in Immortality*, I, 24–5.
33. *Bibliotheca Classica*, ed. John Lemprière (London: T. Cadell, 1788).
34. *Adonis, Attis, Osiris* (1906), citing Strabo, *Geographia*, XIV.5.9. But Athenaeus, XII, gives a more vociferous version:

243	I was the king, and while I lived on earth,
244	And saw the bright rays of the genial sun.
245	I ate and drank and loved; and know full well
246	The time that men do live on earth was brief
247	And liable to many changes. Now others
248	Will have the enjoyment of my luxuries
249	Which I do now leave behind me. For this reason
250	I never ceased one single day from pleasure.

35. F. C. Movers, *Die Phoenizier* (Bonn, 1841), I, 490ff, cited by Frazer in *GB* 3, IX, 368.

36. Byron, Sardanapalus, I.ii.179.
37. GB 3, IX, 373–4.
38. Adonis, Attis, Osiris (1906), p. 4.
39. GB 3, IV, 265ff.

CHAPTER XII   THE FLUTES OF TAMMUZ

1. Firmicus Maternus, De Errore, XXII.1–2.
2. Frazer to Macmillan, 8 March 1906, BL Add. 55136.
3. Adonis, Attis, Osiris (1906), p. 154.
4. Ibid., pp. 154–5.
5. Ibid., pp. 153–4. For the date of the festival in Cyprus and a description of the rite there, see Smith, Religion of the Semites, pp. 391–4.
6. Ernest Renan, Mission de Phénicie (Paris: Imprimerie Impériale, 1864), p. 283.
7. Lucian, De Dea Syria, 8.
8. Charles Vellay, "Le Culte et les fêtes d'Adônis-Thammouz dans l'Orient antique", Annales du Musée Guinet, XVI (1904), 131.
9. Macrobius, Saturnalia, I.21.5. Cf. also Renan, Mission de Phénicie, pl. 38.
10. Adonis, Attis, Osiris (1906), p. 126.
11. Shelley, "Adonais", iii.
12. Ezekiel 8.14.
13. Plutarch, Alcibiades, 18; Nicias, 13.
14. Thucydides, VI. 30. Cf. Adonis, Attis, Osiris (1906), p. 128.
15. Smith, Religion of the Semites, pp. 391–4.
16. Renan, Mission de Phénicie, p. 12.
17. Adonis, Attis, Osiris (1906), pp. 34–5.
18. Ezekiel 28:14, cited in Adonis, Attis, Osiris (1906), p. 38.
19. Adonis, Attis, Osiris (1906), pp. 87ff.
20. Ibid., pp. 48ff.
21. Ibid., pp. 36ff.
22. Ibid., pp. 23ff.
23. Ibid., pp. 50ff.
24. Livy, xxix.14, Aubrey de Sélincourt in Livy, The War with Hannibal (Harmondsworth: Penguin, 1965), pp. 583–4.
25. Lucian, De Dea Syria, 51.
26. The translation is Grant Allen's: The Attis of Valerius Catullus (London: David Nutt, 1892).
27. Adonis, Attis, Osiris (1914; incorporated in GB 3), I (GB 3, V), 309–10.
28. The Ancient Egyptian Book of the Dead, tr. Raymond O. Faulkner (London: British Museum, 1972), p. 27.
29. Plutarch, Isis and Osiris, 69–71, cited in Adonis, Attis, Osiris (1906), p. 233.
30. Adonis, Attis, Osiris (1906), pp. 234–6.
31. Postcard from Smith to Frazer, August 1889, TCC Frazer 1.86.
32. Diodorus Siculus, I.88.5, amplifying Plutarch, Isis and Osiris, 73, and cited in Adonis, Attis, Osiris (1906), p. 269.
33. Herodotos, II.57.

34. Margaret Murray, *The Osireion at Abydos* (London: Bernard Quantitch, 1904).
35. Ibid., p. 19.
36. Strabo, *Geographia*, XVI. For Frazer's discussion of Meroë, see Chapter IV.
37. W. M. Flinders Petrie, *Researches in Sinai* (London: John Murray, 1906), p. 183.
38. Firmicus Maternus, *De Errore*, XXVII.2.
39. *GB*, Abridged Edition (1922), p. vii.
40. Andrew Lang, *Magic and Religion* (1901), cited in Downie, *Frazer and the Golden Bough*, p. 54. Lang's book is largely an extended attack on the Second Edition of *The Golden Bough*.

CHAPTER XIII "SEXTA LUNA"

1. Virgil, *Aeneid*, VI, 124–211.
2. Christopher Pitt, *The Aeneid of Virgil* (London, 1743), I, 177.
3. Servius on the *Aeneid*, VI.136.
4. *Aeneid*, VI. 205–9.
5. Jacob Grimm, *Teutonic Mythology*, 4th edn, tr. James Steven Stallybras (London: George Bell and Sons, 1900), IV, 1674.
6. Greek Journal 1890, entry for 1 May, TCC R 844 (1).
7. See esp. his remarks in the Preface of the Abridged Edition, p. vii. Also letter to A. B. Cook, 13 December 1914, acknowledging a gift of volume I of Cook's *Zeus* and congratulating the author on avoiding the term "vegetation spirit": "I must confess I wince and shudder when I hear the name pronounced in a public lecture" (TCC Frazer 1.61).
8. Grimm, *Teutonic Mythology*, 1, p. 70.
9. See esp. Mannhardt, *Der Baumkultus der Germanen und ihrer Nachbarstämme*.
10. *Odyssey*, XIV. 325–30, tr. Robert Fitzgerald in Homer, *The Odyssey* (London: Heinemann, 1961), p. 231.
11. Livy, I.10.
12. Grimm, *Teutonic Mythology*, p. 69.
13. *GB 1*, II, 285n. The Welsh information I owe to my wife.
14. Pliny, *Nat. Hist.*, XVI.249ff tr. in *GB 1*, II, 285–6.
15. Mannhardt, *Baumkultus*, pp. 509–13.
16. *GB 1*, II, 245–6.
17. *GB 1*, II, 289.
18. Ackerman, *Frazer*, p. 115.
19. *The Athenaeum*, 21 November 1891.
20. Downie, *Frazer and the Golden Bough*, p. 22 and n.; Ackerman, *Frazer*, p. 116.
21. Frazer to Cook, 19 October 1902, TCC 1.57.
22. Which he subsequently incorporated in his lecture series: *Lectures on the Early History of the Kingship* (London: Macmillan, 1905), pp. 198–202, 207–9, 214, 274, 281.
23. Virgil, *Aeneid*, VI. 772.

24. A. B. Cook, "Zeus, Jupiter and the Oak", *Classical Review*, XVII (1903), 174–86; XVIII (1904), 360ff.
25. Frazer, *Lectures*, p. 274.
26. *GB 3*, II, 308ff.
27. Fowler to Frazer, 30 July 1906, with accompanying "Notes on Lecture VII". Of Frazer's new theory of the Regifugium he says, "I confess that the old explanation seems to me much more natural" (TCC Add b.35.316 and 317).
28. *GB 3*, II, 191–2.
29. The passages in Seligmann used by Frazer are reproduced in full in *Anthologia Anthropologica* (London: Percy Lund Humphries, 1938), I (*The Native Races of Africa and Madagascar*), 509ff.
30. Ibid., I, 510.

CHAPTER XIV   THE DYING SUN

1. T. S. Eliot, "The Interpretation of Primitive Ritual", lecture delivered 9 December 1913, King's College, Cambridge, the Hayward Bequest. Quoted in Piers Gray, *T. S. Eliot's Intellectual and Poetic Development* (Brighton: Harvester, 1982), p. 129.
2. J. G. Frazer, *Aftermath: A Supplement to the Golden Bough* (London: Macmillan, 1936), from which all of the foregoing examples are taken.
3. *Nature*, 19 May 1923, pp. 658–62, repr. as "Science and Superstition of Primitive Mankind" in *Sex, Culture and Myth* (London: Rupert Hart-Davis, 1963), pp. 268ff.
4. Geoffrey Kirk, *Myth: Its Meaning and Function in Ancient and Other Cultures* (Cambridge: Cambridge University Press; Berkeley, Calif.: University of California Press, 1970), p. 4.
5. Notebook "Ancient Law", TCC 0.11.39.
6. Ludwig Wittgenstein, *Remarks on Frazer's Golden Bough*, ed. Rush Rhees (Nottinghamshire: Brynmill Press, 1979), p. 5e.
7. Sir William Hamilton, *Lectures on Metaphysics and Logic* (1860), I, 279.
8. Ludwig Wittgenstein, *Tractatus Logico-philosophicus*, v.1361.
9. Russell's Preface to the 1922 ed, repr. in *Tractatus Logico-philosophicus*, tr. D. F. Pears and B. F. McGuinness (London: Routledge and Kegan Paul, 1961), p. xvi.
10. *GB 1*, I, 212.
11. *GB 1*, I, 212.
12. Frazer, *Belief in Immortality*, pp. 18–19.
13. *GB 2*, III, 461; also *GB 3*, XI, 308.
14. *GB 2*, III, 460–1; also *GB 3*, XI, 306–7. For a fuller treatment of the theme of solar decline in the nineteenth century, and of Lord Kelvin's theories in particular, see Gillian Beer, "'The Death of the Sun': Victorian Solar Physics and Solar Myth", in J. B. Bullen (ed.), *The Sun is God: Painting, Literature and Mythology in the Nineteenth Century* (Oxford: Clarendon Press, 1989), pp. 159–80, to which I am much indebted.
15. Frazer to Jackson, 18 April 1904, TCC Add. c.30.47, quoted in Ackerman, *Frazer*, pp. 188–9.
16. Frazer to Macmillan, 17 May 1906, BL Add. 55136.

17. Frazer, *Belief in Immortality*, pp. 1–2.
18. Byron, *Don Juan*, III. cviii, imitating Dante, Purgatorio, VIII. 1–6. Stanza cvii is a reworking of Sappho.
19. Frazer, *Folklore in the Old Testament*, III, 453–4. Also quoted in "Address to the Ernest Renan Society Delivered at the École du Louvre, December 11th, 1920", repr. in *Garnered Sheaves*, pp. 277–9. Frazer had wished to write to Renan acknowledging his debt, but had been dissuaded. Puzzlingly he states, "dans la dernière edition de mon livre, j'ai remplacé les cloches de Rome par les cloches d'Aricie". Nevertheless, *GB* 3, XI, 309 still has "the church bells of Rome ringing the Angelus".

INDEX

DATE DUE
